W9-BAH-783

Taste of Home

Grandma's
Favorites

Taste of Home

© 2018 RDA Enthusiast Brands, LLC
1610 N. 2nd St., Suite 102, Milwaukee, WI 53212
All rights reserved.

Taste of Home is a registered trademark of RDA Enthusiast Brands, LLC.

EDITORIAL

EDITOR-IN-CHIEF	Catherine Cassidy
EXECUTIVE EDITOR, PRINT AND DIGITAL BOOKS	Stephen C. George
CREATIVE DIRECTOR	Howard Greenberg
EDITORIAL SERVICES MANAGER	Kerri Balliet
EDITOR	Janet Briggs
ASSOCIATE CREATIVE DIRECTOR	Edwin Robles Jr.
ART DIRECTOR	Jessie Sharon, Kristen Stecklein
CONTENT PRODUCTION MANAGER	Julie Wagner
CONTRIBUTING LAYOUT DESIGNER	Holly Patch
LAYOUT DESIGNER	Catherine Fletcher
COPY CHIEF	Deb Warlaumont Mulvey
COPY EDITORS	Joanne Weintraub, Alysse Gear
RECIPE EDITOR	Mary King
RECIPE CONTENT MANAGER	Colleen King
RECIPE TESTING	Taste of Home Test Kitchen
FOOD PHOTOGRAPHY	Taste of Home Photo Studio
EXECUTIVE ASSISTANT	Marie Brannon
EDITORIAL ASSISTANT	Marilyn Iczkowski

BUSINESS

VICE PRESIDENT, PUBLISHER	Jan Studin, jan_studin@rd.com
REGIONAL ACCOUNT DIRECTOR	Donna Lindskog, donna_lindskog@rd.com
EASTERN ACCOUNT DIRECTOR	Joanne Carrara
EASTERN ACCOUNT MANAGER	Kari Nestor
ACCOUNT MANAGER	Gina Minerbi
MIDWEST & WESTERN ACCOUNT DIRECTOR	Jackie Fallon
MIDWEST ACCOUNT MANAGER	Lorna Phillips
MICHIGAN SALES REPRESENTATIVE	Linda C. Donaldson
SOUTHWESTERN ACCOUNT REPRESENTATIVE	Summer Nilsson
CORPORATE DIGITAL AND INTEGRATED SALES DIRECTOR, N.A.	Steve Sottile
ASSOCIATE MARKETING DIRECTOR, INTEGRATED SOLUTIONS	Katie Gaon Wilson
DIGITAL SALES PLANNER	Tim Baarda
GENERAL MANAGER, TASTE OF HOME COOKING SCHOOLS	Erin Puariea
DIRECT RESPONSE ADVERTISING	Katherine Zito, David Geller Associates
VICE PRESIDENT, CREATIVE DIRECTOR	Paul Livornese
EXECUTIVE DIRECTOR, BRAND MARKETING	Leah West
SENIOR MARKETING MANAGER	Vanessa Bailey
ASSOCIATE MARKETING MANAGER	Betsy Connors
VICE PRESIDENT, MAGAZINE MARKETING	Dave Fiegel

READER'S DIGEST NORTH AMERICA

VICE PRESIDENT, BUSINESS DEVELOPMENT	Jonathan Bigham
PRESIDENT, BOOKS AND HOME ENTERTAINING	Harold Clarke
CHIEF FINANCIAL OFFICER	Howard Halligan
VP, GENERAL MANAGER, READER'S DIGEST MEDIA	Marilynn Jacobs
CHIEF CONTENT OFFICER, MILWAUKEE	Mark Jannot
CHIEF MARKETING OFFICER	Renee Jordan
VICE PRESIDENT, CHIEF SALES OFFICER	Mark Josephson
GENERAL MANAGER, MILWAUKEE	Frank Quigley
VICE PRESIDENT, CHIEF CONTENT OFFICER	Liz Vaccariello

THE READER'S DIGEST ASSOCIATION, INC.

PRESIDENT AND CHIEF EXECUTIVE OFFICER	Robert E. Guth

For other Taste of Home books and products, visit us at **tasteofhome.com**.

For more Reader's Digest products and information, visit
rd.com (in the United States) or **rd.ca** (in Canada).

INTERNATIONAL STANDARD BOOK NUMBER	978-1-61765-780-1
LIBRARY OF CONGRESS CONTROL NUMBER	2012948152

COVER PHOTOGRAPHY

PHOTOGRAPHER	Jim Wieland
SENIOR FOOD STYLIST	Kathryn Conrad
SET STYLIST	Melissa Franco

PICTURED ON FRONT COVER Citrus Cranberry Pie, page 249
PICTURED ON BACK COVER Top: Caramel Pecan Monkey Bread, page 34; Cookie Jar Gingersnaps, page 268; Center: Party Potatoes, page 92; Bottom: Mom's Peach Pie, page 248; Roasted Chicken with Rosemary, page 171
PICTURED ON SPINE Classic Beef Stew, page 139

Printed in China.
1 3 5 7 9 10 8 6 4 2

TABLE OF CONTENTS

SNACKS & BEVERAGES

Deviled Eggs with Bacon

These yummy deviled eggs went over so well at our summer cookouts, I started making them for holiday dinners as well. Everyone likes the addition of crumbled bacon.

—**BARBARA REID** MOUNDS, OKLAHOMA

YIELD: 2 DOZEN.

12 hard-cooked eggs
⅓ cup mayonnaise
3 bacon strips, cooked and crumbled
3 tablespoons finely chopped red onion
3 tablespoons sweet pickle relish
¼ teaspoon smoked paprika

1. Cut eggs in half lengthwise. Remove yolks; set whites aside. In a small bowl, mash yolks. Add the mayonnaise, bacon, onion and relish; mix well. Stuff into egg whites. Refrigerate until serving. Sprinkle with paprika.

Pepperoni Pizza Spread

Loaded with popular pizza ingredients, this cheesy concoction is wonderful on crackers of all kinds.

—**CONNIE MILINOVICH** CUDAHY, WISCONSIN

YIELD: 6 CUPS.

2 cups (8 ounces) shredded part-skim mozzarella cheese
2 cups (8 ounces) shredded cheddar cheese
1 cup mayonnaise
1 cup chopped pimiento-stuffed olives
1 cup chopped pepperoni
1 can (6 ounces) ripe olives, drained and chopped
1 can (4 ounces) mushroom stems and pieces, drained and chopped

½ cup chopped onion
½ cup chopped green pepper
Crackers, breadsticks and/or French bread

1. In a large bowl, combine the first nine ingredients. Transfer to an 11-in. x 7-in. baking dish. Bake, uncovered, at 350° for 25-30 minutes or until edges are bubbly and lightly browned. Serve with crackers, breadsticks and/or French bread.

Strawberry Citrus Slushies

Ordinary juice is just fine most of the time, but when you have guests in the morning, try something special. Pretty and refreshing, this festive drink will delight everyone at the table.

—**TASTE OF HOME TEST KITCHEN**

YIELD: 5 SERVINGS.

STRAWBERRY PUREE
½ cup frozen unsweetened sliced strawberries, thawed
2 tablespoons confectioners' sugar
2 tablespoons water

CITRUS SLUSH
¾ cup sugar
¾ cup water
¾ cup lemon juice
⅔ cup orange juice
4½ cups ice cubes

1. Place the strawberries, confectioners' sugar and water in a blender. Cover and process until blended; transfer to a small bowl. Cover and chill until serving.

2. In a small saucepan, bring sugar and water to a boil. Cook and stir until sugar is dissolved. Remove from the heat; cool to room temperature.

3. Just before serving, place the lemon juice, orange juice, ice cubes and sugar syrup in a blender. Cover and process until it reaches a slushy consistency. Divide strawberry puree among four chilled glasses. Top with citrus slush. Serve immediately.

Cheese Rye Appetizers

I enjoy serving this canape at family gatherings. The topping can be mixed ahead of time and refrigerated. Just before serving, spread cheese mixture on bread and bake. Even kids like it.

—JOYCE DYKSTRA LANSING, ILLINOIS

YIELD: 2½ DOZEN.

2 cups (8 ounces) shredded Swiss cheese
1 cup mayonnaise
1 can (4¼ ounces) chopped ripe olives
4 bacon strips, cooked and crumbled
¼ cup chopped green onions
1½ teaspoons minced fresh parsley or ½ teaspoon dried parsley flakes
30 slices snack rye bread

1. In a small bowl, combine first six ingredients. Spread a rounded tablespoonful over each slice of bread. Place on an ungreased baking sheet. Bake at 450° for 6-8 minutes or until the cheese is melted.

Blizzard Party Mix

This sweet-salty combo is sure to be popular. It's perfect for a party, munching at home or giving away as a gift.

—**KELLEY SCOTT** PARMA, OHIO

YIELD: 6 CUPS.

- 2 cups Corn Chex
- 2 cups miniature pretzels
- 1 cup dry roasted peanuts
- 20 caramels, coarsely chopped
- 1 package (10 to 12 ounces) white baking chips

1. In a large bowl, combine the first four ingredients. In a microwave, melt chips; stir until smooth. Pour over cereal mixture and toss to coat.

2. Immediately spread onto waxed paper-lined baking sheet; let stand until set, about 20 minutes.

3. Break into pieces. Store in an airtight container.

Artichoke Spinach Dip in a Bread Bowl

Baking the dip in the actual bread shell makes a very attractive dish, and it's so easy to clean up. Every time I serve my dip, people can't believe how healthy and veggie-filled it is.

—**ELLA HOMEL** CHICAGO, ILLINOIS

YIELD: 4 CUPS.

- 3 jars (7½ ounces each) marinated quartered artichoke hearts, drained and chopped
- 1 cup grated Parmesan cheese
- ¾ cup mayonnaise
- 3 green onions, sliced
- 1 can (4 ounces) chopped green chilies, drained
- 1 package (10 ounces) frozen chopped spinach, thawed and squeezed dry
- 1 cup (4 ounces) shredded Swiss cheese
- 1 round loaf (1 pound) rye or pumpernickel bread

1. In a large bowl, combine the first seven ingredients. Cut a thin slice off the top of bread. Hollow out the bottom half, leaving a ½-in. shell. Cut removed bread into 1-in. cubes.

2. Place cubes on an ungreased baking sheet. Broil 6 in. from the heat for 2-3 minutes or until golden, stirring once.

3. Place bread shell on an ungreased baking sheet. Spoon dip into bread shell. Bake, uncovered, at 350° for 20-25 minutes or until heated through. Serve with bread cubes.

Editor's Note: *Reduced-fat or fat-free mayonnaise is not recommended for this recipe. If any of the dip does not fit in bread shell, bake, uncovered, in a greased small baking dish until heated through.*

Roast Beef Spirals

This savory appetizer is simple, addictive and a nice change of pace from familiar tortilla pinwheels.

—**MARCIA ORLANDO** BOYERTOWN, PENNSYLVANIA

YIELD: 4 DOZEN.

- 2 packages (8 ounces each) cream cheese, softened
- 2 garlic cloves, minced
- 1 teaspoon ground ginger
- 6 thin slices deli roast beef

1. In a small bowl, beat the cream cheese, garlic and ginger until blended. Spread over beef slices; roll up.

2. Wrap each in plastic wrap; refrigerate for at least 2 hours or until firm. Cut into 1-in. slices.

Easy Elephant Ears

You'll love the classic cinnamon-sugar flavor of these crispy bite-size treats. Even more, you'll love that they call for just three ingredients and are so simple to assemble.

—**BOB ROSE** WAUKESHA, WISCONSIN

YIELD: ABOUT 2½ DOZEN.

- 1 package (17.3 ounces) frozen puff pastry, thawed
- ½ cup sugar
- 2 teaspoons ground cinnamon

1. On a lightly floured surface, roll one sheet of puff pastry into an 11-in. x 8-in. rectangle. Combine sugar and cinnamon; sprinkle half of mixture over pastry.

2. Working from the short sides, roll up dough jelly-roll style toward the center. With a sharp knife, cut roll into ½-in. slices. Place on parchment paper-lined baking sheets. Repeat with remaining pastry and sugar mixture.

3. Bake at 375° for 12-15 minutes or until crisp and golden brown. Remove from pans to wire racks.

Cinnamon-Raisin Granola

This granola recipe makes a great late-night snack. I like that it's nutritious, too.

—**TAMMY NEUBAUER** IDA GROVE, IOWA

YIELD: 12 SERVINGS.

- 4 cups old-fashioned oats
- 1 cup flaked coconut
- ¼ cup packed brown sugar
- ¼ cup canola oil
- ¼ cup honey
- 1 teaspoon ground cinnamon
- 1½ teaspoons vanilla extract
- 1 cup raisins

1. In a large bowl, combine oats and coconut; set aside. In a saucepan, combine the brown sugar, oil, honey and cinnamon; bring to a boil. Remove from the heat and stir in vanilla. Pour over oat mixture; stir to coat. Spread in a large shallow baking pan.

2. Bake at 350° for 15-20 minutes, stirring occasionally. Cool. Add raisins. Store in an airtight container.

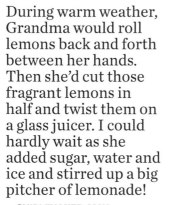

During warm weather, Grandma would roll lemons back and forth between her hands. Then she'd cut those fragrant lemons in half and twist them on a glass juicer. I could hardly wait as she added sugar, water and ice and stirred up a big pitcher of lemonade!

—**SHIRLEY MIER-MAY**
OLYMPIA, WASHINGTON

Tangy Meatballs

These hearty meatballs are a family favorite and a big hit wherever they go! In their delicious barbecue sauce, they're a perfect dish to pass along and also work well as hors d'oeuvres.

—**JANE BARTA** ST. THOMAS, NORTH DAKOTA

YIELD: 12 SERVINGS.

- 2 eggs
- 2 cups quick-cooking or rolled oats
- 1 can (12 ounces) evaporated milk
- 1 cup chopped onion
- 2 teaspoons salt
- ½ teaspoon pepper
- ½ teaspoon garlic powder
- 3 pounds lean ground beef (90% lean)

SAUCE
- 2 cups ketchup
- 1½ cups packed brown sugar
- ½ cup chopped onion
- 1 to 2 teaspoons liquid smoke
- ½ teaspoon garlic powder

1. In a large bowl, beat eggs. Add oats, milk, onion, salt, pepper and garlic powder. Add the ground beef; mix well. Shape into 1½-in. balls. Place meatballs on greased racks in shallow baking pans. Bake, uncovered, at 375° for 30 minutes; drain.

2. Place all of the meatballs in one of the pans. In a saucepan, bring all sauce ingredients to a boil. Pour over meatballs. Return to the oven and bake, uncovered, for 20 minutes or until meatballs are done.

3 large onions, chopped
2 large sweet red peppers, chopped
2 habanero peppers, seeded and finely chopped
1 cup white vinegar
1 can (6 ounces) tomato paste
3 teaspoons salt

1. Fill a Dutch oven two-thirds with water; bring to a boil. Score an X on the bottom of each tomato. Using a slotted spoon, place tomatoes, one at a time, in boiling water for 30-60 seconds. Remove tomatoes and immediately plunge in ice water. Discard peel; chop tomatoes.

2. In a stockpot, combine the remaining ingredients. Stir in tomatoes. Bring to a boil over medium-high heat. Reduce heat; simmer, uncovered, for 15-20 minutes or until desired thickness.

3. Carefully ladle hot mixture into hot 1-pint jars, leaving ½-in. headspace. Remove air bubbles; wipe rims and adjust lids. Process for 15 minutes in a boiling-water canner.

Editor's Note: *We recommend wearing disposable gloves when cutting hot peppers. Avoid touching your face. The processing time listed is for altitudes of 1,000 feet or less. For altitudes up to 3,000 feet, add 5 minutes; 6,000 feet, add 10 minutes; 8,000 feet, add 15 minutes; 10,000 feet, add 20 minutes.*

Cheesy Sun Crisps

These crisps have a great cheesy flavor perfect for snacking.
—MARY DETWEILER MIDDLEFIELD, OHIO

YIELD: 32 SERVINGS.

2 cups (8 ounces) shredded cheddar cheese
½ cup grated Parmesan cheese
½ cup butter, softened
3 tablespoons water
1 cup all-purpose flour
¼ teaspoon salt
1 cup quick-cooking oats
⅔ cup roasted salted sunflower kernels

1. In a bowl, combine cheddar and Parmesan cheeses, butter and water until well mixed. Combine flour and salt; add to cheese mixture. Stir in oats and sunflower kernels. Knead dough until it holds together. Shape into a 12-in. roll. Cover with plastic wrap; chill for 4 hours or overnight.

2. Let stand at room temperature for 10 minutes before cutting into ⅛-in. slices. Place on greased foil-lined baking sheets. Bake at 400° for 8 to 10 minutes or until edges are golden. Slide crackers and foil off baking sheets to wire racks to cool.

Chunky Salsa

My fresh-tasting salsa is wonderfully chunky. If you like it hotter, add more habanero peppers; if you prefer a mild salsa, add fewer.
—DANA HAYES CANTON, OHIO

YIELD: 7 PINT JARS.

5 pounds tomatoes
4 large green peppers, chopped

Spiced Pecans

These crunchy pecans are a family-favorite treat to munch on anytime and are very nice to serve when you have company.

—MIRIAM HERSCHBERGER HOLMESVILLE, OHIO

YIELD: 4 CUPS.

- 1 egg white
- 1 teaspoon cold water
- 4 cups (about 1 pound) pecan halves
- ½ cup sugar
- ½ teaspoon ground cinnamon
- ¼ teaspoon salt

1. In a small bowl, lightly beat egg white. Add water; beat until frothy but not stiff. Add pecans; stir until well coated. Combine the sugar, cinnamon and salt. Sprinkle over pecans; toss to coat.

2. Spread in a 15-in. x 10-in. x 1-in. greased baking pan. Bake at 250° for 1 hour, stirring occasionally.

Easy Hummus

Using sun-dried tomato salad dressing instead of tahini adds a new dimension of flavor to this nutritious predinner snack.

—JEANNETTE JEREMIAS KITCHENER, ONTARIO

YIELD: 1½ CUPS.

- 1 can (15 ounces) garbanzo beans or chickpeas, rinsed and drained
- ½ cup sun-dried tomato salad dressing
- 2 garlic cloves, minced
Baked pita chips or assorted fresh vegetables

1. In a food processor, combine the beans, salad dressing and garlic. Cover and process for 30 seconds or until smooth. Serve with chips.

Cozy Hot Chocolate

Steaming mugs of this smooth, chocolaty drink make a comforting treat anytime, especially during the colder months.

—MARIE HATTRUP SPARKS, NEVADA

YIELD: 2 SERVINGS.

- 2 tablespoons baking cocoa
- 2 tablespoons sugar
- ¼ cup water
- 2 cups 2% milk
- ½ teaspoon vanilla extract
- ¼ cup whipped cream
Ground cinnamon, optional

1. In a small saucepan, mix the cocoa and sugar; add water and stir until smooth. Bring to a boil, stirring constantly. Boil for 1 minute. Reduce heat; stir in milk and heat through.

2. Remove from the heat and stir in vanilla. Pour into 2 cups; top with whipped cream and sprinkle with cinnamon if desired.

Cozy Hot Mocha: Reduce milk to 1 cup. Add 1 cup strong brewed coffee. Proceed as directed.

Maple Hot Chocolate: Omit whipped cream and cinnamon. Add 1 tablespoon butter to cocoa mixture before bringing it to a boil. Add 3 large marshmallows with the milk and heat until marshmallows are melted. Add ½ teaspoon maple flavoring with the vanilla. Pour into mugs and top with additional marshmallows.

Banana Brunch Punch

A cold glass of refreshing punch really brightens a brunch or other gathering. It's nice to serve a beverage like this that's more special than plain juice. With bananas, orange juice and lemonade, it can add tropical flair to a winter day.

—MARY ANNE MCWHIRTER PEARLAND, TEXAS

YIELD: 60-70 SERVINGS (10 QUARTS).

- 6 medium ripe bananas
- 1 can (12 ounces) frozen orange juice concentrate, thawed
- ¾ cup thawed lemonade concentrate
- 3 cups warm water, divided
- 2 cups sugar, divided
- 1 can (46 ounces) pineapple juice, chilled
- 3 bottles (2 liters each) lemon-lime soda, chilled
Orange slices, optional

1. In a blender, cover and process the bananas, orange juice and lemonade until smooth. Remove half of the mixture and set aside. Add 1½ cups warm water and 1 cup sugar to blender; blend until smooth.

2. Place in a large freezer container. Repeat with remaining banana mixture, water and sugar; add to container. Cover and freeze until solid.

3. One hour before serving, remove punch base from freezer. Just before serving, place in a large punch bowl. Add pineapple juice and soda; stir until well blended. Garnish with orange slices if desired.

Mini Hamburgers

I guarantee these delicious little burgers will be the first snack cleared from your table. These hearty snacks are perfect for Sunday afternoon football games and teen parties. The mini buns are actually store-purchased pan dinner rolls available everywhere.

—JUDY LEWIS STERLING HEIGHTS, MICHIGAN

YIELD: 40 SERVINGS.

½ cup chopped onion
1 tablespoon butter
1 egg, lightly beaten
¼ teaspoon seasoned salt
¼ teaspoon ground sage
¼ teaspoon salt
⅛ teaspoon pepper
1 pound ground beef
40 mini rolls, split

8 ounces process American cheese slices, cut into 1½-inch squares, optional
40 dill pickle slices, optional

1. In a large skillet, saute onion in butter. Transfer to large bowl; add egg and seasonings. Crumble beef over mixture and mix well. Spread over bottom halves of the rolls; replace tops. Place on baking sheets; cover with foil.

2. Bake at 350° for 20 minutes or until a meat thermometer reads 160° and juices run clear. If desired, place a cheese square and pickle on each hamburger; replace tops and foil and return to the oven for 5 minutes.

BLT Bites

These quick hors d'oeuvres may be mini, but their bacon and tomato flavor is full size. I serve them at parties, brunches and picnics, and they're always a hit...even my kids love them.

—KELLIE REMMEN DETROIT LAKES, MINNESOTA

YIELD: 16-20 APPETIZER SERVINGS.

- 16 **to 20 cherry tomatoes**
- 1 **pound sliced bacon, cooked and crumbled**
- ½ **cup mayonnaise**
- ⅓ **cup chopped green onions**
- 3 **tablespoons grated Parmesan cheese**
- 2 **tablespoons snipped fresh parsley**

1. Cut a thin slice off of each tomato top. Scoop out and discard pulp. Invert the tomatoes on a paper towel to drain.

2. In a small bowl, combine the remaining ingredients. Spoon into tomatoes. Refrigerate for several hours.

Sweet Minglers

This snack mix is perfect for a late-night treat or a pick-me-up any time of the day. I sometimes take a batch to work, and it's always eaten up quickly. It's a slightly different cereal snack because of the chocolate and peanut butter.

—MARY OBEILIN SELINSGROVE, PENNSYLVANIA

YIELD: ABOUT 6 CUPS.

- 1 **cup (6 ounces) semisweet chocolate chips**
- ¼ **cup creamy peanut butter**
- 6 **cups Corn or Rice Chex**
- 1 **cup confectioners' sugar**

1. In a large microwave-safe bowl, melt chocolate chips on high for 30 seconds. Stir; microwave 30 seconds longer or until the chips are melted. Stir in peanut butter. Gently stir in cereal until well coated; set aside.

2. Place confectioners' sugar in a 2-gallon plastic storage bag. Add cereal mixture and shake until well coated. Store in an airtight container in the refrigerator.

Editor's Note: *This recipe was tested in a 1,100-watt microwave.*

Sweet Gingered Chicken Wings

I first enjoyed this delicious chicken dish many years ago when I attended a class on using honey in cooking. When I prepare this recipe for a party, it's one of the first dishes to disappear.

—DEBBIE DOUGAL ROSEVILLE, CALIFORNIA

YIELD: 2 DOZEN.

  1 **cup all-purpose flour**
  2 **teaspoons salt**
  2 **teaspoons paprika**
  ¼ **teaspoon pepper**
 24 **chicken wings**
SAUCE
  ¼ **cup honey**
  ¼ **cup thawed orange juice concentrate**
  ½ **teaspoon ground ginger**
Minced fresh parsley, optional

1. In a large resealable plastic bag, combine the flour, salt, paprika and pepper. Add chicken wings, a few at a time; seal bag and toss to coat.

2. Place wings on a large greased baking sheet. Bake at 350° for 30 minutes. Remove from the oven and drain.

3. Combine the honey, orange juice concentrate and ginger; brush generously over chicken wings. Reduce heat to 325°.

4. Bake for 30-40 minutes or until chicken juices run clear, basting occasionally with more sauce. Sprinkle with parsley before serving if desired.

Buttermilk Shakes

These creamy, rich shakes taste just like liquid cheesecake! It's so easy to whip up a couple of satisfying servings.

—GLORIA JARRETT LOVELAND, OHIO

YIELD: 2 SERVINGS.

  1 **pint vanilla ice cream**
  1 **cup buttermilk**
  1 **teaspoon grated lemon peel**
  ½ **teaspoon vanilla extract**
  1 **drop lemon extract**

1. Place all ingredients in a blender container. Cover and process on high until smooth. Pour into glasses. Refrigerate any leftovers.

> How my grandma managed to turn out the good food she did on a woodstove is beyond me. I guess, like everything else, practice makes perfect. Most everything she cooked was what she raised on the farm. For a special treat, she parched corn. She placed ears of corn in the oven and left them until they became crispy and brown. That corn tasted wonderful.
>
> **—SHELBY TEANEY** ROCKY MOUNT, MISSOURI

Fresh Vegetable Dip

This cool and creamy dip is a real family favorite for snacking, especially when paired with fresh garden vegetables. It's also perfect for parties.

—**DENISE GOEDEKEN**
PLATTE CENTER, NEBRASKA

YIELD: 8 SERVINGS.

- 1½ cups (12 ounces) sour cream
- ¾ cup mayonnaise
- 1 tablespoon dried minced onion
- 1 teaspoon dill weed
- 1 teaspoon dried parsley flakes
- 1 teaspoon garlic salt
- Dash Worcestershire sauce
- Fresh vegetables

1. In a small bowl, combine sour cream, mayonnaise, onion, dill, parsley, garlic salt and Worcestershire sauce. Chill for at least 1 hour. Serve with fresh vegetables.

Mini Apple Pizzas

My four children are now grown, but they still enjoy snacking on these sweet little pizzas...and so do my five grandchildren. We use fresh apples from the small orchard on our dairy farm, and they're so easy to make. The warm cinnamon flavor and light crust make them delicious!

—**HELEN LAMB** SEYMOUR, MISSOURI

YIELD: 10 SERVINGS.

- 1 tube refrigerator biscuits (about 10 biscuits)
- ½ cup packed brown sugar
- 2 tablespoons all-purpose flour
- 1 teaspoon ground cinnamon
- 2 medium tart apples, peeled and shredded
- 1 cup (4 ounces) shredded cheddar cheese, optional

1. Roll or pat biscuits into 3½-in. circles; place on a lightly greased baking sheet. In a bowl, combine brown sugar, flour and cinnamon. Add apples and mix well; spoon rounded tablespoonfuls onto biscuits.

2. Bake at 350° for 15-20 minutes or until edges begin to brown. If desired, sprinkle each pizza with 1 tablespoon cheese. Serve warm.

> I remember Grandma's moist spice cakes. She'd bake on Monday, and even several days later her cakes were still fresh. I think they stayed moist because she used real cream, butter and the juice of canned fruits.
>
> —**GEORGE BURKE** BONNERDALE, ARKANSAS

Aunt Frances' Lemonade

My sister and I spent a week each summer with our Aunt Frances, who always had this thirst-quenching lemonade in a stoneware crock in the refrigerator. It tastes so much like fresh cirtus and makes a refreshing drink after a hot day of running around.

—DEBBIE REINHART NEW CUMBERLAND, PENNSYLVANIA

YIELD: 12-16 SERVINGS (1 GALLON).

5 **lemons**
5 **limes**
5 **oranges**
3 **quarts water**
1½ **to 2 cups sugar**

1. Squeeze the juice from four of the lemons, limes and oranges; pour into a gallon container.

2. Thinly slice the remaining fruit and set aside for garnish. Add water and sugar; mix well. Store in the refrigerator. Serve over ice with fruit slices.

Puffed Wheat Balls

My Grandma Hunt is almost 90 years old and she still makes her famous Puffed Wheat Balls by the dozen whenever she comes over. Her 82 grandchildren and 168 great-grandchildren all love them.

—LUCILE PROCTOR PANGUITCH, UTAH

YIELD: 2½ TO 3 DOZEN.

12	**cups unsweetened puffed wheat cereal**
2	**cups packed brown sugar**
1	**cup light corn syrup**
2	**tablespoons butter**
1	**cup evaporated milk**
⅓	**cup sugar**

1. Place cereal in a large bowl; set aside.

2. In a heavy saucepan, bring brown sugar and corn syrup to a boil. Add butter. Combine evaporated milk and sugar; add to boiling mixture. Cook until candy thermometer reads 240° (soft-ball stage). Pour over cereal and stir to coat. Shape into 2-in. balls.

Editor's Note: *We recommend that you test your candy thermometer before each use by bringing water to a boil; the thermometer should read 212°. Adjust your recipe temperature up or down based on your test.*

Homemade Orange Refresher

Family and friends will thank you for serving this cool, tangy orange drink on warm evenings. It tastes a little like oranger sherbet.

—IOLA EGLE BELLA VISTA, ARKANSAS

YIELD: 4 SERVINGS.

- 1 **can (6 ounces) frozen orange juice concentrate, thawed**
- ⅓ **cup sugar**
- ¼ **cup instant nonfat dry milk powder**
- 2 **teaspoons vanilla extract**
- ¾ **cup cold water**
- 10 **to 12 ice cubes**

Orange slices and mint, optional

1. In a blender, combine the first five ingredients; cover and process on high speed until smooth. Add the ice cubes, a few at a time, blending until slushy. Serve in chilled glasses. Garnish with the orange slices and mint if desired. Serve immediately.

Editor's Note: *For a fancy glass edge, invert glass and dip into orange juice and then sugar; let dry 1 hour before filling glass.*

Tater-Dipped Veggies

Deep-fried vegetables are terrific, but it's not always convenient to prepare them for company. Here's a recipe that produces the same deliciously crisp results in the oven. Serve with your favorite ranch-style dressing as a dip.

—EARLEEN LILLEGARD PRESCOTT, ARIZONA

YIELD: 6-8 SERVINGS.

- 1 **cup instant potato flakes**
- ⅓ **cup grated Parmesan cheese**
- ½ **teaspoon celery salt**
- ¼ **teaspoon garlic powder**
- ¼ **cup butter, melted and cooled**
- 2 **eggs**
- 4 **to 5 cups raw bite-size vegetables (mushrooms, peppers, broccoli, cauliflower, zucchini and/or parboiled carrots)**

Prepared ranch salad dressing or dip, optional

1. In a small bowl, combine potato flakes, Parmesan cheese, celery salt, garlic powder and butter. In another bowl, beat eggs. Dip vegetables, one at a time, into egg, then into potato mixture; coat well.

2. Place on an ungreased baking sheet. Bake at 400° for 20-25 minutes. Serve with dressing or dip if desired.

> My grandma and grandpa lived on a farm in Arkansas. My cousins and I liked to visit them. We'd climb up into the loft of the barn where Grandpa stored his peanut crop. Then we'd sit in the middle of the peanut vines and eat raw peanuts until we were about to burst!
>
> **—JEAN HAYGOOD** MINDEN, LOUISIANA

Caramel Corn

For years I've taken this snack to our church retreat. I take it in two containers—one for each night—so it doesn't all disappear the first night. Other church members tell us that if we can't attend, we should just send the caramel corn.

—NANCY BREEN CANASTOTA, NEW YORK

YIELD: 48 SERVINGS
(1 CUP PER SERVING).

- 12 **quarts plain popped popcorn**
- 1 **pound peanuts**
- 2 **cups butter, cubed**
- 2 **pounds brown sugar**
- ½ **cup dark corn syrup**
- ½ **cup molasses**

1. Place popcorn in two large bowls. Stir ½ pound nuts into each bowl. In a Dutch oven, combine the remaining ingredients. Bring to a boil over medium heat; cook and stir for 5 minutes.

2. Pour half of syrup over each bowl of popcorn and stir to coat. Transfer coated popcorn into a large roasting pan. Bake at 250° for 1 hour. Remove from the oven and break apart while warm. Cool. Store in airtight containers.

Crisp and Nutty Mix

On those busy days when running on the track or running to class, this mixture of dried fruit, cereal, nuts and more is the ultimate combination for munching.

—MIKE TCHOU PEPPER PIKE, OHIO

YIELD: 2 QUARTS.

- 1 **cup Wheat Chex**
- 1 **cup Multi Grain Cheerios**
- 1 **cup reduced-fat Triscuits, broken**
- 1 **cup yogurt-covered pretzels**
- ½ **cup blanched almonds**
- ½ **cup dried apples, chopped**
- ½ **cup dried banana chips**
- ½ **cup dried blueberries**
- ½ **cup salted cashews**
- ½ **cup dark chocolate M&M's**
- ⅓ **cup finely shredded unsweetened coconut**
- ⅓ **cup sunflower kernels**
- ⅓ **cup salted pumpkin seeds or pepitas**

1. In a large bowl, combine all ingredients. Store in an airtight container.

Editor's Note: *Look for unsweetened coconut in the baking or health food section.*

Jungle Float

This fun float lets kids (and adults, too) be the masters of their own creations. What a tasty way to experiment!

—TASTE OF HOME TEST KITCHEN

YIELD: 1 SERVING.

- 3 **tablespoons chocolate syrup**
- 3 **scoops chocolate or vanilla ice cream**
- 1 **cup chilled club soda**

Optional toppings: sliced banana, honey-roasted peanuts, cut-up peanut butter cups, animal crackers, whipped cream and maraschino cherries

1. Place 2 tablespoons chocolate syrup in a tall glass. Add ice cream and remaining chocolate syrup. Top with club soda. Garnish with toppings of your choice. Serve immediately.

Mock Champagne

Everyone can join in the toast with this light and refreshing drink. It tastes just like Champagne, complete with bubbles!

—**PAM ION** GAITHERSBURG, MARYLAND

YIELD: 8 SERVINGS.

- 3 **cups white grape juice, divided**
- 2 **cans (12 ounces each) ginger ale, chilled**
- ½ **cup club soda, chilled**

Orange slices and sliced fresh strawberries

1. Pour 2 cups juice into ice cube trays; freeze until set.

2. Transfer ice cubes to a pitcher; add remaining juice. Slowly stir in ginger ale and club soda. Garnish with oranges and strawberries. Serve immediately.

Horseradish Cheese Spread

I got the recipe for this zippy, irresistible cheese spread from a friend. It makes a creamy, delicious evening snack.

—**CONNIE SIMON** DURAND, MICHIGAN

YIELD: 4 CUPS.

- 2 **pounds process American cheese, cubed**
- ½ **cup prepared horseradish**
- ⅓ **cup mayonnaise**
- 1 **teaspoon hot pepper sauce**

¼ **teaspoon garlic salt**
¼ **teaspoon Worcestershire sauce**

1. Melt cheese in the top of a double boiler over simmering water until smooth. Add remaining ingredients and stir until smooth. Spoon into containers and refrigerate. Serve with crackers or raw vegetables.

Olive-Stuffed Celery

My grandmother taught both me and my mom this appetizer recipe. We always serve it at Christmas and Thanksgiving. The stuffing is so yummy that even if you don't normally care for the ingredients on their own, you'll love the end result.

—**STACY POWELL** SANTA FE, TEXAS

YIELD: 2 DOZEN.

- 1 **dill pickle spear plus 1 teaspoon juice**
- 3 **sweet pickles plus 1 teaspoon juice**
- 6 **pitted ripe olives plus 1 teaspoon juice**
- 6 **pimiento-stuffed olives plus 1 teaspoon juice**
- 1 **package (8 ounces) cream cheese, softened**
- ⅓ **cup Miracle Whip**
- ¼ **teaspoon salt**
- ¼ **cup finely chopped pecans, toasted**
- 6 **celery ribs, cut into 2-inch pieces**

1. Finely chop the pickles and olives; set aside. In a small bowl, beat the cream cheese, Miracle Whip, juices and salt until blended. Stir in the pickles, olives and pecans.

2. Transfer to a small resealable plastic bag. Cut a small hole in the corner of the bag; pipe or stuff into celery sticks. Store in the refrigerator.

BREAKFAST & BRUNCH

Polynesian Parfaits

Pack one of these refreshing, tropical treats in a plastic container to take with you. They're great for lunch boxes, too.

—JANICE MITCHELL AURORA, COLORADO

YIELD: 4 SERVINGS.

- 2 cups (16 ounces) pineapple yogurt
- 1 tablespoon sugar
- ⅛ teaspoon ground nutmeg
- 1 cup granola without raisins
- 1 can (11 ounces) mandarin oranges, drained
- ¾ cup unsweetened pineapple tidbits
- ⅓ cup fresh raspberries

1. Combine the yogurt, sugar and nutmeg; spoon into four dishes. Top with granola and fruit.

Overnight Raisin French Toast

This recipe came from a colleague years ago and has become a potluck, brunch and family favorite! My staff used to ask for it every holiday. I love the convenience of great make-ahead recipes and this is one I turn to all the time. I like to sprinkle it with cinnamon and sugar when removing it from the oven.

—STEPHANIE WEAVER SLIGO, PENNSYLVANIA

YIELD: 12 SERVINGS.

- 1 loaf (1 pound) cinnamon-raisin bread, cubed
- 1 package (8 ounces) cream cheese, cubed
- 8 eggs, lightly beaten
- 1½ cups half-and-half cream
- ½ cup sugar
- ½ cup maple syrup
- 2 tablespoons vanilla extract
- 1 tablespoon ground cinnamon
- ⅛ teaspoon ground nutmeg

1. Place half of the bread cubes in a greased 13-in. x 9-in. baking dish. Top with cream cheese and remaining bread.

2. In a large bowl, whisk the remaining ingredients. Pour over top. Cover and refrigerate overnight.

3. Remove from the refrigerator 30 minutes before baking. Cover and bake at 350° for 30 minutes. Uncover; bake 15-20 minutes longer or until a knife inserted near the center comes out clean.

Cherry Syrup

My mom and grandma have been making this fruity syrup to serve with fluffy waffles and pancakes ever since I was a little girl. Now I make it for my sons, who love it as much as me!

—SANDRA HARRINGTON NIPOMO, CALIFORNIA

YIELD: 3 CUPS.

- 1 package (12 ounces) frozen pitted dark sweet cherries, thawed
- 1 cup water
- 2½ cups sugar
- 2 tablespoons butter
- ½ teaspoon almond extract

Dash ground cinnamon

1. Bring cherries and water to a boil in a small saucepan. Reduce heat; simmer, uncovered, for 20 minutes.

2. Add sugar and butter; cook and stir until sugar is dissolved. Remove from the heat; stir in extract and cinnamon. Cool; transfer to airtight containers. Store in the refrigerator for up to 2 weeks.

Elephant Ears

Reaction from those who eat them makes them worth the effort!

—SUZANNE MCKINLEY LYONS, GEORGIA

YIELD: 15 SERVINGS.

- 1 package (¼ ounce) active dry yeast
- 1 cup warm water (110° to 115°)
- 1 cup warm milk (110° to 115°)
- 3 tablespoons sugar
- 1 tablespoon salt
- 3 tablespoons shortening
- 4 to 4½ cups all-purpose flour

Oil for deep-fat frying

GLAZE

- ½ cup sugar
- 1 teaspoon ground cinnamon

1. Dissolve yeast in water. Add milk, sugar, salt, shortening and 2 cups flour; beat until smooth. Stir in enough remaining flour to form a soft dough.

2. On a floured surface, knead until smooth and elastic, 6-8 minutes. Place in a greased bowl; turn once to grease top. Cover and let rise in a warm place until doubled, about 1 hour.

3. Punch down and shape into 15 ovals, 5½ in. round by ⅛ in. thick. Heat 3-4 in. of oil to 375° in deep-fat fryer. Fry ovals, one at a time, 3 minutes per side or until golden brown. Drain. Mix sugar and cinnamon; sprinkle over warm pastries.

Peanut Butter & Jelly Waffles

Don't count out the grown-ups when it comes to craving these golden-brown waffles flavored with peanut butter and just a sprinkling of cinnamon. These are guaranteed crowd-pleasers!

—HELENA GEORGETTE MANN SACRAMENTO, CALIFORNIA

YIELD: 10 WAFFLES.

- 1¼ cups all-purpose flour
- 3 tablespoons sugar
- 1 tablespoon baking powder
- ¼ teaspoon baking soda
- ¼ teaspoon ground cinnamon
- 2 eggs, separated
- 1¼ cups milk
- ⅓ cup peanut butter
- 3 tablespoons butter, melted

Jelly of your choice

1. In a large bowl, combine the flour, sugar, baking powder, baking soda and cinnamon. In another bowl, whisk the egg yolks, milk, peanut butter and butter; stir mixture into dry ingredients just until moistened.

2. In a small bowl, beat egg whites until stiff peaks form; fold into batter. Bake in a preheated waffle iron according to manufacturer's directions until golden brown. Serve with jelly.

To freeze: Arrange waffles in a single layer on sheet pans. Freeze overnight or until frozen. Transfer to a resealable plastic freezer bag. Waffles may be frozen for up to 2 months.

To use frozen waffles: Reheat the waffles in a toaster. Serve with jelly.

Hash Brown Quiche

We love to have guests stay with us, and this is a great dish to serve for breakfast. To save time in the morning, I make the hash brown crust and chop the ham, cheese and peppers the night before.

—**JAN PETERS** CHANDLER, MINNESOTA

YIELD: 6 SERVINGS.

3 cups frozen loose-pack shredded hash browns, thawed
⅓ cup butter, melted
1 cup diced fully cooked ham
1 cup (4 ounces) shredded cheddar cheese
¼ cup diced green pepper
2 eggs
½ cup milk
½ teaspoon salt
¼ teaspoon pepper

1. Press hash browns between paper towel to remove excess moisture. Press onto the bottom and up the sides of an ungreased 9-in. pie plate. Drizzle with butter. Bake at 425° for 25 minutes.

2. Combine the ham, cheese and green pepper; spoon over crust. In a small bowl, beat eggs, milk, salt and pepper. Pour over all. Reduce heat to 350°; bake for 25-30 minutes or until a knife inserted near the center comes out clean. Let stand for 10 minutes before cutting.

Ambrosia Fruit

You can capture the flavor of fresh fruit any time of year with this recipe. With its combination of canned pineapple, fresh apples and flaky coconut, it's the perfect dish to rely on no matter the season.

—**MARSHA RANSOM** SOUTH HAVEN, MICHIGAN

YIELD: 6 SERVINGS.

1 can (20 ounces) pineapple tidbits
¼ cup packed brown sugar
½ teaspoon grated orange peel
2 medium oranges
2 medium unpeeled apples, diced
1 tablespoon flaked coconut

1. Drain pineapple, reserving ¼ cup juice in a saucepan, set pineapple aside. Add brown sugar and orange peel to the juice; heat until sugar dissolves. Peel and section oranges into a large bowl, reserving any juice; add the apples and pineapple. Add pineapple juice mixture and stir gently. Chill. Just before serving, sprinkle with coconut.

Feather-Light Muffins

Your family will likely gobble up these airy muffins; they won a blue ribbon at our county fair. Pretty as well as tasty, their hint of spice will brighten any breakfast.

—**SONJA BLOW** NIXA, MISSOURI

YIELD: 8-10 MUFFINS.

⅓ cup shortening
½ cup sugar
1 egg
1½ cups cake flour
1½ teaspoons baking powder
½ teaspoon salt
¼ teaspoon ground nutmeg
½ cup milk
TOPPING
½ cup sugar
1 teaspoon ground cinnamon
½ cup butter, melted

1. In a bowl, cream shortening, sugar and egg. Combine dry ingredients; add to creamed mixture alternately with milk. Fill greased muffin cups two-thirds full.

2. Bake at 325° for 20-25 minutes or until golden. Let cool for 3-4 minutes. Meanwhile, combine sugar and cinnamon in a small bowl. Roll warm muffins in melted butter, then in sugar mixture. Serve warm.

Cinnamon Coffee Cake

I love the excellent texture of this old-fashioned streusel-topped coffee cake. I find that everyone enjoys it. The pleasing vanilla flavor enriched by sour cream will remind you of breakfast at Grandma's!

—ELEANOR HARRIS CAPE CORAL, FLORIDA

YIELD: 16-20 SERVINGS.

1	**cup butter, softened**
2¾	**cups sugar, divided**
4	**eggs**
2	**teaspoons vanilla extract**
3	**cups all-purpose flour**
1	**teaspoon baking soda**
1	**teaspoon salt**
2	**cups (16 ounces) sour cream**
2	**tablespoons ground cinnamon**
½	**cup chopped walnuts**

1. In a large bowl, cream butter and 2 cups sugar until light and fluffy. Add eggs, one at a time, beating well after each addition. Beat in vanilla. Combine flour, baking soda and salt; add alternately with sour cream, beating just enough after each addition to keep batter smooth.

2. Spoon a third of batter into a greased 10-in. tube pan. Combine cinnamon, nuts and remaining sugar; sprinkle a third over batter in pan. Repeat layers two more times. Bake at 350° for 60-65 minutes or until a toothpick inserted near the center comes out clean. Cool for 15 minutes before removing from pan to a wire rack to cool completely.

Crunchy Granola

This crisp, lightly sweet mixture is great just eaten out of hand or as an ice cream topping. My husband and I grow wheat, barley and canola.

—LORNA JACOBSEN
ARROWWOOD, ALBERTA

YIELD: 10 CUPS.

- ⅔ **cup honey**
- ½ **cup canola oil**
- ⅓ **cup packed brown sugar**
- 2 **teaspoons vanilla extract**
- 4 **cups old-fashioned oats**
- 1 **cup sliced almonds**
- 1 **cup flaked coconut**
- ½ **cup sesame seeds**
- ½ **cup salted sunflower kernels**
- 2 **cups raisins**

1. In a small saucepan, combine the honey, oil and brown sugar; cook and stir over medium heat until sugar is dissolved. Remove from the heat; stir in vanilla.

2. In a bowl, combine oats, almonds, coconut, sesame seeds and sunflower kernels. Add honey mixture, stirring until evenly coated. Spread onto two ungreased baking pans.

3. Bake at 300° for 20 minutes, stirring frequently. Stir in the raisins. Bake 10 minutes longer. Cool, stirring occasionally. Store the granola in an airtight container.

Overnight Apple French Toast

My in-laws own and operate an orchard, so we have an abundance of fruit fresh from the trees. This dish includes fresh apples, apple jelly and applesauce all in one recipe. It's a warm, hearty breakfast for busy days.

—DEBRA BLAZER HEGINS, PENNSYLVANIA

YIELD: 9 SERVINGS.

- 1 **cup packed brown sugar**
- ½ **cup butter, cubed**
- 2 **tablespoons light corn syrup**
- 2 **large tart apples, peeled and sliced ¼ inch thick**
- 3 **eggs**
- 1 **cup milk**
- 1 **teaspoon vanilla extract**
- 9 **slices day-old French bread (¾ inch thick)**

SYRUP
- 1 **cup applesauce**
- 1 **jar (10 ounces) apple jelly**
- ½ **teaspoon ground cinnamon**
- ⅛ **teaspoon ground cloves**

1. In a small saucepan, cook brown sugar, butter and syrup until thick, about 5-7 minutes. Pour into an ungreased 13-in. x 9-in. baking pan; arrange apples on top.

2. In a large bowl, beat eggs, milk and vanilla. Soak bread slices in the egg mixture for 1 minute; place over apples. Cover and refrigerate overnight.

3. Remove from the refrigerator 30 minutes before baking. Bake, uncovered, at 350° for 35-40 minutes.

4. Meanwhile combine syrup ingredients in a medium saucepan; cook and stir until hot. Serve with French toast.

I loved spending the night at Grandmother's, as I knew her breakfast the next day was a special treat. Her cornmeal pancakes topped with homemade syrup were the best!

—**ROSE LEE** CITRA, FLORIDA

Hearty Egg Scramble

Scrambled eggs with meat and potatoes for breakfast is always a satisfying choice. Switch up the veggies to your family's liking.

—**MARSHA RANSOM** SOUTH HAVEN, MICHIGAN

YIELD: 6 SERVINGS.

- ⅓ cup chopped onion
- ¼ cup chopped green pepper
- ¼ cup butter, cubed
- 2 medium potatoes, peeled, cooked and cubed
- 1½ cups julienned fully cooked ham
- 6 eggs
- 2 tablespoons water

Dash pepper

1. In a large skillet, saute the onion and green pepper in butter until crisp-tender. Add the potatoes and ham; cook and stir for 5 minutes.

2. In a large bowl, whisk the eggs, water and pepper; pour over ham mixture. Cook and stir over medium heat until eggs are completely set.

Sheepherder's Breakfast

My sister-in-law always made this delicious breakfast dish when we were camping. Served with toast, juice and milk or coffee, it's a sure hit with the breakfast crowd! One-dish casseroles like this were a big help while I was raising my nine children. Now I've passed this recipe on to them.

—**PAULETTA BUSHNELL** ALBANY, OREGON

YIELD: 10 SERVINGS.

- 1 pound sliced bacon, diced
- 1 medium onion, chopped
- 32 ounces frozen shredded hash brown potatoes, thawed
- 10 eggs

Salt and pepper to taste

- 2 cups (8 ounces) shredded cheddar cheese, optional

Chopped fresh parsley

1. In a large skillet, cook bacon and onion over medium heat until bacon is crisp. Drain all but ½ cup of the drippings. Add hash browns to skillet; mix well.

2. Cook over medium heat for 10 minutes, turning when browned. Make 10 "wells" evenly spaced in hash browns. Place one egg in each well. Sprinkle with salt and pepper. Sprinkle with cheese if desired.

3. Cover and cook over low heat for about 10 minutes or until eggs are set. Garnish with parsley; serve immediately.

Sweet Broiled Grapefruit

I was never a fan of grapefruit until I had it broiled at a Florida restaurant—it was so tangy and delicious! I finally got the recipe and now make it often for husband Ron, myself and our children and grandchildren.

—**TERRY BRAY** AUBURNDALE, FLORIDA

YIELD: 2 SERVINGS.

- 1 large grapefruit
- 2 tablespoons butter, softened
- 2 tablespoons sugar
- ½ teaspoon ground cinnamon
- **Maraschino cherry for garnish, optional**

1. Cut each grapefruit in half. With a sharp knife, cut around the membrane in the center of each half and discard. Cut around each section to loosen fruit.

2. Place 1 tablespoon butter in the center of each half. Combine sugar and cinnamon; sprinkle over each. Place on a baking pan. Broil 4 in. from heat until butter is melted and sugar is bubbly. Garnish with a cherry if desired. Serve immediately.

Overnight Blueberry Coffee Cake

This cake, made with our own berries, stars at "Welcome to Washington" breakfasts I serve summer company.

—**MARIAN PLATT** SEQUIM, WASHINGTON

YIELD: 9 SERVINGS.

- 1 egg
- ½ cup plus 2 tablespoons sugar, divided
- 1¼ cups all-purpose flour
- 2 teaspoons baking powder
- ¾ teaspoon salt
- ⅓ cup milk
- 3 tablespoons butter, melted
- 1 cup fresh blueberries

1. In a bowl, beat egg and ½ cup sugar. Combine flour, baking powder and salt; add alternately with milk to sugar mixture, beating well after each addition. Stir in butter. Fold in berries.

2. Pour batter into greased 8-in. square baking pan; sprinkle with the remaining sugar. Cover and chill overnight. Remove from the refrigerator 30 minutes before baking. Bake at 350° for 30-35 minutes.

Stuffed Apricot French Toast

In our family, this special recipe is often served for our Christmas Day brunch. I was always looking for something unique to serve, and this rich, colorful dish made my dreams come true. It tastes so good!

—DEB LELAND THREE RIVERS, MICHIGAN

YIELD: 8 SERVINGS.

    1 package (8 ounces) cream cheese, softened
 1½ teaspoons vanilla extract, divided
    ½ cup finely chopped walnuts
    1 loaf (1½ pounds) French bread
    4 eggs
    1 cup heavy whipping cream
    ½ teaspoon ground nutmeg
    1 jar (12 ounces) apricot preserves
    ½ cup orange juice

1. In a bowl, beat cream cheese and 1 teaspoon vanilla until fluffy. Stir in nuts; set aside.

2. Cut bread into 1½-in. slices; cut a pocket in the top of each slice. Fill each pocket with about 2 tablespoons cream cheese mixture. In another bowl, beat eggs, cream, nutmeg and remaining vanilla. Dip both sides of bread into egg mixture, being careful not to squeeze out the filling.

3. Cook on a lightly greased griddle until lightly browned on both sides. Place on an ungreased baking sheet; bake at 325° for 15-20 minutes or until a knife inserted near the middle comes out clean.

4. Meanwhile, combine preserves and orange juice in a small saucepan; heat through. Drizzle over hot French toast.

Sausage Gravy

This savory sausage gravy is a specialty among country folks in our area. It's best served over fresh, hot biscuits. It makes a real "stick to the ribs" dish that we always enjoy, and carries a traditional flavor that can showcase locally produced sausage.

—MRS. J. N. STINE ROANOKE, VIRGINIA

YIELD: 4-6 SERVINGS.

    1 pound sage-flavored bulk pork
       sausage
    2 tablespoons finely chopped onion
    6 tablespoons all-purpose flour
    1 quart milk
    ½ teaspoon poultry seasoning
    ½ teaspoon ground nutmeg
    ¼ teaspoon salt
Dash Worcestershire sauce
Dash hot pepper sauce
Biscuits

1. Crumble sausage into a large saucepan; cook over medium-low heat. Add onion; cook and stir until transparent. Drain, discarding all but 2 tablespoons of drippings.

2. Stir in flour; cook over medium-low heat about 6 minutes or until mixture bubbles and turns golden. Stir in milk. Add seasonings; cook, stirring, until thickened.

3. To serve, slice biscuits and spoon gravy over halves.

Oh-So-Good Oatmeal

Add extra nutrition to fiber-rich oatmeal by adding chopped apple with the peel and chopped almonds. My two boys demand seconds! At 1½ cups per serving, it's hearty and filling; and at zero cholesterol, what's not to love?

—DANIELLE PEPA ELGIN, ILLINOIS

YIELD: 4 SERVINGS.

- 3 **cups water**
- 2 **medium tart apples, chopped**
- 1½ **cups old-fashioned oats**
- Dash salt
- ¼ **cup packed brown sugar**
- ½ **teaspoon ground cinnamon**
- ½ **teaspoon vanilla extract**
- ¼ **cup chopped almonds**
- Maple syrup and/or fat-free milk, optional

1. In a large saucepan over medium heat, bring water to a boil. Add the apples, oats and salt; cook and stir for 5 minutes.

2. Remove from the heat; stir in the brown sugar, cinnamon and vanilla. Cover and let stand for 2 minutes. Sprinkle each serving with almonds. Serve with maple syrup and/or milk if desired.

Grandma's Cinnamon Rolls

The secret to these rolls is the brown sugar sauce they're baked in. I serve them as dinner rolls as well as for a special breakfast treat.

—DELLA TALBERT HOWARD, COLORADO

YIELD: 15 ROLLS.

DOUGH
- 1 **package (¼ ounce) active dry yeast**
- ¼ **cup sugar, divided**
- 1 **cup warm water (110° to 115°), divided**
- 2 **tablespoons butter, softened**
- 1 **egg**
- 1 **teaspoon salt**
- 3¼ to 3¾ **cups all-purpose flour**

TOPPING
- 1 **cup heavy whipping cream**
- 1 **cup packed brown sugar**

FILLING
- ½ **cup sugar**
- 2 **teaspoons ground cinnamon**
- ½ **cup butter, softened**

1. In a large bowl, dissolve yeast and ½ teaspoon sugar in ¼ cup warm water. Let stand for 5 minutes. Add the remaining sugar and water, butter, egg, salt and 1½ cups of flour; beat until smooth. Stir in enough remaining flour to form a soft dough.

2. Turn onto a lightly floured surface; knead until smooth and elastic, about 6-8 minutes. Place in a greased bowl, turning once to grease top. Cover and let rise in a warm place until doubled, about 1 hour.

3. Meanwhile, combine topping ingredients; pour into a greased 13-in. x 9-in. baking pan; set aside. Combine filling ingredients; set aside.

4. Punch dough down and turn onto a lightly floured surface. Roll into a 15-in. x 8-in. rectangle; spread filling over dough. Roll up from the long side. Seal seam. Slice into 15 rolls; place with cut side down over topping. Cover and let rise until nearly doubled, about 30-45 minutes.

5. Bake at 375° for 25 minutes or until golden brown. Cool 3 minutes; invert pan onto a serving plate.

Cream Cheese Coffee Cake

These impressive loaves really sparkle on the buffet. You can't just eat one slice of this treat.
—MARY ANNE MCWHIRTER PEARLAND, TEXAS

YIELD: 20-24 SERVINGS.

1 cup (8 ounces) sour cream
½ cup sugar
½ cup butter, cubed
1 teaspoon salt
2 packages (¼ ounce each) active dry yeast
½ cup warm water (110° to 115°)
2 eggs, lightly beaten
4 cups all-purpose flour

FILLING
2 packages (8 ounces each) cream cheese, softened
¾ cup sugar
1 egg, lightly beaten
2 teaspoons vanilla extract
⅛ teaspoon salt

GLAZE
2½ cups confectioners' sugar
¼ cup milk
1 teaspoon vanilla extract
Toasted sliced almonds, optional

1. In a small saucepan, combine the sour cream, sugar, butter and salt. Cook over medium-low heat, stirring constantly, for 5-10 minutes or until well blended. Cool to room temperature.

2. In a large bowl, dissolve yeast in warm water. Add sour cream mixture and eggs. Beat until smooth. Gradually stir in flour to form a soft dough (dough will be very soft). Cover and refrigerate overnight.

3. Punch dough down. Turn dough onto a floured surface; knead 5-6 times. Divide into fourths. Roll each piece into a 12-in. x 8-in. rectangle. In a large bowl, combine the filling ingredients until well blended. Spread over each rectangle to within 1 in. of edges.

4. Roll up jelly-roll style, starting with a long side; pinch seams and ends to seal. Place seam side down on greased baking sheets. Cut six X's on top of loaves. Cover and let rise until nearly doubled, about 1 hour.

5. Bake at 375° for 20-25 minutes or until golden brown. Remove from pans to wire racks to cool. In a bowl, combine confectioners' sugar, milk and vanilla; drizzle over warm loaves. Sprinkle with almonds if desired. Store in the refrigerator.

Caramel-Pecan Monkey Bread

You can either cut this bread into generous slices, or let everyone pick off the gooey pieces themselves. No one can resist this tender, caramel-coated bread.

—TASTE OF HOME TEST KITCHEN

YIELD: 1 LOAF (20 SERVINGS).

 1 package (¼ ounce) active dry yeast
 ¼ cup water (110° to 115°)
 1¼ cups warm 2% milk (110° to 115°)
 ⅓ cup butter, melted
 ¼ cup sugar
 2 eggs
 1 teaspoon salt
 5 cups all-purpose flour
CARAMEL
 ⅔ cup packed brown sugar
 ¼ cup butter, cubed
 ¼ cup heavy whipping cream
ASSEMBLY
 ¾ cup chopped pecans
 1 cup sugar
 1 teaspoon ground cinnamon
 ½ cup butter, melted

1. In a large bowl, dissolve yeast in warm water. Add the milk, butter, sugar, eggs, salt and 3 cups flour. Beat on medium speed for 3 minutes. Stir in enough of the remaining flour to form a firm dough.

2. Turn onto a floured surface; knead until smooth and elastic, about 6-8 minutes. Place in a greased bowl, turning once to grease the top. Cover and refrigerate overnight.

3. For caramel, in a small saucepan, bring the brown sugar, butter and cream to a boil. Cook and stir for 3 minutes. Pour half into a greased 10-in. fluted tube pan; sprinkle with half of the pecans.

4. Punch dough down; shape into 40 balls (about 1¼-in. diameter). In a shallow bowl, combine sugar and cinnamon. Place melted butter in another bowl. Dip balls in butter, then roll in sugar mixture.

5. Place 20 balls in the tube pan; top with remaining caramel and pecans. Top with remaining balls. Cover and let rise until doubled, about 45 minutes.

6. Bake at 350° for 30-35 minutes or until golden brown. (Cover loosely with foil if top browns too quickly.) Cool for 10 minutes before inverting onto a serving plate. Serve warm.

Sweet Potato Muffins

This is my own recipe, and I make it often. My five grandchildren think these are a delicious treat.

—CHRISTINE JOHNSON RICETOWN, KENTUCKY

YIELD: 2 DOZEN.

 2 cups self-rising flour
 2 cups sugar
 2 teaspoons ground cinnamon
 1 egg
 2 cups cold mashed sweet potatoes (without added butter or milk)
 1 cup canola oil
GLAZE
 1 cup confectioners' sugar
 2 tablespoons plus 1½ teaspoons 2% milk
 1½ teaspoons butter, melted
 1 teaspoon vanilla extract
 ½ teaspoon ground cinnamon

1. In a small bowl, combine the flour, sugar and cinnamon. In another bowl, whisk the egg, sweet potatoes and oil. Stir into dry ingredients just until moistened.

2. Fill greased muffin cups two-thirds full. Bake at 375° for 15-18 minutes or until a toothpick comes out clean. Cool for 5 minutes before removing from pans to wire racks. In a small bowl, combine glaze ingredients; drizzle over warm muffins.

Editor's Note: *As a substitute for each cup of self-rising flour, place 1½ teaspoons baking powder and ½ teaspoon salt in a measuring cup. Add all-purpose flour to measure 1 cup.*

Banana Chip Pancakes

Perfect for weekends or a birthday-morning special, these fluffy pancakes can be flavor-adjusted to your heart's content! One of my kids eats the plain banana pancakes, another likes just chocolate chips added, and a third one goes for the works.

—CHRISTEEN PRZEPIOSKI NEWARK, CALIFORNIA

YIELD: 12 PANCAKES.

- 2 **cups biscuit/baking mix**
- 1 **egg**
- 1 **cup milk**
- 1 **cup mashed ripe bananas**
- ¾ **cup swirled milk chocolate and peanut butter chips**

Maple syrup and additional swirled milk chocolate and peanut butter chips, optional

1. Place biscuit mix in a large bowl. Combine the egg, milk and bananas; stir into biscuit mix just until moistened. Stir in chips.

2. Pour batter by ¼ cupfuls onto a greased hot griddle; turn when bubbles form on top. Cook until the second side is golden brown. Serve with syrup and additional chips if desired.

Sausage Hash

I created this recipe by trying to work with what I had in the refrigerator. Regular or spicy sausage can be used, and red potatoes make it more colorful.

—KARI CAVEN POST FALLS, IDAHO

YIELD: 2 SERVINGS.

- ½ **pound bulk pork sausage**
- 2½ **cups cubed cooked potatoes**
- 1 **cup thinly sliced sweet onion**
- 1 **cup sliced fresh mushrooms**
- 2 **tablespoons butter**
- ¼ **teaspoon salt**
- ¼ **teaspoon pepper**

1. In a large heavy skillet over medium heat, cook the sausage until no longer pink; drain and set aside.

2. In the same skillet, cook the potatoes, onion and mushrooms in butter until potatoes are lightly browned. Stir in the sausage, salt and pepper; heat through.

Apple Fritters

My kids love these fritters year-round, but I get even more requests in the fall when there are plenty of apples in season. I like to serve them as a special breakfast treat when they host friends for sleepovers.

—KATIE BEECHY SEYMOUR, MISSOURI

YIELD: 40 FRITTERS.

- 2½ **cups all-purpose flour**
- ½ **cup nonfat dry milk powder**
- ⅓ **cup sugar**
- 2 **teaspoons baking powder**
- 1 **teaspoon salt**
- 2 **eggs**
- 1 **cup water**
- 2 **cups chopped peeled apples**

Oil for deep-fat frying
Sugar

1. In a large bowl, combine first five ingredients. Whisk eggs and water; add to the dry ingredients just until moistened. Fold in apples.

2. In an electric skillet, heat oil to 375°. Drop batter by teaspoonfuls, a few at a time, in hot oil. Fry until golden brown, about 1½ minutes on each side. Drain on paper towels. Roll warm fritters in sugar. Serve warm.

Delicious Potato Doughnuts

I first tried these tasty treats at my sister's house and thought they were the best I've ever had. They're easy to make, and the fudge frosting tops them off well.

—PAT DAVIS BEULAH, MICHIGAN

YIELD: 4 DOZEN.

2	**cups hot mashed potatoes (with added milk and butter)**
2½	**cups sugar**
2	**cups buttermilk**
2	**eggs, lightly beaten**
2	**tablespoons butter, melted**
2	**teaspoons baking soda**
2	**teaspoons baking powder**
1	**teaspoon salt**
1	**teaspoon ground nutmeg**
6½	**to 7 cups all-purpose flour**

Oil for deep-fat frying

FAST FUDGE FROSTING

3¾	**cups confectioners' sugar**
½	**cup baking cocoa**
¼	**teaspoon salt**
⅓	**cup boiling water**
⅓	**cup butter, melted**
1	**teaspoon vanilla extract**

1. In a large bowl, combine the potatoes, sugar, buttermilk and eggs. Stir in the butter, baking soda, baking powder, salt, nutmeg and enough of the flour to form a soft dough. Turn onto a lightly floured surface; pat out to ¾-in. thickness. Cut with a 2½-in. floured doughnut cutter.

2. In an electric skillet, heat 1 in. of oil to 375°. Fry the doughnuts for 2 minutes on each side or until browned. Place on paper towels.

3. For frosting, combine the confectioners' sugar, cocoa and salt in a large bowl. Stir in the water, butter and vanilla. Dip tops of warm doughnuts in frosting.

Spinach Bacon Quiche

My versatile dish fits nicely into a menu for brunch or supper. The colorful pie slices easily.

—LOIS SUNDHEIM FAIRVIEW, MONTANA

YIELD: 6 SERVINGS.

- 4 eggs
- 2 cups milk
- 1¼ cups shredded cheddar cheese, divided
- ¼ cup finely chopped onion
- 4 bacon strips, cooked and crumbled
- ½ teaspoon salt
- ½ teaspoon ground mustard
- ¼ teaspoon paprika
- 1 package (10 ounces) frozen chopped spinach, cooked and drained
- 1 unbaked pastry shell (9 inches)

1. In a large bowl, beat eggs; whisk in milk, 1 cup cheese, onion, bacon, salt, mustard and paprika. Add spinach. Pour into pie shell. Sprinkle with the remaining cheese. Bake at 400° for 40 minutes or until a knife inserted halfway between the center and the edge comes out clean.

Jellied Biscuits

These biscuits are a pleasure to serve because they look so lovely with the colorful jelly.

—MARSHA RANSOM SOUTH HAVEN, MICHIGAN

YIELD: ABOUT 1 DOZEN.

- 2 cups all-purpose flour
- 4 teaspoons baking powder
- 2 teaspoons sugar
- ½ teaspoon salt
- ½ teaspoon cream of tartar
- ½ cup shortening
- ¾ cup milk
- ⅓ cup jelly

1. In a bowl, combine the flour, baking powder, sugar, salt and cream of tartar. Cut in shortening until the mixture resembles coarse crumbs. Add milk; stir quickly with a fork just until mixed. Drop by rounded tablespoonfuls onto a greased baking sheet. Make a deep thumbprint in tops; fill each with 1 teaspoon of jelly. Bake at 450° for 10-12 minutes or until browned.

Scrambled Egg Casserole

There's nothing nicer than a delicious egg dish you can prepare the night before so you're not "scrambling" when guests arrive. With satisfying ingredients like ham and a creamy cheese sauce, this dish is really special.

—MARY ANNE MCWHIRTER PEARLAND, TEXAS

YIELD: 6-8 SERVINGS.

- ½ cup butter, divided
- 2 tablespoons all-purpose flour
- ½ teaspoon salt
- ⅛ teaspoon pepper
- 2 cups milk
- 1 cup (4 ounces) shredded process American cheese
- 1 cup cubed fully cooked ham
- ¼ cup sliced green onions
- 12 eggs, beaten
- 1 jar (4 ounces) sliced mushrooms, drained
- 1½ cups soft bread crumbs
- Additional sliced green onions, optional

1. In a large saucepan, melt 2 tablespoons butter. Whisk in the flour, salt and pepper until smooth. Gradually stir in milk. Bring to a boil. Cook and stir for 2 minutes or until thickened and bubbly. Remove from the heat. Stir in cheese; set aside.

2. In a large skillet, saute the ham and onions in 3 tablespoons butter until onions are tender. Add eggs; cook and stir until eggs are almost set. Stir in mushrooms and cheese sauce. Transfer to a greased 11-in. x 7-in. baking dish. Melt remaining butter; toss with bread crumbs. Sprinkle over top. Cover and refrigerate for 2-3 hours or overnight.

3. Remove from the refrigerator 30 minutes before baking. Bake, uncovered, at 350° for 25-30 minutes or until top is golden brown. Sprinkle with additional green onions if desired.

Buttermilk Pecan Waffles

I like cooking with buttermilk. These nutty, golden waffles are my husband's favorite breakfast, so we enjoy them often. They're as easy to prepare as regular waffles, but their unique taste makes them exceptional.

—EDNA HOFFMAN HEBRON, INDIANA

YIELD: 7 WAFFLES
(ABOUT 8 INCHES EACH).

- 2 cups all-purpose flour
- 1 tablespoon baking powder
- 1 teaspoon baking soda
- ½ teaspoon salt
- 4 eggs
- 2 cups buttermilk
- ½ cup butter, melted
- 3 tablespoons chopped pecans

1. In a large bowl, combine the flour, baking powder, baking soda and salt; set aside.

2. In a large bowl, beat eggs until light. Add buttermilk; mix well. Add dry ingredients and beat until batter is smooth. Stir in butter.

3. Pour about ¾ cup batter onto a lightly greased preheated waffle iron. Sprinkle with a few pecans. Bake according to the manufacturer's directions until golden brown. Repeat until batter and pecans are gone.

Ham 'n' Cheese Pie

There's no need to make a crust for this delicious and easy quiche. My family and friends love it for dinner, brunch or any other time.

—IRIS POSEY ALBANY, GEORGIA

YIELD: 6-8 SERVINGS.

- 1 cup diced fully cooked ham
- ¾ cup shredded Swiss cheese
- 5 bacon strips, cooked and crumbled
- ¾ cup shredded sharp cheddar cheese
- 3 tablespoons chopped onion
- 3 tablespoons chopped green pepper
- 1 cup milk
- ¼ cup biscuit/baking mix
- 2 eggs
- ¼ teaspoon salt
- ⅛ teaspoon pepper

1. In a greased 10-in. quiche dish or pie plate, layer the ham, Swiss cheese, bacon, cheddar cheese, onion and green pepper. Place remaining ingredients in blender in the order given; cover and process for 35-40 seconds. Pour over the meat, cheese and vegetables; do not stir.

2. Bake, uncovered at 350° for 30-35 minutes or until set and lightly browned. Let stand for 5 minutes before cutting.

Quiche Lorraine

Ideal for a brunch or luncheon, this classic recipe highlights a delicious meal. Try serving a wedge with fresh fruit of the season and homemade muffins for a plate that will look as good as the food tastes!

—**MARCY CELLA** L'ANSE, MICHIGAN

YIELD: 6 SERVINGS.

CRUST
- 2 **cups sifted all-purpose flour**
- ½ **teaspoon salt**
- ¾ **cup butter-flavored shortening**
- 3 **to 4 tablespoons cold water**

FILLING
- 12 **bacon strips, cooked and crumbled**
- 4 **eggs**
- 2 **cups half-and-half cream**
- ¼ **teaspoon salt**
- ⅛ **teaspoon ground nutmeg**
- 1¼ **cups shredded Swiss cheese**

1. Combine flour and salt in a bowl. Cut in shortening with a pastry blender until mixture resembles coarse crumbs. Add water, a little at a time, until dough comes away from the bowl. Form dough into a ball. Divide in half.

2. On a lightly floured surface, roll half of dough to fit a 9-in. pie plate; transfer to pie plate. Trim and flute edges. Chill. Wrap remaining dough; chill or freeze for another use.

3. For filling, sprinkle crumbled bacon into the chilled pie crust. In a bowl, beat eggs, cream, salt and nutmeg. Stir in cheese. Pour into crust.

4. Bake at 425° for 15 minutes. Reduce temperature to 325°; continue to bake for 30 to 40 minutes or until a knife inserted near the center comes out clean. Let stand 10 minutes before cutting.

Zucchini Scramble

I like this recipe because I can change it through the year as other fresh vegetables become available. It also makes a tasty light lunch or dinner.

—**BETTY CLAYCOMB**
ALVERTON, PENNSYLVANIA

YIELD: 4-6 SERVINGS.

- 2 **to 3 small zucchini (about 1 pound), sliced**
- 1 **medium onion, chopped**
- 2 **tablespoons butter**

Salt and pepper to taste
- 6 **to 8 eggs, beaten**
- ½ **cup shredded cheddar cheese**

Tomato wedges, optional

1. In a skillet, sauté zucchini and onion in butter until tender. Season with salt and pepper. Add the eggs; cook and stir until set. Sprinkle with cheese. Remove from the heat; cover until cheese melts. Serve with tomato wedges if desired.

Apple-Topped Oatcakes

During the week we have quick breakfasts, but on Saturday I like to make something special. This is one of our favorite recipes because the oatcakes and apple topping are a tasty, wholesome combination. They also can be made ahead so a hungry family doesn't have to wait long.

—**LOIS HOFMEYER** AURORA, ILLINOIS

YIELD: 6-8 SERVINGS.

- 1½ cups hot milk
- ¾ cup old-fashioned oats
- 1 egg, lightly beaten
- 2 tablespoons canola oil
- 2 tablespoons molasses
- 1 cup all-purpose flour
- 1½ teaspoons baking powder
- ¾ teaspoon ground cinnamon
- ¼ teaspoon ground ginger
- ¼ teaspoon baking soda
- ¼ teaspoon salt
- 3 egg whites

LEMON APPLES
- 2 tablespoons butter
- 5 medium tart apples, peeled and sliced
- 1 tablespoon lemon juice
- 1 teaspoon grated lemon peel
- ½ cup sugar
- 1 tablespoon cornstarch
- ⅛ teaspoon ground nutmeg

1. In a large bowl, combine milk and oats; let stand for 5 minutes. Stir in the egg, oil and molasses. Combine dry ingredients; stir into oat mixture just until moistened. Beat egg whites until soft peaks form; fold gently into batter. Set aside.

2. Heat the butter in a skillet until foamy. Add the apples, lemon juice and peel; cook, uncovered, for 8-10 minutes, stirring occasionally.

3. Meanwhile, cook oatcakes. Pour batter by ¼ cupfuls onto a hot greased griddle. Cook until bubbles form; turn and cook until browned on other side.

4. For apples, combine sugar, cornstarch and nutmeg; add to apple mixture and cook 2 minutes longer or until tender. Serve warm over oatcakes.

Breakfast Biscuit Cups

The first time I made these biscuit cups, my husband and his assistant basketball coach came in as I was pulling them out of the oven. They loved them!

—**DEBRA CARLSON** COLUMBUS JUNCTION, IOWA

YIELD: 8 SERVINGS.

- ⅓ pound bulk pork sausage
- 1 tablespoon all-purpose flour
- ⅛ teaspoon salt
- ½ teaspoon pepper, divided
- ¾ cup plus 1 tablespoon 2% milk, divided
- ½ cup frozen cubed hash brown potatoes, thawed
- 1 tablespoon butter
- 2 eggs
- ⅛ teaspoon garlic salt
- 1 can (16.3 ounces) large refrigerated flaky biscuits
- ½ cup shredded Colby-Monterey Jack cheese

1. In a large skillet, cook sausage over medium heat until no longer pink; drain. Stir in the flour, salt and ¼ teaspoon pepper until blended; gradually add ¾ cup milk. Bring to a boil; cook and stir for 2 minutes or until thickened. Remove from the heat and set aside.

2. In another large skillet over medium heat, cook potatoes in butter until tender. Whisk the eggs, garlic salt and remaining milk and pepper; add to skillet. Cook and stir until almost set.

3. Press each biscuit onto the bottom and up the sides of eight ungreased muffin cups. Spoon the egg mixture, half of the cheese and sausage into cups; sprinkle with remaining cheese.

4. Bake at 375° for 18-22 minutes or until golden brown. Cool for 5 minutes before removing from pan. Serve immediately or allow to cool completely. Tightly wrap individual biscuit cups in foil; freeze for up to 3 months.

To use one frozen biscuit cup: Unwrap; microwave on high for 50-60 seconds or until heated through.

Pork Patties

These patties provide a taste bud wake-up call with a variety of herbs and spices. To save some time, combine all the seasonings the night before, then stir in the ground pork just before frying in the morning.

—LOIS FETTING NELSON, WISCONSIN

YIELD: 6 SERVINGS.

<pre>
 1 pound lean ground pork
 2 tablespoons water
1½ teaspoons salt
 ½ teaspoon dried sage
 ¼ teaspoon pepper
 ¼ teaspoon ground nutmeg
 ¼ teaspoon dried thyme
Pinch of ground ginger
</pre>

1. In a bowl, combine all of the ingredients; mix well. Shape into six patties. Fry in a skillet until meat is browned and cooked through.

Breakfast Bread Pudding

I assemble this dish the day before our grandchildren visit. It gives me more time for fun with them!

—ALMA ANDREWS LIVE OAK, FLORIDA

YIELD: 6-8 SERVINGS.

<pre>
12 slices white bread
 1 package (8 ounces) cream cheese, cubed
12 eggs
 2 cups milk
 ⅓ cup maple syrup
 ¼ teaspoon salt
</pre>

1. Remove and discard crusts from bread; cut bread into cubes. Toss lightly with cream cheese cubes; place in a greased 13-in. x 9-in. baking pan. In a large bowl, beat eggs. Add milk, syrup and salt; mix well. Pour over bread mixture. Cover and refrigerate 8 hours or overnight.

2. Remove from refrigerator 30 minutes before baking. Bake, uncovered, at 375° for 40-45 minutes or until a knife inserted near the center comes out clean. Let stand 5 minutes before cutting.

SOUPS

Creamy Vegetable Soup

I tasted this delicious soup in a restaurant, and when I couldn't persuade the chef to share the recipe, I began to experiment on my own. Finally, I came up with this blend, which is very close to what I'd tasted. The secret ingredient, I think, is sweet potatoes!

—**AUDREY NEMETH** MT. VERNON, MAINE

YIELD: 12-16 SERVINGS (4 QUARTS).

1	**large onion, chopped**
¼	**cup butter**
3	**medium sweet potatoes, peeled and chopped**
3	**medium zucchini, chopped**
1	**bunch broccoli, chopped**
2	**cartons (32 ounces each) chicken broth**
2	**medium potatoes, peeled and shredded**
1	**teaspoon celery seed**
1	**to 2 teaspoons ground cumin**
2	**teaspoons salt**
1	**teaspoon pepper**
2	**cups half-and-half cream**

1. In a stockpot, saute onion in butter until transparent but not browned. Add the sweet potatoes, zucchini and broccoli; saute lightly for 5 minutes or until crisp-tender. Stir in the broth; simmer for a few minutes. Add the potatoes and seasonings; cook 10 minutes longer or until the vegetables are tender. Stir in the cream and heat through.

Three-Bean Soup

When I was growing up, my mother prepared many different soups, each seasoned just right. She often made this colorful combination that's chock-full of harvest-fresh goodness. It showcases an appealing assortment of beans, potatoes, carrots and spinach.

—**VALERIE LEE** SNELLVILLE, GEORGIA

YIELD: 12 SERVINGS (ABOUT 3 QUARTS).

1	**medium onion, chopped**
1	**tablespoon canola oil**
3	**small potatoes, peeled and cubed**
2	**medium carrots, sliced**
3	**cans (14½ ounces each) chicken or vegetable broth**
3	**cups water**
2	**tablespoons dried parsley flakes**
2	**teaspoons dried basil**
1	**teaspoon dried oregano**
1	**garlic clove, minced**
½	**teaspoon pepper**
1	**can (15½ ounces) great northern beans, rinsed and drained**
1	**can (15 ounces) pinto beans, rinsed and drained**
1	**can (15 ounces) garbanzo beans or chickpeas, rinsed and drained**
3	**cups chopped fresh spinach**

1. In a Dutch oven, saute onion in oil. Add the next nine ingredients. Simmer, uncovered, until vegetables are tender. Add beans and spinach; heat through.

Italian-Style Onion Soup

On a chilly winter's day, warm everyone from head to toe with a steaming pot of this veggie soup. Each bowlful is crowned with a slice of cheesy tomato-topped toast.

—**DEBBIE MILLER** OLDSMAR, FLORIDA

YIELD: 5 SERVINGS.

- 2 **tablespoons butter**
- 1 **tablespoon olive oil**
- 6 **medium sweet onions, thinly sliced (about 6 cups)**
- ½ **teaspoon minced fresh rosemary**
- ¼ **teaspoon salt, divided**
- ¼ **teaspoon pepper, divided**
- 6 **cups beef broth**
- ½ **cup white wine or additional beef broth**
- 1 **tablespoon balsamic vinegar**
- 1 **cup grape tomatoes, quartered**
- ½ **cup fresh basil leaves, thinly sliced**
- ¼ **cup grated Parmesan cheese**
- ½ **teaspoon garlic powder**
- 5 **slices day-old French bread (1½ inches thick), toasted**
- 5 **slices part-skim mozzarella cheese**

1. In a Dutch oven over medium heat, melt butter with the oil. Add the onions, rosemary, ⅛ teaspoon salt and ⅛ teaspoon pepper. Cook for 30 minutes or until lightly browned, stirring occasionally. Add the broth, wine and vinegar; heat through.

2. Meanwhile, in a small bowl, combine the tomatoes, basil, Parmesan cheese, garlic powder and remaining salt and pepper. Spoon tomato mixture over bread slices; top with mozzarella. Place on a baking sheet.

3. Broil 3-4 in. from the heat for 2-3 minutes or until the cheese is melted. Ladle the soup into bowls; top with toast. Serve immediately.

Tomato Soup with Cheese Tortellini

Tortellini gives this garden-fresh tomato soup an extra stick-to-your-ribs bonus. It's a staple on my family's table.

—**SUSAN PECK** REPUBLIC, MISSOURI

YIELD: 8 SERVINGS (2 QUARTS).

- 1 **large onion, chopped**
- 1 **tablespoon butter**
- 2 **pounds plum tomatoes, seeded and quartered**
- 3 **cups reduced-sodium chicken broth or vegetable broth**
- 1 **can (8 ounces) tomato sauce**
- 1 **tablespoon minced fresh basil**
- ¼ **teaspoon salt**

Dash pepper
- 1 **cup dried cheese tortellini**
- ⅓ **cup shredded Parmesan cheese**

1. In a large saucepan, saute the onion in butter until tender. Add the tomatoes, broth, tomato sauce, basil, salt and pepper. Bring to a boil. Reduce heat; cover and simmer for 30 minutes. Cool slightly.

2. Cook tortellini according to package directions; drain well and set aside. In a blender, cover and process soup in batches until smooth. Return to the saucepan; add tortellini and heat through. Garnish with cheese.

Cheesy Chicken Chowder

I like to serve this hearty chowder with garlic bread and a salad. It's a wonderful dish to prepare when company drops in. The rich, mild flavor and tender chicken and vegetables appeal even to children and picky eaters.

—**HAZEL FRITCHIE** PALESTINE, ILLINOIS

YIELD: 6-8 SERVINGS.

- 3 **cups chicken broth**
- 2 **cups diced peeled potatoes**
- 1 **cup diced carrots**
- 1 **cup diced celery**
- ½ **cup diced onion**
- 1½ **teaspoons salt**
- ¼ **teaspoon pepper**
- ¼ **cup butter, cubed**
- ⅓ **cup all-purpose flour**
- 2 **cups milk**
- 2 **cups (about 8 ounces) shredded cheddar cheese**
- 2 **cups diced cooked chicken**

1. In a 4-quart saucepan, bring chicken broth to a boil. Reduce heat; add the potatoes, carrots, celery, onion, salt and pepper. Cover and simmer for 12-15 minutes or until vegetables are tender.

2. Meanwhile, melt butter in a medium saucepan; stir in flour until smooth. Gradually stir in the milk. Bring to a boil over medium heat; cook and stir for 2 minutes or until thickened. Reduce heat; add cheese, stirring until melted; add to broth along with chicken. Cook and stir until heated through.

Country Italian Soup

My mom gave me this recipe a few years back, and it quickly became a family favorite. It's so rustic and flavorful, and loaded with veggies.

—**KIM L'HOTE** VIOLA, WISCONSIN

YIELD: 10 SERVINGS (2½ QUARTS).

- 1 **pound bulk Italian sausage**
- 1 **large onion, sliced**
- 2 **celery ribs, sliced**
- 2 **garlic cloves, minced**
- 5 **cups water**
- 2 **medium potatoes, peeled and chopped**
- 1 **can (14½ ounces) diced tomatoes, undrained**
- 2 **medium carrots, sliced**
- 2 **teaspoons salt**
- 1 **teaspoon dried basil**
- 1 **teaspoon dried thyme**
- ½ **teaspoon dried oregano**
- ½ **teaspoon pepper**
- ¼ **teaspoon cayenne pepper, optional**
- 1 **bay leaf**
- 2 **medium zucchini, sliced**

1. In a Dutch oven, cook the sausage, onion and celery over medium heat until meat is no longer pink; drain. Add garlic; cook 1 minute longer.

2. Add the water, potatoes, tomatoes, carrots and seasonings. Bring to a boil. Reduce heat; cover and simmer for 15 minutes. Stir in the zucchini; simmer 8-10 minutes longer or until the vegetables are tender. Discard the bay leaf.

Chicken Soup with Spaetzle

Here's a new and interesting twist to traditional chicken soup. Everyone who samples it can't resist the delicious soup paired with homemade spaetzle.
—**ELAINE LANGE** GRAND RAPIDS, MICHIGAN

YIELD: 8-10 SERVINGS (2 ½ QUARTS).

- 1 broiler/fryer chicken (2 to 3 pounds), cut into pieces
- 2 tablespoons canola oil
- 8 cups chicken broth
- 2 bay leaves
- ½ teaspoon dried thyme
- ¼ teaspoon pepper
- 1 cup sliced carrots
- 1 cup sliced celery
- ¾ cup chopped onion
- 1 garlic clove, minced
- ⅓ cup medium pearl barley
- 2 cups sliced fresh mushrooms

SPAETZLE
- 1¼ cups all-purpose flour
- ⅛ teaspoon baking powder
- ⅛ teaspoon salt
- 1 egg, lightly beaten
- ¼ cup water
- ¼ cup 2% milk

1. In a stockpot or Dutch oven, brown chicken pieces in oil. Add the broth, bay leaves, thyme and pepper. Bring to a boil; skim foam. Reduce heat; cover and simmer for 45-60 minutes or until chicken is tender. Remove chicken and set aside until cool enough to handle. Remove meat from bones; discard bones and skin and cut chicken into bite size pieces. Cool broth and skim off fat.

2. Return chicken to broth along with the carrots, celery, onion, garlic and barley. Bring to a boil. Reduce heat; cover and simmer for 35 minutes. Add mushrooms and simmer 8-10 minutes longer. Discard bay leaves.

3. In a small bowl, combine first three spaetzle ingredients. Stir in the egg, water and milk; blend well. Drop batter by ½ teaspoonfuls into simmering soup. Cook for 10 minutes.

French Onion Soup

I adapted a basic recipe to copy the onion soup served at my favorite restaurant. No matter what my entree, I always ordered the soup. Now I can make it at home. It can be a meal in itself or an impressive beginning to a full-course meal.
—**BARBARA BRUNNER** STEELTON, PENNSYLVANIA

YIELD: 2 SERVINGS.

- 2 medium onions, chopped
- 1 teaspoon sugar
- 6 tablespoons butter, divided
- 1 tablespoon all-purpose flour
- ⅛ teaspoon pepper
- Dash ground nutmeg
- 2½ cups beef or vegetable broth
- 2 tablespoons grated Parmesan cheese
- 2 slices French bread (1 inch thick)
- 4 slices provolone cheese

1. In a large saucepan, saute onions and sugar in 3 tablespoons of butter until golden brown. Stir in the flour, pepper and nutmeg until blended. Gradually stir in the broth. Bring to a boil; cook and stir for 2 minutes. Reduce heat; cover and simmer for 30 minutes. Stir in Parmesan cheese.

2. Meanwhile, in a large skillet, melt remaining butter; add bread. Cook until golden brown on both sides. Ladle soup into two oven-proof bowls. Place a slice of cheese in each bowl; top with bread and remaining cheese. Bake at 375° for 10 minutes or until the cheese is bubbly.

Gnocchi Chicken Minestrone

My Italian heritage—and my mother, who was an excellent soup maker—inspired my take on minestrone. Using frozen gnocchi saves time and adds extra heartiness to this chunky soup.

—BARBARA ESTABROOK RHINELANDER, WISCONSIN

YIELD: 8 SERVINGS (2¾ QUARTS).

1¼ pounds chicken tenderloins, cut into ½-inch pieces
¾ teaspoon dried oregano
¼ teaspoon salt
¼ teaspoon pepper
2 tablespoons olive oil, divided
1 each small green, sweet red and yellow peppers, finely chopped
1 medium zucchini, finely chopped
1 cup chopped fresh baby portobello mushrooms
⅓ cup chopped red onion
⅓ cup chopped prosciutto or deli ham
4 garlic cloves, minced
2 cans (14½ ounces each) chicken broth
1 can (14½ ounces) Italian diced tomatoes, undrained

¾ cup canned white kidney or cannellini beans, rinsed and drained
½ cup frozen peas
3 tablespoons tomato paste
1 package (16 ounces) potato gnocchi
½ cup shredded Asiago cheese
8 fresh basil leaves, thinly sliced

1. Sprinkle chicken with oregano, salt and pepper. In a Dutch oven, saute chicken in 1 tablespoon oil until no longer pink. Remove from the pan and set aside.

2. In the same pan, cook the peppers, zucchini, mushrooms and onion in remaining oil until tender. Add prosciutto and garlic; cook 1 minute longer. Add the broth, tomatoes, beans, peas, tomato paste and chicken. Bring to a boil. Reduce heat; simmer, uncovered, for 20 minutes, stirring occasionally.

3. Meanwhile, cook gnocchi according to package directions. Drain; stir into the soup. Garnish each serving with cheese and basil.

Editor's Note: *Look for potato gnocchi in the pasta or frozen foods section.*

Italian Wedding Soup

You don't have to be Italian to love this easy-to-make soup! I find it's very popular when I serve it, and makes a great meal with hot crusty Italian bread or garlic bread.

—MARY SHEETZ CARMEL, INDIANA

YIELD: 9 SERVINGS (2¼ QUARTS).

- 2 eggs, lightly beaten
- ½ cup dry bread crumbs
- ¼ cup minced fresh parsley
- 2 tablespoons grated Parmesan cheese
- 1 tablespoon raisins, finely chopped
- 3 garlic cloves, minced
- ¼ teaspoon crushed red pepper flakes
- ½ pound lean ground beef (90% lean)
- ½ pound bulk spicy pork sausage
- 2 cartons (32 ounces each) reduced-sodium chicken broth
- ½ teaspoon pepper
- 1½ cups cubed rotisserie chicken
- ⅔ cup uncooked acini di pepe pasta
- ½ cup fresh baby spinach, cut into thin strips

Shredded Parmesan cheese, optional

1. In a large bowl, combine the first seven ingredients. Crumble beef and sausage over mixture and mix well. Shape into ½-in. balls.

2. In a Dutch oven, brown the meatballs in small batches; drain. Add the broth and pepper; bring to a boil. Reduce heat; simmer, uncovered, for 10 minutes. Stir in chicken and pasta; cook 5-7 minutes longer or until pasta is tender. Stir in the spinach; cook until wilted. Sprinkle with shredded Parmesan cheese if desired.

Knoephla Soup

While I was growing up, my mom would make this traditional German soup. It tasted so good on chilly fall days. Knoephla (pronounced nip-fla) Soup is still a warm and comforting meal.

—LORRAINE MEYERS WILLOW CITY, NORTH DAKOTA

YIELD: 8-10 SERVINGS (2½ QUARTS).

- ½ cup butter, cubed
- 3 medium potatoes, peeled and cubed
- 1 small onion, grated
- 3 cups milk
- 6 cups water
- 6 teaspoons chicken bouillon granules or 3 vegetable bouillon cubes

KNOEPHLA

- 1½ cups all-purpose flour
- 1 egg, beaten
- 5 to 6 tablespoons milk
- ½ teaspoon salt

Minced fresh parsley, optional

1. In a large skillet, melt butter; cook potatoes and onion for 20-25 minutes or until tender. Add the milk; heat through but do not boil. Set aside. In a Dutch oven, bring water and bouillon to a boil.

2. Combine the first four knoephla ingredients to form a stiff dough. Roll into a ½-in. rope; cut into ¼-in. pieces. Drop into boiling broth. Reduce heat; cover and simmer for 10 minutes. Add the potato mixture; heat through. Sprinkle with parsley if desired.

Rocky Ford Chili

When my brother and sister were in grade school in little Rocky Ford, Colorado, this satisfying chili dish was served in the school cafeteria. My siblings described it to my mother so she could duplicate it at home. We all enjoy preparing it for our own families now.

—**KAREN SIKORA** PHOENIX, ARIZONA

YIELD: 4 SERVINGS.

- 2 cans (14.3 ounces each) chili with beans
- 1 package (10 ounces) frozen corn
- 4 cups corn chips
- 1 cup shredded lettuce
- 1 cup (4 ounces) shredded Mexican cheese blend
- 1 can (2¼ ounces) sliced ripe olives, drained
- ¼ cup sour cream
- ¼ cup salsa

1. In a large microwave-safe bowl, cook chili and corn on high for 2-4 minutes or until heated through. Place corn chips in four large soup bowls; top with chili mixture, lettuce, cheese, olives, sour cream and salsa.

Editor's Note: *This recipe was tested in a 1,100-watt microwave.*

Mushroom Barley Soup

Here's a hearty soup that is delicious and full of vegetables. I like to eat it with warm bread smothered in butter.

—**CONSTANCE SULLIVAN** OCEANSIDE, CALIFORNIA

YIELD: 12 SERVINGS (3 QUARTS).

- ½ cup dried great northern beans
- 1 pound sliced fresh mushrooms
- 2 cups chopped onions
- 1 medium leek (white portion only), sliced
- 2 tablespoons butter
- 1 to 2 garlic cloves, minced
- 2 cartons (32 ounces each) chicken broth
- 3 celery ribs, thinly sliced
- 3 large carrots, chopped
- ½ cup medium pearl barley
- 2 teaspoons dried parsley flakes
- 1½ teaspoons salt
- 1 bay leaf
- ¼ teaspoon white pepper

1. Soak beans according to package directions. In a large skillet, cook the mushrooms, onions and leek in butter over medium heat until tender. Add garlic; cook 1 minute longer.

2. Transfer to a 6-quart slow cooker. Drain and rinse beans, discarding liquid. Add the beans, broth, celery, carrots, barley, parsley, salt, bay leaf and pepper. Cover and cook on low for 5-6 hours or until beans and vegetables are tender. Discard bay leaf.

Mulligatawny Soup

I learned to cook and bake from my mom and grandmother, and always try to use fresh fruits, vegetables and herbs. This is a delicious and satisfying soup, which I make with leftover chicken, turkey and sometimes beef, pork or lamb. My family enjoys this on a crisp fall or winter day.

—MARY ANN MARINO WEST PITTSBURGH, PENNSYLVANIA

YIELD: 8 SERVINGS (2 QUARTS).

1 carton (32 ounces) chicken broth
1 can (14½ ounces) diced tomatoes
2 cups cubed cooked chicken
1 large tart apple, peeled and chopped
¼ cup finely chopped onion
¼ cup chopped carrot
¼ cup chopped green pepper
1 tablespoon minced fresh parsley
2 teaspoons lemon juice
1 teaspoon salt
1 teaspoon curry powder
½ teaspoon sugar
¼ teaspoon pepper
2 whole cloves

1. In a 3- or 4-qt. slow cooker, combine all ingredients. Cover and cook on low for 6-8 hours or until vegetables are tender. Discard cloves.

Hearty Minestrone

Packed with sausage and veggies, this soup is not only nutritious, it's also a great way to put your garden bounty to use.

—DONNA SMITH FAIRPORT, NEW YORK

YIELD: 9 SERVINGS.

- 1 **pound bulk Italian sausage**
- 2 **cups sliced celery**
- 1 **cup chopped onion**
- 6 **cups chopped zucchini**
- 1 **can (28 ounces) diced tomatoes, undrained**
- 1½ **cups chopped green pepper**
- 1½ **teaspoons Italian seasoning**
- 1½ **teaspoons salt**
- 1 **teaspoon dried oregano**
- 1 **teaspoon sugar**
- ½ **teaspoon dried basil**
- ¼ **teaspoon garlic powder**

1. In a large saucepan, cook the sausage until no longer pink. Remove with a slotted spoon to paper towel to drain, reserving 1 tablespoon of drippings. Saute celery and onion in drippings for 5 minutes. Add sausage and remaining ingredients; bring to a boil. Reduce heat; cover and simmer for 20-30 minutes or until the vegetables are tender.

Spinach Garlic Soup

During the years I owned and operated a deli, this was one of the most popular soups I served.

—MARILYN PARADIS WOODBURN, OREGON

YIELD: 4-6 SERVINGS.

- 1 **package (10 ounces) fresh spinach, trimmed and coarsely chopped**
- 4 **cups chicken broth**
- ½ **cup shredded carrots**
- ½ **cup chopped onion**
- 8 **garlic cloves, minced**

- ⅓ **cup butter, cubed**
- ¼ **cup all-purpose flour**
- ¾ **cup heavy whipping cream**
- ¼ **cup milk**
- ½ **teaspoon pepper**
- ⅛ **teaspoon ground nutmeg**

1. In a 5-qt. Dutch oven, bring spinach, broth and carrots to a boil. Reduce heat; simmer for 5 minutes, stirring occasionally. Remove from heat; cool to lukewarm.

2. Meanwhile, in a large skillet, saute the onion and garlic in butter until onion is soft, about 5-10 minutes. Add flour; cook and stir over low heat for 3-5 minutes. Add to spinach mixture. Cool slightly.

3. Puree in small batches in a blender until finely chopped. Place in a large saucepan. Add the cream, milk, pepper and nutmeg; heat through but do not boil.

Creamy Carrot Soup

When I set this creamy soup on the table, people are amazed by the bright carrot color and are hooked by the deliciously different flavor. A hint of rosemary adds a nice spark to a slightly sweet soup.

—GRACE YASKOVIC LAKE HIAWATHA, NEW JERSEY

YIELD: 10 SERVINGS (2½ QUARTS).

- 1 **cup chopped onion**
- ¼ **cup butter, cubed**
- 4½ **cups sliced fresh carrots**
- 1 **large potato, peeled and cubed**
- 2 **cans (14½ ounces each) chicken broth**
- 1 **teaspoon ground ginger**
- 2 **cups heavy whipping cream**
- 1 **teaspoon dried rosemary, crushed**
- ½ **teaspoon salt**
- ⅛ **teaspoon pepper**

1. In a Dutch oven, saute onion in butter until tender. Add the carrots, potato, broth and ginger. Cover and cook over medium heat for 30 minutes or until the vegetables are tender. Cool for 15 minutes.

2. In a blender, cover and puree the vegetable mixture in batches. Return all to the pan; stir in the cream, rosemary, salt and pepper. Cook over low heat until heated through.

Five-Bean Soup

One of my family's favorite soups, this tasty recipe was one I discovered years ago. Served with a salad and bread or rolls, it makes a savory supper.

—LYNNE DODD MENTOR, OHIO

YIELD: 14 SERVINGS (3½ QUARTS).

> 5 packages (16 ounces each) dried beans: lima, great northern, kidney, pinto and split peas (enough for four batches of soup)

For one batch of soup

> 3 tablespoons minced chives
> 1 teaspoon dried savory
> 1 teaspoon salt, optional
> ½ teaspoon ground cumin
> ½ teaspoon pepper
> 1 bay leaf
> 3 beef bouillon cubes
> 2½ quarts water
> 1 can (14½ ounces) stewed tomatoes

1. Combine beans; divide into four even batches, about 3¾ cups each.

To make one batch of soup:

2. Wash one batch of beans. Place in a stockpot; add enough water to cover. Bring to a boil; cook for 3-4 minutes. Remove from the heat; cover and let stand 1 hour.

3. Tie spices in a cheesecloth bag. Drain and rinse beans. Return to stockpot; add bouillon, spices and water. Bring to a boil. Reduce heat; cover and simmer 1½ hours or until beans are tender, stirring occasionally. Discard spice bag. Add tomatoes and heat through.

Mushroom and Potato Chowder

My daughter shared this delightful recipe with me. Its rich broth, big mushroom taste and medley of vegetables make this chowder a little different from ordinary mushroom soup.

—ROMAINE WETZEL RONKS, PENNSYLVANIA

YIELD: 4-6 SERVINGS.

> ½ cup chopped onion
> ¼ cup butter, cubed
> 2 tablespoons all-purpose flour
> 1 teaspoon salt
> ½ teaspoon pepper
> 3 cups water
> 1 pound fresh mushrooms, sliced
> 1 cup chopped celery
> 1 cup diced peeled potatoes
> ½ cup chopped carrots
> 1 cup half-and-half cream
> ¼ cup grated Parmesan cheese

1. In a stockpot, saute onion in butter until tender. Add the flour, salt and pepper; stir to make a smooth paste. Gradually add the water, stirring constantly. Bring to a boil; cook and stir for 1 minute. Add the mushrooms, celery, potatoes and carrots. Reduce heat; cover and simmer for 30 minutes or until vegetables are tender. Add cream and Parmesan cheese; heat through (do not boil).

Old-World Tomato Soup

This hearty soup has been in our family for four generations, and I've never seen another recipe like it. Each spoonful brings back memories.

—LINDA PANDOLFO
EAST HADDAM, CONNECTICUT

YIELD: 16-20 SERVINGS.

- 3 quarts water
- 4 bone-in beef short ribs (2 pounds)
- 2 to 3 meaty soup bones, beef shanks or short ribs (about 2 pounds)
- 1 can (28 ounces) diced tomatoes, undrained
- 3 celery ribs, halved
- 1 large onion, quartered
- ½ cup chopped fresh parsley, divided
- 1 tablespoon salt
- 1½ teaspoons pepper
- 4 carrots, cut into 1-inch pieces
- 2 parsnips, peeled and quartered
- 2 cups (16 ounces) sour cream
- ½ cup all-purpose flour
- ½ teaspoon ground nutmeg, optional
- 1 package (8 ounces) egg noodles, cooked and drained

1. In a stockpot, combine water, ribs, soup bones, tomatoes, celery, onion, ¼ cup parsley, salt and pepper. Cover and simmer for 2 hours. Add carrots and parsnips; cover and simmer for 1 hour or until the meat and vegetables are tender.

2. With a slotted spoon, remove meat, bones and vegetables. Strain broth and skim off fat; return all but 1 cup broth to stockpot. Set reserved broth aside. Remove meat from the bones; dice and return to stockpot. Discard celery and onion. Cut parsnips, carrots and tomatoes into ½-in. pieces and return to pot. Add the remaining parsley.

3. In a large bowl, combine the sour cream, flour, nutmeg if desired and reserved broth; stir into soup. Add noodles. Cook and stir until thickened and heated through (do not boil).

Potato Cheese Soup

My father was Swiss, so cheese has been a basic food in our family as long as I can remember. With its big cheese taste, you'll want to prepare this soup often. A steaming bowl plus a salad and a slice of bread makes a wonderful light meal.

—CAROL SMITH NEW BERLIN, WISCONSIN

YIELD: 6 SERVINGS (1½ QUARTS).

- 3 medium potatoes (about 1 pound), peeled and quartered
- 1 small onion, finely chopped
- 1 cup water
- 1 teaspoon salt
- 3 cups milk
- 3 tablespoons butter, melted
- 2 tablespoons all-purpose flour
- 2 tablespoons minced fresh parsley
- ⅛ teaspoon white pepper
- 1 cup (4 ounces) shredded Swiss cheese

1. In a large saucepan, bring potatoes, onion, water and salt to a boil. Reduce heat; cover and simmer until potatoes are tender. Do not drain; mash slightly. Stir in milk.

2. Meanwhile, in a small bowl, blend the butter, flour, parsley and pepper; stir into the potato mixture. Bring to a boil over medium heat. Cook and stir for 2 minutes. Remove from the heat; add cheese and stir until almost melted.

Grandma almost always had a pot of soup simmering on the woodstove. When my brother and I came in from sledding, we'd get a bowl, and sometimes Grandma would ask all the neighbor kids in for soup. Hoboes would stop by for a bowl, too. Grandma fed her soup to anyone who was hungry, any time, day or night.

—JOE SNYDER BELLEVUE, WASHINGTON

Grandma's Chicken 'n' Dumpling Soup

I've enjoyed making this rich soup for over 40 years. Every time I serve it, I remember my grandma, who was very special to me and was known as a great cook.

—PAULETTE BALDA PROPHETSTOWN, ILLINOIS

YIELD: 12 SERVINGS (3 QUARTS).

- 1 broiler/fryer chicken (3½ to 4 pounds), cut up
- 2¼ quarts cold water
- 5 chicken bouillon cubes
- 6 whole peppercorns
- 3 whole cloves
- 1 can (10¾ ounces) condensed cream of chicken soup, undiluted
- 1 can (10¾ ounces) condensed cream of mushroom soup, undiluted
- 1½ cups chopped carrots
- 1 cup fresh or frozen peas
- 1 cup chopped celery
- 1 cup chopped peeled potatoes
- ¼ cup chopped onion
- 1½ teaspoons seasoned salt
- ¼ teaspoon pepper
- 1 bay leaf

DUMPLINGS
- 2 cups all-purpose flour
- 4 teaspoons baking powder
- 1 teaspoon salt
- ¼ teaspoon pepper
- 1 egg, beaten
- 2 tablespoons butter, melted
- ¾ to 1 cup milk

Snipped fresh parsley, optional

1. Place the chicken, water, bouillon, peppercorns and cloves in a stockpot. Cover and bring to a boil; skim foam. Reduce heat; cover and simmer 45-60 minutes or until chicken is tender. Strain broth; return to stockpot.

2. Remove chicken and set aside until cool enough to handle. Remove meat from bones; discard bones and skin and cut chicken into chunks. Cool broth and skim off fat.

3. Return chicken to stockpot with soups, vegetables and seasonings; bring to a boil. Reduce heat; cover and simmer for 1 hour. Uncover; increase heat to a gently boil. Discard bay leaf.

4. For dumplings, combine dry ingredients in a medium bowl. Stir in egg, butter and enough milk to make a moist, stiff batter. Drop by teaspoonfuls into soup. Cover and cook without lifting the lid for 18-20 minutes. Sprinkle with parsley if desired.

Vegetable Beef Soup

When we come in from playing in the snow, I serve this warming, economical soup. Because the recipe makes a lot, you'll have plenty to freeze or to share with friends.

—NANCY SODERSTROM
ROSEVILLE, MINNESOTA

YIELD: 18-20 SERVINGS (6 QUARTS).

- 1 boneless beef chuck roast (2½ to 3 pounds)
- 4 quarts water
- 1 cup medium pearl barley
- 1½ cups chopped onion
- 1½ cups chopped celery
- 1 teaspoon salt
- 1 teaspoon pepper
- 1 can (28 ounces) diced tomatoes, undrained
- 1½ cups chopped carrots
- 1 package (16 ounces) frozen mixed vegetables
- ¼ cup minced fresh parsley
- ½ teaspoon dried basil
- ¼ teaspoon dried thyme
- ¼ teaspoon garlic salt

1. Place roast in a large Dutch oven. Add the water, barley, onion, celery, salt and pepper; bring to a boil. Reduce heat; cover and simmer for 1¼ hours or until meat is tender.

2. Remove the meat; cool. Cut into bite-size pieces. Skim fat from broth. Add beef and remaining ingredients; bring to a boil. Reduce heat; cover and simmer for 45 minutes or until the vegetables are tender.

Scotch Broth

Early in winter, I make up big pots of this hearty soup to freeze in plastic containers. Then I can bring out one or two containers at a time. I heat the frozen soup in a saucepan on low all morning. By lunchtime, it's hot and ready to serve!

—**ANN MAIN** MOOREFIELD, ONTARIO

YIELD: 6-8 SERVINGS (2 QUARTS).

    2 pounds meaty beef soup bones
       (beef shanks or short ribs)
    8 cups water
    6 whole peppercorns
 1½ teaspoons salt
    1 cup chopped carrots
    1 cup chopped turnips
    1 cup chopped celery
 ½ cup chopped onion
 ¼ cup medium pearl barley

1. In a stockpot, combine soup bones, water, peppercorns and salt. Cover and simmer for 2½ hours or until the meat comes easily off the bones.

2. Remove bones. Strain broth; cool and chill. Skim off fat. Remove meat from bones; dice. Place the meat, broth and remaining ingredients in stockpot. Bring to a boil. Reduce heat; cover and simmer about 1 hour or until vegetables and barley are tender.

Creamy Squash Soup

I make my smooth, full-flavored soup featuring whatever winter squash is available.

—**GAYLE LEWIS** YUCAIPA, CALIFORNIA

YIELD: 6-8 SERVINGS.

    3 bacon strips
    1 cup finely chopped onion
    2 garlic cloves, minced
    2 cups mashed cooked winter squash
    2 tablespoons all-purpose flour
    1 can (12 ounces) evaporated milk, divided
    3 cups chicken broth
 ½ teaspoon curry powder
 ½ teaspoon salt
 ¼ teaspoon pepper
 ⅛ teaspoon ground nutmeg
Sour cream, optional

1. In a large saucepan or Dutch oven, cook bacon over medium heat until crisp. Remove to paper towels; crumble and set aside. Drain all but 1 tablespoon drippings; saute onion and garlic in drippings until tender.

2. In a blender or food processor, puree squash, flour, ⅓ cup milk and onion mixture; add to pan. Add the broth, curry powder, salt, pepper, nutmeg and remaining milk; bring to a boil over medium heat. Boil for 2 minutes. Top servings with a dollop of sour cream if desired. Sprinkle with bacon.

Beef Noodle Soup

This takes minutes—but tastes like it simmered all day.

—**MARGERY BRYAN** MOSES LAKE, WASHINGTON

YIELD: 6-8 SERVINGS (2 QUARTS).

    1 pound ground beef
 ½ cup chopped onion
    2 cans (14½ ounces each) Italian stewed tomatoes
    2 cans (10½ ounces each) beef broth
    1 can (15 ounces) mixed vegetables, drained
    1 teaspoon salt
 ¼ teaspoon pepper
    1 cup uncooked medium egg noodles

1. In a Dutch oven, cook beef and onion over medium heat until meat is no longer pink; drain.

2. Add the tomatoes, broth, vegetables and seasonings. Bring to a boil; add the noodles. Reduce heat to medium-low; cover and cook for 10-15 minutes to until noodles are tender.

Basic Turkey Soup

I cook up a batch of this rich broth using a turkey carcass, then add my favorite vegetables and sometimes noodles to this soup.
—**KATIE KOZIOLEK** HARTLAND, MINNESOTA

YIELD: 8-10 SERVINGS.

TURKEY BROTH
- 1 leftover turkey carcass
- 8 cups water
- 1 teaspoon chicken bouillon granules
- 1 celery rib with leaves
- 1 small onion, halved
- 1 carrot
- 3 whole peppercorns
- 1 garlic clove
- 1 teaspoon seasoned salt
- 1 teaspoon dried thyme

TURKEY VEGETABLE SOUP
- 8 cups turkey broth
- 2 teaspoons chicken bouillon granules
- ½ to ¾ teaspoon pepper
- 4 cups sliced carrots, celery, green beans and/or other vegetables
- ¾ cup chopped onion
- 4 cups diced cooked turkey

1. Place all broth ingredients in a large stockpot; cover and bring to a boil. Reduce heat; simmer for 25 minutes. Strain broth; discard bones and vegetables. Cool; skim fat. Use immediately for turkey vegetable soup or refrigerate and use within 24 hours.

2. For soup, combine the broth, bouillon, pepper, vegetables and onion in a large stockpot. Cover and simmer for 15-20 minutes or until the vegetables are tender. Add turkey and heat through.

Dumpling Vegetable Soup

Fabulous rice dumplings give a homemade touch to this speedy soup that takes advantage of canned goods, frozen vegetables and dry soup mix. My mom found this to be a quick, nourishing all-in-one-pot meal, and so do I.
—**PEGGY LINTON** COBOURG, ONTARIO

YIELD: 6-8 SERVINGS (2 QUARTS).

- ½ pound ground beef
- 4 cups water
- 1 can (28 ounces) diced tomatoes, undrained
- 1 package (10 ounces) frozen mixed vegetables
- 1 envelope onion soup mix
- ½ teaspoon dried oregano
- ¼ teaspoon pepper

RICE DUMPLINGS
- 1¼ cups all-purpose flour
- 1 teaspoon baking powder
- ½ teaspoon salt
- 1 tablespoon shortening
- ⅓ cup cooked rice, room temperature
- 1 tablespoon minced fresh parsley
- 1 egg, lightly beaten
- ½ cup milk

1. In a Dutch oven, cook beef over medium heat until no longer pink; drain. Add the water, tomatoes, vegetables, soup mix, oregano and pepper; bring to a boil. Reduce heat; cover and simmer for 30-40 minutes or until the vegetables are tender.

2. For dumplings, combine the flour, baking powder and salt in a bowl. Cut in shortening until the mixture resembles coarse crumbs. Add rice and parsley; toss. In a small bowl, combine egg and milk. Stir into rice mixture just until moistened.

3. Drop the dough by teaspoonfuls onto the simmering soup. Cover and simmer for 15 minutes or until a toothpick inserted in a dumpling comes out clean (do not lift lid while simmering).

Broccoli Soup

This thick, creamy soup has wonderful broccoli flavor with just a hint of nutmeg. When it comes to broccoli recipes, this is one of my favorites.

—MARION TIPTON PHOENIX, ARIZONA

YIELD: 4 SERVINGS.

- 4 **cups chicken broth**
- 2 **to 2½ pounds fresh broccoli spears, cut into florets**
- ½ **cup chopped green onions**
- 1 **tablespoon canola oil**
- ¼ **cup all-purpose flour**
- 1 **teaspoon salt**
- ¼ **teaspoon ground nutmeg**
- ⅛ **teaspoon pepper**
- 1 **cup half-and-half cream**

1. In a large saucepan, bring broth to a boil; add broccoli. Reduce heat; cover and simmer until broccoli is tender, about 10 minutes.

2. Meanwhile, in a small skillet, saute the onions in oil until tender; stir into the broth. Remove from heat; cool 10-15 minutes. Puree soup in small batches in a blender or food processor until smooth.

3. In the saucepan, combine flour, salt, nutmeg and pepper. Slowly add cream, stirring constantly. Gradually stir in broccoli mixture. Bring to a boil over medium heat. Coook and stir for 2 minutes or until thickened.

Creamy Corn Chowder

Corn really stars in this delectable recipe—it hits the spot whenever you crave a rich, hearty soup. I make it each year for a luncheon at our church's flea market, where it's always a big seller.

—CAROL SUNDQUIST ROCHESTER, NEW YORK

YIELD: 6-8 SERVINGS (2 QUARTS).

- 2 **chicken bouillon cubes**
- 1 **cup hot water**
- 5 **bacon strips**
- 1 **cup chopped green pepper**
- ½ **cup chopped onion**
- ¼ **cup all-purpose flour**
- 3 **cups milk**
- 1½ **cups fresh or frozen whole kernel corn**
- 1 **can (14¾ ounces) cream-style corn**
- 1½ **teaspoons seasoned salt**
- ¼ **teaspoon salt**
- ⅛ **teaspoon white pepper**
- ⅛ **teaspoon dried basil**

1. Dissolve bouillon in water; set aside. In a large Dutch oven, cook bacon over medium heat until crisp. Remove bacon to paper towels to drain; crumble and set aside.

2. In a large skillet, saute green pepper and onion in the drippings until tender. Add flour; cook and stir until smooth. Gradually stir in milk and dissolved bouillon. Bring to a boil; cook and stir for 2 minutes or until thickened. Add corn and seasonings. Cook for 10 minutes or until heated through. Sprinkle with bacon.

Tomato Dill Bisque

My family really enjoys this soup when we make it from our garden tomatoes. When those tomatoes are plentiful, I make a big batch (without mayonnaise) and freeze it. Then we can enjoy it even after the garden is gone for the season.

—SUSAN BRECKBILL LINCOLN UNIVERSITY, PENNSYLVANIA

YIELD: 5 SERVINGS (5 CUPS).

- 2 **medium onions, chopped**
- 1 **garlic clove, minced**
- 2 **tablespoons butter**
- 2 **pounds tomatoes, peeled and chopped**
- ½ **cup water**
- 1 **chicken bouillon cube**
- 1 **teaspoon sugar**
- 1 **teaspoon dill weed**
- ½ **teaspoon salt**
- ¼ **teaspoon pepper**
- ½ **cup mayonnaise, optional**

1. In a large saucepan, saute onions and garlic in butter until tender. Add the tomatoes, water, bouillon, sugar and seasonings. Cover and simmer 10 minutes or until tomatoes are tender. Remove from heat; cool slightly.

2. Place tomato mixture in a blender, cover and process until pureed. Return to saucepan. If creamy soup is desired, stir in mayonnaise. Cook and stir over low heat until heated through. Serve warm.

Savory Cheese Soup

This delicious soup recipe was shared by a friend and instantly became a hit with my husband. Its big cheese flavor blends wonderfully with the flavor of the vegetables. I first served this creamy soup as part of a holiday meal, but now we enjoy it throughout the year.

—DEE FALK STROMSBURG, NEBRASKA

YIELD: 4 SERVINGS.

- ¼ **cup chopped onion**
- 3 **tablespoons butter**
- ¼ **cup all-purpose flour**
- ¼ **teaspoon salt**
- ⅛ **teaspoon garlic powder**
- ⅛ **teaspoon pepper**
- 2 **cups 2% milk**
- 1 **can (14½ ounces) chicken or vegetable broth**
- ½ **cup shredded carrot**
- ½ **cup finely chopped celery**
- 1½ **cups (6 ounces) shredded cheddar cheese**
- ¾ **cup shredded part-skim mozzarella cheese**

Minced chives, optional

1. In a large saucepan, saute onion in butter until tender. Add the flour, salt, garlic powder and pepper; stir until smooth. Gradually add milk; bring to a boil over medium heat. Cook and stir for 2 minutes or until thickened.

2. Meanwhile, in a small saucepan, bring broth to a boil. Add the carrot and celery; simmer for 5 minutes or until vegetables are tender. Add to the milk mixture and stir until blended. Add cheeses. Cook and stir until melted (do not boil). Garnish with chives if desired.

Hearty Potato Soup

Having grown up on a dairy farm in Holland, I love our country life here in Idaho's "potato country." My favorite potato soup originally called for heavy cream and bacon fat, but I've trimmed it down.

—GLADYS DE BOER CASTLEFORD, IDAHO

YIELD: 8-10 SERVINGS (ABOUT 2½ QUARTS).

- 6 **medium potatoes, peeled and sliced**
- 2 **carrots, chopped**
- 6 **celery ribs, chopped**
- 8 **cups water**
- 1 **onion, chopped**
- 6 **tablespoons butter, cubed**
- 6 **tablespoons all-purpose flour**
- 1 **teaspoon salt**
- ½ **teaspoon pepper**
- 1½ **cups 2% milk**

1. In a Dutch oven, cook the potatoes, carrots and celery in water until tender, about 15-20 minutes. Drain, reserving liquid and setting vegetables aside.

2. In the same pan, saute onion in butter until tender. Stir in the flour, salt and pepper; gradually add milk. Bring to a boil, cook and stir for 2 minutes or until thickened. Gently stir in cooked vegetables. Add 1 cup or more of reserved cooking liquid until soup is desired consistency.

U.S. Senate Bean Soup

Chock-full of ham, beans and celery, this hearty soup makes a wonderful meal at any time of year. Freeze the bone from a holiday ham until you're ready to make soup. Plus, once prepared, it freezes well for a great make-ahead supper!

—ROSEMARIE FORCUM HEATHSVILLE, VIRGINIA

YIELD: 8-10 SERVINGS (2½ QUARTS).

- 1 **pound dried great northern beans**
- 1 **meaty ham bone or 2 smoked ham hocks**
- 3 **medium onions, chopped**
- 3 **garlic cloves, minced**
- 3 **celery ribs, chopped**
- ¼ **cup minced fresh parsley**
- 1 **cup mashed potatoes or ⅓ cup instant potato flakes**

Salt and pepper to taste
Minced parsley or chives

1. Rinse and sort beans. Place beans in a Dutch oven or stockpot; add water to cover by 2 in. Bring to a boil; boil for 2 minutes. Remove from the heat; cover and let stand for 1 to 4 hours or until beans are softened.

2. Drain and rinse beans, discarding liquid. In a large Dutch oven or stockpot, bring the beans, ham bone and 3 quarts water to boil. Reduce heat; cover and simmer for 2 hours.

3. Skim fat if necessary. Add the onions, garlic, celery, parsley, potatoes, salt and pepper; simmer 1 hour longer.

4. Set aside ham bones until cool enough to handle. Remove meat from bones; discard bones. Cut meat into bite-size pieces and return to Dutch oven. Heat through. Sprinkle with parsley or chives.

> The scent of dill takes me back to Grandma's kitchen. She always spent much time tending the coal cookstove and the pot of dill-flavored chicken soup, which seemed to be constantly simmering on the back burner.
>
> **—HELEN CATHERINE SMITH** TAMPA, FLORIDA

Stuffed Roast Pepper Soup

After sampling a similar soup at a summer resort, my daughter and I experimented to create this version. Using a colorful variety of peppers gives it plenty of eye appeal.

—BETTY VIG VIROQUA, WISCONSIN

YIELD: 14-16 SERVINGS (4 QUARTS).

- 2 **pounds ground beef**
- ½ **medium onion, chopped**
- 6 **cups water**
- 8 **beef bouillon cubes**
- 2 **cans (28 ounces each) diced tomatoes, undrained**
- 2 **cups cooked rice**
- 2 **teaspoon salt**
- ½ **teaspoon pepper**
- ½ **teaspoon paprika**
- 3 **green, sweet yellow or red peppers, seeded and chopped**

1. In a large Dutch oven, cook ground beef and onion over medium heat, until the meat is no longer pink and onion is tender; drain. Add water, bouillon cubes, tomatoes, rice and seasonings. Bring to a boil; reduce heat and simmer, covered, for 1 hour.

2. Add peppers; cook, uncovered, for 10-15 minutes or just until tender.

SALADS

Banana Fruit Compote

My mother used to make this recipe when I was a child. My four kids always eat more fruit when I serve it up this way.

—**MAXINE OTIS** HOBSON, MONTANA

YIELD: 2 SERVINGS.

- 1 cup apricot nectar, divided
- Dash to ⅛ teaspoon ground cloves
- Dash to ⅛ teaspoon ground cinnamon
- 1 tablespoon cornstarch
- 2 tablespoons lemon juice
- 1 firm banana, cut into ½-inch slices
- 4 fresh strawberries, sliced
- 1 kiwifruit, halved and thinly sliced

1. In a small saucepan, bring ¾ cup apricot nectar, cloves and cinnamon to a boil. Combine the cornstarch and remaining apricot nectar until smooth; gradually whisk into nectar mixture. Return to a boil; cook and stir for 1-2 minutes or until thickened . Remove from heat; stir in the lemon juice. Cool.

2. Stir in the banana, strawberries and kiwi. Cover and refrigerate for at least 1 hour before serving.

Seven-Layer Gelatin Salad

Here's an eye-catching salad that my mother makes for Christmas dinner each year. You can choose different flavors to make other color combinations for specific holidays or other gatherings.

—**JAN HEMNESS** STOCKTON, MISSOURI

YIELD: 15-20 SERVINGS.

- 7 packages (3 ounces each) assorted flavored gelatin
- 4½ cups boiling water, divided
- 4½ cups cold water, divided
- 1 can (12 ounces) evaporated milk, divided
- 1 carton (8 ounces) frozen whipped topping, thawed
- Fresh mint, sliced strawberries and kiwifruit, optional

1. In a small bowl, dissolve one package of gelatin in ¾ cup boiling water. Add ¾ cup cold water; stir. Spoon into a 13-in. x 9-in. dish coated with cooking spray. Chill until set but not firm, about 40 minutes.

2. In another bowl, dissolve another package of gelatin in ½ cup boiling water. Add ½ cup cold water and ½ cup milk; stir. Spoon over the first layer. Chill until set but not firm, about 40 minutes.

3. Repeat five times, alternating plain gelatin layers with creamy gelatin layers. Chill each layer until set but not firm before spooning next layer on top. Refrigerate the entire salad overnight. Just before serving, spread top with the whipped topping. Cut into squares to serve. Garnish with mint and fruit if desired.

Editor's Note: *This recipe takes time to prepare since each layer must be set before the next layer is added.*

Tasty Tossed Salad

My mom got this recipe from a friend; it's a re-creation of a salad at a favorite restaurant. It's crisp, crunchy and colorful, with a slightly sweet homemade dressing everyone will enjoy.

—EMILY DENNIS HANCOCK, MICHIGAN

YIELD: 6 SERVINGS.

2   **cups torn iceberg lettuce**
1   **cup fresh cauliflowerets**
1   **cup fresh broccoli florets**
1   **cup shredded carrots**
⅓   **cup chopped red onion**
6   **bacon strips, cooked and crumbled**
1   **cup (4 ounces) shredded cheddar cheese**

DRESSING
¾   **cup mayonnaise**
3   **tablespoons sugar**
3   **tablespoons lemon juice**

1. In a large salad bowl, combine the lettuce, cauliflower, broccoli, carrots, onion and bacon. Top with cheese.

2. In a bowl, combine the mayonnaise, sugar and lemon juice. Pour over lettuce mixture and toss to coat.

Hearty Eight-Layer Salad

I'm a great-grandmother and have been making this satisfying salad for years. It's my most requested recipe for family gatherings. It's simple to make ahead of time and looks lovely with all of its tasty layers. Dijon mustard gives a nice kick to the dressing.

—**NOREEN MEYER** MADISON, WISCONSIN

YIELD: 10 SERVINGS.

- 1½ cups uncooked small pasta shells
- 1 tablespoon canola oil
- 3 cups shredded lettuce
- 3 hard-cooked eggs, sliced
- ¼ teaspoon salt
- ⅛ teaspoon pepper
- 1 cup julienned fully cooked ham
- 1 cup julienned hard salami
- 1 package (10 ounces) frozen peas, thawed
- 1 cup mayonnaise
- ¼ cup sour cream
- ¼ cup chopped green onions
- 2 teaspoons Dijon mustard
- 1 cup (4 ounces) shredded Colby or Monterey Jack cheese
- 2 tablespoons minced fresh parsley

1. Cook macaroni according to package directions; drain and rinse with cold water. Drizzle with oil; toss to coat.

2. Place the lettuce in a 2½-qt. glass serving bowl; top with macaroni and eggs. Sprinkle with salt and pepper. Layer with ham, salami and peas. Combine mayonnaise, sour cream, green onions and mustard. Spread over the top. Cover and refrigerate for several hours or overnight.

3. Just before serving, sprinkle with cheese and parsley.

Creamy German Potato Salad

My mom's recipe for potato salad has been a staple in our family for years. The whipping cream makes it taste like no other.

—**TRACY ZETTELMEIER** MUKWONAGO, WISCONSIN

YIELD: 13 SERVINGS (¾ CUP EACH).

- 4½ pounds red potatoes (about 18 medium)
- ½ pound bacon strips, diced
- 1 medium onion, chopped
- 4 teaspoons all-purpose flour
- ¾ cup sugar
- ¾ cup cider vinegar
- 1 cup heavy whipping cream

1. Cut potatoes into ½-in. cubes; place in a stockpot and cover with water. Bring to a boil. Reduce heat; cover and simmer for 10-12 minutes or until tender.

2. In a Dutch oven, cook bacon over medium heat until crisp. Using a slotted spoon, remove to paper towels; drain, reserving 5 tablespoons drippings. Set bacon aside.

3. In the same pan, saute onion in drippings until tender. Stir in flour until blended. Gradually stir in sugar and vinegar. Bring to a boil; cook and stir for 2 minutes until thickened.

4. Remove from the heat; gradually whisk in cream. Set aside. Drain potatoes. Transfer to a large bow; add reserved onion mixture and bacon. Stir gently to coat. Serve warm.

Watercress with Fennel & Berries

I like to experiment when I'm cooking. This surprising combination of watercress and fennel creates a fresh-tasting summer salad, which was a success with my family.
—**JIM RUDE** JANESVILLE, WISCONSIN

YIELD: 6 SERVINGS.

4 **cups watercress**
1 **cup thinly sliced fennel bulb**
½ **cup fresh blueberries**
¼ **cup chopped fennel fronds**
¼ **cup pistachios, toasted**
⅓ **cup refrigerated spinach salad dressing with bacon**
1 **tablespoon orange juice**
1 **teaspoon grated orange peel**
1 **teaspoon teriyaki sauce**

1. In a salad bowl, combine the first five ingredients. In a small bowl, whisk the remaining ingredients. Drizzle over salad; toss to coat. Serve immediately.

Editor's Note: *This recipe was tested with Marie's brand salad dressing.*

Sweet 'n' Creamy Coleslaw

My grandmother taught me how to make the dressing for this coleslaw when I was very young. It's not too tart and not too sweet. Sometimes I make 8 gallon jars a week at the restaurant where I work! It gets lots of compliments.
—**DENISE ELDER** HANOVER, ONTARIO

YIELD: 32 (¾-CUP) SERVINGS.

½ **cup plus 2 tablespoons sugar**
2¼ **teaspoons all-purpose flour**
2¼ **teaspoons cornstarch**
1 **teaspoon ground mustard**
½ **teaspoon salt**
½ **teaspoon pepper**
½ **cup plus 2 tablespoons cider vinegar**
½ **cup water**
1 **egg, lightly beaten**
½ **cup milk**
¼ **cup packed brown sugar**
½ **cup half-and-half cream**
2 **cups mayonnaise**
3 **medium heads cabbage (6 to 7 pounds), shredded**
2 **medium carrots, shredded**
2 **celery ribs, chopped**
7 **green onions, thinly sliced**

1. In a large saucepan, combine the sugar, flour, cornstarch, mustard, salt and pepper. Gradually stir in vinegar and water. Add egg and milk. Cook and stir until mixture comes to a boil. Cook 2 minutes longer or until slightly thickened. Cool to room temperature, stirring several times.

2. In a large bowl, combine the brown sugar and cream. Stir in mayonnaise. Add cooked dressing; mix well. In several large bowls, combine the cabbage, carrots, celery and green onions. Add dressing and toss to coat.

Summer Squash Salad

This is a colorful and tasty alternative to coleslaw. Like most gardeners, we usually have an abundance of squash and zucchini in summer, so this dish is inexpensive to prepare and a great way to put this fresh produce to use.

—**DIANE HIXON** NICEVILLE, FLORIDA

YIELD: 12-16 SERVINGS.

- 4 cups julienned zucchini
- 4 cups julienned yellow squash
- 2 cups sliced radishes
- 1 cup canola oil
- ⅓ cup cider vinegar
- 2 tablespoons Dijon mustard
- 2 tablespoons snipped fresh parsley
- 1½ teaspoons salt
- 1 teaspoon dill weed
- ½ teaspoon pepper

1. In a large bowl, toss the zucchini, squash and radishes. In a small bowl, whisk the remaining ingredients. Pour over vegetables. Cover and refrigerate for at least 2 hours.

Gazpacho Salad

Here's a beautiful and tasty way to use garden vegetables. This fresh, savory salad is great to make ahead and take to a potluck later, after the flavors have had a chance to blend. It's sure to be a success!

—**FLORENCE JACOBY**
GRANITE FALLS, MINNESOTA

YIELD: 10-12 SERVINGS.

- 4 tomatoes, diced and seeded
- 2 cucumbers, peeled and diced
- 2 green peppers, seeded and diced
- 1 medium onion, diced
- 1 can (2¼ ounces) sliced ripe olives, drained
- 1 teaspoon salt
- ½ teaspoon pepper

DRESSING

- ½ cup olive oil
- ¼ cup white vinegar
- Juice of 1 lemon (about ¼ cup)
- 1 tablespoon chopped fresh parsley
- 2 garlic cloves, minced
- 2 teaspoons chopped green onions
- ½ teaspoon salt
- ¼ teaspoon ground cumin

1. In a 1½-quart bowl, layer one-third to one-half of the tomatoes, cucumbers, green peppers, onion, olives, salt and pepper. Repeat layers two or three more times.

2. In a small bowl, combine all dressing ingredients. Pour over vegetables. Cover and chill several hours or overnight. Serve with a slotted spoon.

Pineapple Gelatin Salad

My family enjoys this lovely layered salad in the summer with grilled hamburgers. Although I haven't used the recipe long, it's already become a favorite. A good friend shared it with me, and every time I make it, I think of her.
—**SUSAN KIRBY** TIPTON, INDIANA

YIELD: 12-16 SERVINGS.

- 1 can (20 ounces) crushed pineapple
- 1 package (6 ounces) lemon gelatin
- 3 cups boiling water
- 1 package (8 ounces) cream cheese, softened
- 1 carton (16 ounces) frozen whipped topping, thawed
- ¾ cup sugar
- 3 tablespoons lemon juice
- 3 tablespoons water
- 2 tablespoons all-purpose flour
- 2 egg yolks, lightly beaten

1. Drain pineapple, reserving juice. Dissolve gelatin in boiling water; add pineapple. Pour into a 13-in. x 9-in. dish; chill until almost set, about 45 minutes.

2. In a bowl, beat cream cheese and whipped topping until smooth. Carefully spread over gelatin; chill for 30 minutes. Meanwhile, in a saucepan over medium heat, combine sugar, lemon juice, water, flour, egg yolks and reserved pineapple juice; bring to a boil, stirring constantly. Cook for 1 minute or until thickened. Cool. Carefully spread over cream cheese layer. Chill for at least 1 hour.

Corn Bread Layered Salad

My mother's corn bread salad is so complete, it can be a meal in itself. The recipe has been in our family for years and is great for potlucks or large family gatherings.
—**JODY MILLER** OKLAHOMA CITY, OKLAHOMA

YIELD: 6-8 SERVINGS.

- 1 package (8½ ounces) corn bread/muffin mix
- 6 green onions, chopped

- 1 medium green pepper, chopped
- 1 can (15¼ ounces) whole kernel corn, drained
- 1 can (15 ounces) pinto beans, rinsed and drained
- ¾ cup mayonnaise
- ¾ cup sour cream
- 2 medium tomatoes, seeded and chopped
- ½ cup shredded cheddar cheese

1. Prepare and bake corn bread according to package directions. Cool on a wire rack.

2. Crumble corn bread into a 2-qt. glass serving bowl. Layer with onions, green pepper, corn and beans.

3. In a small bowl, combine mayonnaise and sour cream; spread over the vegetables. Sprinkle with tomatoes and cheese. Refrigerate until serving.

Garden Bean Salad

My mother gave me this crunchy bean salad recipe many years ago, and I often take it to covered-dish dinners. It looks especially attractive served in a glass bowl to show off the colorful vegetables.
—**BERNICE MCFADDEN** EATON, OHIO

YIELD: 12-16 SERVINGS.

- 1 can (16 ounces) kidney beans, rinsed and drained
- 2 cans (15¼ ounces each) lima beans
- 1 can (14½ ounces) cut green beans
- 1 can (14½ ounces) cut wax beans, drained
- 1 can (15 ounces) garbanzo beans or chickpeas, rinsed and drained
- 1 large green pepper, chopped
- 3 celery ribs, chopped
- 1 jar (2 ounces) sliced pimientos, drained
- 1 bunch green onions, sliced
- 2 cups white vinegar
- 2 cups sugar
- ½ cup water
- 1 teaspoon salt

1. Drain all beans; place in a large bowl. Add the green pepper, celery, pimientos and green onions; set aside. Bring remaining ingredients to a boil in a heavy saucepan; boil for 5 minutes. Remove from heat and immediately pour over vegetables.

2. Refrigerate the salad several hours or overnight. Serve with a slotted spoon.

Favorite Broccoli Salad

"Fresh-tasting…so colorful…delicious dressing." Those are some of the compliments I get when I serve this broccoli salad with a meal or take it to a church dinner. Although I have many other good salad recipes, I'm especially fond of this one.

—**ESTHER SHANK** HARRISONBURG, VIRGINIA

YIELD: 6-8 SERVINGS.

  1 **bunch broccoli, separated into florets**
  1 **head cauliflower, separated into florets**
  8 **bacon strips, cooked and crumbled**
  1 **cup chopped seeded tomatoes**
  ⅓ **cup chopped onion**
  2 **hard-cooked eggs, sliced**
  1 **cup mayonnaise**
  ⅓ **cup sugar**
  2 **tablespoons cider vinegar**

1. In a large salad bowl, combine the broccoli, cauliflower, bacon, tomatoes, onion and eggs; set aside.

2. In another bowl, combine the mayonnaise, sugar and vinegar. Just before serving, pour dressing over salad and toss to coat.

Tomato Basil Salad

Tomatoes team up with red onion and fresh basil in a pleasant salad.

—**JOYCE BROWN** GENESEE, IDAHO

YIELD: 2 SERVINGS.

  6 **tomato slices (¼ inch thick)**
  6 **red onion slices**
  2 **tablespoons olive oil**
  4 **teaspoons red wine vinegar**
  2 **tablespoons chopped fresh basil**
  1 **teaspoon sugar**

1. Place tomatoes in a shallow dish; top each slice with an onion. In a small jar with tight-fitting lid, combine remaining ingredients; shake well. Pour over tomatoes and onions. Cover and refrigerate for at least 1 hour.

Lime Gelatin Salad

I've made this refreshing recipe hundreds of times! It can be a salad or dessert. When I take it to a potluck, it's always one of the first things to disappear.
—**LOUISE HARDING** NEWBURGH, NEW YORK

YIELD: 16-20 SERVINGS.

- 1 **package (6 ounces) lime gelatin**
- 1 **cup boiling water**
- 1 **package (8 ounces) cream cheese, softened**
- ½ **teaspoon vanilla extract**
- 1 **can (15 ounces) mandarin oranges, drained**
- 1 **can (8 ounces) crushed pineapple, drained**
- 1 **cup lemon-lime soda**
- ½ **cup chopped pecans**
- 1 **carton (8 ounces) frozen whipped topping, thawed, divided**

1. Dissolve gelatin in water. In a bowl, beat cream cheese until fluffy. Stir in gelatin mixture and beat until smooth. Stir in vanilla, oranges, pineapple, soda and pecans. Chill until mixture mounds slightly when dropped from a spoon.

2. Fold in three-fourths of the whipped topping. Pour into a 13-in. x 9-in. dish. Refrigerate for 3-4 hours or until firm. Cut into squares; garnish with the remaining whipped topping.

> Grandma would make the most delicious dishes from so little. One of my favorites was "old field lettuce" picked behind the house and wilted with a cooked creamy-white dressing. It was a delightful taste that I haven't experienced since.
> —**JACK ZINN** LONG BEACH, NORTH CAROLINA

Overnight Coleslaw

This has been a very popular salad from my recipe box for a long, long time! Before I retired, when my office had a covered-dish get-together, I was always asked to bring my tangy coleslaw. My family loves it, too.
—**FERN HAMMOCK** GARLAND, TEXAS

YIELD: 12-16 SERVINGS.

- 12 **cups shredded cabbage (1 medium head)**
- 1 **green pepper, chopped**
- 1 **medium red onion, chopped**
- 2 **carrots, shredded**
- 1 **cup sugar**

DRESSING
- 2 **teaspoons sugar**
- 1 **teaspoon ground mustard**
- 1 **teaspoon celery seed**
- 1 **teaspoon salt**
- 1 **cup white vinegar**
- ¾ **cup canola oil**

1. In a large bowl, combine first four ingredients. Sprinkle with sugar; set aside.

2. In a large saucepan, combine dressing ingredients; bring to a boil. Remove from the heat and pour over vegetables; toss to coat.

3. Cover and refrigerate overnight. Stir well before serving. Serve with a slotted spoon.

Special Potato Salad

Vinegar and yogurt give this salad a refreshing tang that's unlike typical potato salads with heavy dressings. My family loves the crispness of the onion and celery and the heartiness that comes from the eggs and crumbled bacon.

—PAGE ALEXANDER BALDWIN CITY, KANSAS

YIELD: 6-8 SERVINGS.

- 2½ **pounds red potatoes**
- 2 **tablespoons red wine vinegar**
- 1 **tablespoon olive oil**
- 1 **tablespoon Dijon mustard**
- ½ **teaspoon dried basil**
- ½ **teaspoon pepper**
- ¼ **teaspoon salt**
- ½ **cup plain yogurt**
- ¼ **cup sour cream**
- 1 **teaspoon garlic salt**
- ¾ **cup chopped red onion**
- ½ **cup diced celery**
- 4 **bacon strips, cooked and crumbled**
- 2 **hard-cooked eggs, chopped**

1. In a saucepan, cook potatoes in boiling salted water until tender. Meanwhile, in a large bowl, combine the vinegar, oil, mustard, basil, pepper and salt. Drain potatoes; cut into 1-in. chunks and add to vinegar and oil mixture while still warm. Toss to coat; cool completely.

2. In another bowl, combine yogurt, sour cream and garlic salt. Add onion, celery, bacon and eggs; mix well. Add to potato mixture; toss gently. Cover and chill for several hours.

Summer Apple Salad

It is a good thing this serves 12 because my family can't get enough of it! The salad tastes great, looks nice on the table and combines a mixture of healthy fruits and vegetables with a sweet dressing—a deliciously different idea.

—KIM STOLLER SMITHVILLE, OHIO

YIELD: 12 SERVINGS.

- 3 **medium tart red apples, diced**
- ¾ **cup pineapple tidbits, drained**
- 1½ **cups sliced celery**
- 1 **cup grape halves**
- 1 **medium carrot, shredded**
- ½ **cup coarsely chopped almonds**
- ¾ **cup sour cream**
- 1 **tablespoon sugar**
- ½ **teaspoon lemon juice**

1. In a large salad bowl, combine the apples, pineapple, celery, grapes, carrot and almonds. In a small bowl, combine the sour cream, sugar and lemon juice. Add to the apple mixture and toss to coat. Chill.

Molded Peach Gelatin

The outstanding orange color of this gelatin makes it a perfect addition to any Halloween party table. It's a convenient do-ahead dish when preparing for a busy day.

—BETTY HOWARD WHEELER, TEXAS

YIELD: 4-6 SERVINGS.

- 1 **can (15¼ ounces) sliced peaches**
- ½ **cup sugar**
- ¼ **to ½ teaspoon ground nutmeg**
- 1 **package (3 ounces) peach or orange gelatin**

1. Drain peaches, reserving juice; add enough water to juice to measure 1 cup. Place peaches in a blender. Cover and process until smooth; set aside.

2. In a large saucepan, combine the sugar, nutmeg and reserved juice mixture. Bring to a boil over medium heat; cook and stir for 1 minute or until sugar is dissolved. Remove from the heat; stir in gelatin until dissolved. Stir in the peach puree.

3. Pour mixture into a 3-cup mold coated with cooking spray. Refrigerate the salad until set. Just before serving, unmold onto a serving plate.

Emily's Spinach Salad

I've always loved eating spinach—it's grown here in our area. When I saw an announcement of a spinach cooking contest, I made up this recipe to enter. I was delighted when my colorful, tangy salad took the grand prize!

—EMILY FIELDS SANTA ANA, CALIFORNIA

YIELD: 6-8 SERVINGS.

⅔ cup canola oil
¼ cup red wine vinegar
2 teaspoons lemon juice
2 teaspoons soy sauce
1 teaspoon sugar
1 teaspoon ground mustard
½ teaspoon curry powder
½ teaspoon salt
½ teaspoon seasoned pepper
¼ teaspoon garlic powder

1 package (10 ounces) fresh spinach, torn
5 bacon strips, cooked and crumbled
2 hard-cooked eggs, sliced

1. In a small bowl, whisk the first 10 ingredients; set aside. Place spinach in a large salad bowl.

2. Just before serving, whisk dressing again and drizzle over spinach; toss gently. Garnish with bacon and egg slices.

Pat's Potato Salad

I developed this recipe while working at a restaurant. We wanted a salad that would complement a barbecue sandwich and use up day-old baked potatoes. It keeps well and tastes even better after it's chilled.

—PATRICIA MAUL
BARTLESVILLE, OKLAHOMA

YIELD: 12-16 SERVINGS.

- 12 **medium red potatoes, cooked, peeled and cubed**
- 1 **medium red onion, chopped**
- 1 **cup chopped fresh parsley**
- 1½ **cups mayonnaise**
- 1 **cup (8 ounces) sour cream**
- ¼ **cup sugar**
- ¼ **cup vinegar**
- 4 **teaspoons ground mustard**
- 1 **teaspoon salt**

1. In a large bowl, combine potatoes, onion and parsley. In a small bowl, combine the remaining ingredients. Pour dressing over the potatoes and mix well. Refrigerate at least 1 hour before serving. Salad can be prepared a day ahead.

Layered Fruit Salad

Fresh fruit is layered into an appealing salad that's a welcome side dish not only in summer but all year long.

—PAGE ALEXANDER BALDWIN CITY, KANSAS

YIELD: 8 SERVINGS.

- ½ **cup orange juice**
- ¼ **cup lemon juice**
- ¼ **cup packed brown sugar**
- ½ **teaspoon grated orange peel**
- ½ **teaspoon grated lemon peel**
- 1 **cinnamon stick (3 inches)**
- 2 **cups fresh or drained canned pineapple chunks**
- 1 **cup seedless red grapes**
- 2 **medium bananas, sliced**
- 2 **medium oranges, sectioned**
- 1 **medium grapefruit, sectioned**
- 1 **pint fresh strawberries, sliced**
- 2 **medium kiwifruit, peeled and sliced**

1. In a large saucepan, combine the juices, sugar, peels and cinnamon stick; bring to a boil. Reduce heat; simmer, uncovered, for 5 minutes. Remove from the heat; cool completely.

2. Meanwhile, layer fruit in a glass serving bowl. Remove cinnamon stick from the sauce; pour sauce over fruit. Cover and refrigerate for several hours.

Vegetable Pasta Salad

This light, multicolored salad is an original. When I serve it at potlucks, I'm always asked for the recipe. It's also a standby for the snowbirds who gather with us in Arizona each winter.

—**KATHY CROW** CORDOVA, ALASKA

YIELD: 16-18 SERVINGS.

- 12 ounces spiral pasta, cooked and drained
- 6 green onions, thinly sliced
- 1 to 2 small zucchini, thinly sliced
- 2 cups frozen broccoli and cauliflower, thawed and drained
- 1½ cups thinly sliced carrots, parboiled
- 1 cup thinly sliced celery
- ½ cup frozen peas, thawed
- 1 jar (2¼ ounces) sliced ripe olives, drained
- 1 jar (6 ounces) marinated artichoke hearts, drained and quartered

DRESSING
- ½ cup mayonnaise
- ½ cup bottled Italian salad dressing
- ½ cup sour cream
- 1 tablespoon prepared mustard
- ½ teaspoon Italian seasoning

1. In a large bowl, combine pasta, onions, zucchini, broccoli and cauliflower, carrots, celery, peas, olives and artichoke hearts. In a small bowl, combine dressing ingredients. Pour over pasta and vegetables and toss. Cover and refrigerate for at least 1 hour.

Curried Walnut Rice Salad

As a busy wife and mother of eight, I'm always on the lookout for appetizing and nutritious recipes. With its mild curry flavor, nutty crunch and veggie garnish, this one easily passed my test!

—**RHODA WENGER** PILOT MOUNTAIN, NORTH CAROLINA

YIELD: 10 SERVINGS.

- 1¾ cups brown rice, cooked and cooled
- 1 medium cucumber, diced
- ½ cup chopped onion
- 1 large carrot, shredded

- 1 tablespoon minced fresh parsley
- 3 tablespoons fat-free mayonnaise
- 2 tablespoons canola oil
- 1 tablespoon lemon juice
- 2 teaspoons honey
- 1 teaspoon curry powder
- 2 garlic cloves, minced
- 1 teaspoon salt
- ¼ teaspoon pepper
- ½ cup chopped walnuts, toasted
- 4 medium tomatoes, cut into wedges

1. In a large bowl, combine the first five ingredients. In another bowl, whisk mayonnaise, oil, lemon juice, honey, curry powder, garlic, salt and pepper; stir into rice mixture. Just before serving, stir in nuts. Garnish with tomatoes.

Caesar Salad

Here's a great salad to perk up any spring or summer meal. The zesty dressing provides a fresh burst of flavor with each bite.

—**SCHELBY THOMPSON** CAMDEN WYOMING, DELAWARE

YIELD: 6-8 SERVINGS.

- 1 large bunch romaine, torn
- ¾ cup olive oil
- 3 tablespoons red wine vinegar
- 1 teaspoon Worcestershire sauce
- ½ teaspoon salt
- ¼ teaspoon ground mustard
- 1 large garlic clove, minced
- ½ fresh lemon

Dash pepper
- ¼ to ½ cup shredded Parmesan cheese

Caesar-flavored or garlic croutons

1. Place lettuce in a large salad bowl. Combine the next six ingredients in a blender; process until smooth. Pour over lettuce and toss to coat.

2. Squeeze lemon over lettuce. Sprinkle with pepper, cheese and croutons.

Sweet and Tangy Pasta Salad

I'm a retired farmwife and one of 16 children. I learned lots about cooking from my mother. This recipe is my version of her pasta salad.

—JUNE HERKE WATERTOWN, SOUTH DAKOTA

YIELD: 16 SERVINGS.

1 package (16 ounces) spiral pasta
1 medium cucumber, finely chopped
1 jar (8 ounces) whole baby corn,
   drained and cut into ½-inch pieces
1 jar (7½ ounces) marinated
   artichoke hearts, drained
1 cup sliced pimiento-stuffed olives
1 cup sliced ripe olives
½ cup finely chopped sweet red
   pepper
¼ cup finely chopped onion

DRESSING
1 cup canola oil
1 cup cider vinegar
1 cup sugar
½ teaspoon pepper
2 tablespoons minced fresh parsley

1. Cook pasta according to package directions. Meanwhile, in a large bowl, combine the cucumber, corn, artichokes, olives, red pepper and onion. Drain pasta and rinse in cold water; stir into vegetable mixture.

2. In a small bowl, whisk the dressing ingredients. Pour over salad; toss to coat. Cover and refrigerate for at least 2 hours. Serve with a slotted spoon.

Greens with Vinaigrette

This pretty salad topped with a sweet and savory dressing is a refreshing addition to any meal. It's a perfect example of how Mother could turn even simple ingredients into something special.

—**NANCY DUTY** JACKSONVILLE, FLORIDA

YIELD: 6 SERVINGS (ABOUT ⅔ CUP VINAIGRETTE).

- 6 cups torn romaine
- 1 cup sliced radishes
- ⅓ cup olive oil
- ¼ cup honey
- 2 teaspoons white wine vinegar
- 1½ teaspoons lemon juice
- 1 teaspoon Dijon mustard
- 1 teaspoon poppy seeds
- 2 garlic cloves, minced
- Dash hot pepper sauce
- Pinch sugar
- Salt and pepper to taste

1. In a large bowl, combine the romaine and radishes. In a jar with tight-fitting lid, combine the remaining ingredients; shake well. Just before serving, pour the vinaigrette over salad; toss to coat.

Cheddar-Almond Lettuce Salad

Sugared almonds and a honey-mustard dressing make this salad a real standout. In fact, I keep slivered almonds in my freezer just so I can whip it up on the spur of the moment. For more nutrition, color or variety, I sometimes add broccoli and tomatoes.

—**JULIA MUSSER** LEBANON, PENNSYLVANIA

YIELD: 9 SERVINGS.

- ½ cup slivered almonds
- 3 tablespoons sugar
- 9 cups torn romaine

- 2 hard-cooked eggs, sliced
- 1 cup (4 ounces) shredded cheddar cheese

HONEY-MUSTARD DRESSING
- ¼ cup sugar
- 2 tablespoons white vinegar
- 2 tablespoons honey
- 1 tablespoon lemon juice
- ½ teaspoon onion powder
- ½ teaspoon celery seed
- ½ teaspoon ground mustard
- ½ teaspoon paprika
- ¼ teaspoon salt
- ½ cup canola oil

1. In a small heavy skillet, combine almonds and sugar. Cook and stir over medium heat for 5-6 minutes or until nuts are coated and golden. Spread onto foil to cool. Divide romaine among salad plates; top with eggs and cheese.

2. In a blender, combine the sugar, vinegar, honey, lemon juice, onion powder, celery seed, mustard, paprika and salt. While processing, gradually add oil in a steady stream. Drizzle over salads; sprinkle with almonds.

Southwestern Rice Salad

The recipe for this delicious salad has been in my family for years. My mother used to bring it to many different functions, and I'm carrying on her tradition.

—**RUTH BIANCHI** APPLE VALLEY, MINNESOTA

YIELD: 12 SERVINGS.

- 1⅓ cups water
- ⅔ cup uncooked long grain rice
- ¾ cup chopped green pepper
- ½ cup chopped red onion
- 1 medium carrot, chopped
- 1 tablespoon canola oil
- 3 garlic cloves, minced
- 1 package (16 ounces) frozen corn, thawed
- 1 can (15 ounces) black beans, rinsed and drained
- 2 medium plum tomatoes, chopped
- 1 cup salted peanuts
- ⅓ cup minced fresh cilantro
- ⅔ cup olive oil
- ⅓ cup lemon juice
- ½ to 1½ teaspoons cayenne pepper
- ½ teaspoon ground cumin

1. In a large saucepan, bring water and rice to a boil. Reduce heat; cover and simmer for 15 minutes. Remove from the heat. Let stand for 5 minutes or until rice is tender. Rinse rice with cold water and drain. Place in a large bowl.

2. In a small skillet, saute the green pepper, onion and carrot in oil until crisp-tender. Add garlic; cook 1 minute longer. Add to rice. Stir in the corn, beans, tomatoes, peanuts and cilantro.

3. In a small bowl, combine the oil, lemon juice, cayenne and cumin. Pour over the rice mixture; stir to coat. Cover and refrigerate until serving.

Tomato Spinach Salad

When I serve my fresh spinach tossed with a creamy dill dressing, I receive plenty of compliments. The recipe is a longtime favorite.

—**RUTH SEITZ** COLUMBUS JUNCTION, IOWA

YIELD: 6-8 SERVINGS.

- ½ cup mayonnaise
- ½ cup grated Parmesan cheese

- ¼ cup milk
- 1½ teaspoons dill weed
- 1½ teaspoons dried minced onion
- 1½ teaspoons lemon-pepper seasoning
- 1 package (10 ounces) fresh spinach, torn
- 2 cups cherry tomatoes

1. In a jar with tight-fitting lid, combine first six ingredients; shake well. Refrigerate for at least 1 hour. Just before serving, combine spinach and tomatoes in a large salad bowl. Shake dressing; drizzle over salad and toss.

Editor's Note: *If the dressing thickens, thin with additional milk if desired.*

Ruby Red Raspberry Salad

A refreshing and attractive side dish, this salad adds a festive touch to any table. Children especially like this slightly sweet salad.

—**MARGE CLARK** WEST LEBANON, INDIANA

YIELD: 12-16 SERVINGS.

- 1 package (3 ounces) raspberry gelatin
- 2 cups boiling water, divided
- 1 package (10 ounces) frozen sweetened raspberries
- 1½ cups sour cream
- 1 package (3 ounces) cherry gelatin
- 1 can (20 ounces) crushed pineapple, drained
- 1 can (14 ounces) whole-berry cranberry sauce

Mayonnaise and mint sprigs, optional

1. Dissolve raspberry gelatin in 1 cup boiling water. Add raspberries and stir until berries are thawed and separated. Pour into a 13-in. x 9-in. dish; chill until set.

2. Carefully spread with sour cream; chill. Dissolve cherry gelatin in remaining boiling water. Add pineapple and cranberry sauce; mix well. Allow to thicken slightly.

3. Carefully spoon over sour cream mixture; chill. If desired, garnish with mayonnaise and mint.

Dilly Bean Potato Salad

Green beans, dill pickles and a refreshing Italian-style dressing perk up this potato salad. My Irish grandmother made it for family gatherings. Even though I've changed it a bit, Nanny always comes to mind when I dish it up.

—MARGUERITE NOVICKE VINELAND, NEW JERSEY

YIELD: 14-16 SERVINGS.

- 1 **pound fresh green beans, trimmed**
- 4 **pounds red potatoes**
- 1 **medium red onion, thinly sliced and separated into rings**
- 1 **medium Vidalia or sweet onion, thinly sliced and separated into rings**
- 1 **cup chopped celery**
- 8 **dill pickles, sliced**
- 2 **tablespoons snipped fresh dill or 2 teaspoons dill weed**
- 2 **tablespoons minced fresh parsley**
- 4 **garlic cloves, minced**

VINAIGRETTE

- ¾ **cup olive oil**
- ⅓ **to ½ cup tarragon vinegar**
- 1 **envelope Italian salad dressing mix**
- 2 **tablespoons sugar**
- 1 **teaspoon salt**
- 1 **teaspoon pepper**

Celery salt and seasoned salt to taste

1. Place 1 in. of water and beans in a skillet; bring to a boil. Reduce heat. Cover and simmer for 8-10 minutes or until crisp-tender; drain and set aside.

2. Meanwhile, place potatoes in a large saucepan or Dutch oven and cover with water. Bring to a boil. Reduce heat. Cover and cook for 15-20 minutes or until tender; drain and cool.

3. Cut potatoes into ¼-in. slices; transfer to a large bowl. Add the onions, celery, pickles, dill, parsley and garlic.

4. In a jar with a tight-fitting lid, combine the vinaigrette ingredients; shake well. Drizzle over potato mixture. Add beans; gently toss.

> After he finished lunch, Grandpa would say to Grandma, "That was the best meal I ever ate!" Then, turning to me, he'd say, "Your grandmother has cooked me 16,425 meals so far and every one of them has been delicious!"
>
> **—SUZANNE BEARD** KINGS MOUNTAIN, NORTH CAROLINA

Festive Fruit Salad

Everyone who tries this refreshing, beautiful salad loves it. My bowl always comes home empty when I take it to a party or cookout. The recipe is an excellent way to take advantage of fresh fruit at its best.

—GAIL SELLERS SAVANNAH, GEORGIA

YIELD: 16-20 SERVINGS.

- 1 **medium fresh pineapple**
- 3 **medium apples (red, yellow and green), cubed**
- 1 **small cantaloupe, cubed**
- 1 **large firm banana, sliced**
- 1 **pint strawberries, halved**
- 1 **pint blueberries**
- 4 **cups seedless red and green grapes**
- 3 **kiwifruit, peeled and sliced**

DRESSING

- 1 **package (3 ounces) cream cheese, softened**
- ½ **cup confectioners' sugar**
- 2 **teaspoons lemon juice**
- 1 **carton (8 ounces) frozen whipped topping, thawed**

Additional berries for garnish, optional

1. Peel and core pineapple; cut into cubes. Place in a 3- or 4-qt. glass serving bowl. Stir in remaining fruit.

2. In a large bowl, beat cream cheese until fluffy. Gradually add sugar and lemon juice and mix well. Fold in the whipped topping.

3. Spread over fruit. Garnish with additional berries if desired. Store leftovers in the refrigerator.

SIDE DISHES

Root for Winter Vegetables

This medley is an updated version of a recipe my mom had while growing up. It's my favorite way to prepare veggies and is marvelous with a batch of hot rolls.

—JULIE BUTLER PUYALLUP, WASHINGTON

YIELD: 13 SERVINGS (¾ CUP EACH).

1	**whole garlic bulb**
3	**tablespoons olive oil, divided**
1	**pound fresh beets**
3	**medium parsnips**
2	**small rutabagas**
2	**medium turnips**
4	**medium carrots**
2	**large red onions, cut into wedges**
1	**teaspoon salt**
15	**whole peppercorns**
3	**bay leaves**
½	**cup white wine or vegetable broth**
½	**cup vegetable broth**
2	**tablespoons butter**

1. Remove papery outer skin from garlic (do not peel or separate cloves). Cut top off garlic bulb. Brush with ½ teaspoon oil. Wrap bulb in heavy-duty foil.

2. Peel the beets, parsnips, rutabagas, turnips and carrots; cut into 2-in. pieces. Place in a large bowl; add the onions, salt, peppercorns, bay leaves and remaining oil. Toss to coat.

3. Transfer to three greased 15-in. x 10-in. x 1-in. baking pans. Place garlic on one of the pans.

4. Bake at 400° for 35 minutes or until garlic is softened, stirring once. Remove garlic; set aside to cool. Drizzle wine and broth over vegetables. Bake vegetables 20-30 minutes longer or until tender. Squeeze softened garlic over vegetables; dot with butter. Transfer to a serving platter.

Summer Risotto

My mom always made this hearty dish to use up late-summer garden vegetables. Often, I'll add sauteed mushrooms and serve it as an entree with crusty bread and a salad.

—SHIRLEY HODGE BANGOR, PENNSYLVANIA

YIELD: 12 SERVINGS.

5½ to 6 cups reduced-sodium chicken broth
  1 small onion, finely chopped
  2 tablespoons olive oil
  1 tablespoon butter
  2 cups uncooked arborio rice
  3 large tomatoes, chopped
  2 cups fresh or frozen corn, thawed
  ½ cup crumbled feta cheese
  2 tablespoons minced fresh thyme or 2 teaspoons dried thyme
  2 tablespoons minced fresh rosemary or 2 teaspoons dried rosemary, crushed
  2 tablespoons minced fresh basil or 2 teaspoons dried basil
  ¼ teaspoon salt
  ¼ teaspoon pepper
Shredded Parmesan cheese

1. In a large saucepan, heat broth and keep warm. In a large skillet, saute onion in oil and butter until tender. Add rice; cook and stir for 2-3 minutes or rice is until lightly browned. Stir in 1 cup warm broth. Cook and stir until all the liquid is absorbed.

2. Add remaining broth, ½ cup at a time, stirring constantly. Allow the liquid to be absorbed between additions. Cook until risotto is creamy and rice is almost tender (total cooking time will be about 20 minutes).

3. Add tomatoes, corn, feta cheese, herbs, salt and pepper; heat through. Sprinkle with Parmesan cheese. Serve immediately.

Succotash

You can't get more Southern than succotash. This recipe comes from my mother, who was a fantastic cook. Her dish made her famous with everyone who ever tasted it.

—ROSA BOONE MOBILE, ALABAMA

YIELD: 12-16 SERVINGS.

  1 smoked ham hock (about 1½ pounds)
  4 cups water
  1 can (28 ounces) diced tomatoes, undrained
1½ cups frozen lima beans, thawed
  1 package (10 ounces) crowder peas, thawed or 1 can (15½ ounces) black-eyed peas, drained
  1 package (10 ounces) frozen corn, thawed
  1 medium green pepper, chopped
  1 medium onion, chopped
  ⅓ cup ketchup
1½ teaspoons salt
1½ teaspoons dried basil
  1 teaspoon rubbed sage
  1 teaspoon paprika
  ½ teaspoon pepper
  1 bay leaf
  1 cup sliced fresh or frozen okra

1. In a Dutch oven or large saucepan, simmer ham hock in water for 1½ hours or until tender. Cool; remove meat from the bone and return to pan. (Discard bone and broth or save for another use.) Add the tomatoes, beans, peas, corn, green pepper, onion, ketchup and seasonings. Simmer, uncovered, for 45 minutes. Add okra; simmer, uncovered, 15 minutes longer. Discard bay leaf before serving.

Maple Baked Beans

My mother's baked beans were always a hit. You'll get a touch of heat from the chopped jalapeno pepper. Once you make it, you'll know it off the top of your head—it's just a half-cup of this and a half-cup of that!

—**NADINE BRISSEY** JENKS, OKLAHOMA

YIELD: 8 SERVINGS.

- 3 **cans (15 ounces each) pork and beans**
- ½ **cup finely chopped onion**
- ½ **cup chopped green pepper**
- ½ **cup ketchup**
- ½ **cup maple syrup**
- 2 **tablespoons finely chopped seeded jalapeno pepper**
- ½ **cup crumbled cooked bacon**

1. In a 3-qt. slow cooker, combine the first six ingredients. Cover and cook on low for 6-8 hours or until vegetables are tender. Just before serving, stir in bacon.

Editor's Note: *Wear disposable gloves when cutting hot peppers; the oils can burn skin. Avoid touching your face.*

Sage Dressing for Chicken

My family just loves this chicken stuffed with delicious sage dressing. They always ask for seconds.

—**BOBBIE TALBOTT** VENETA, OREGON

YIELD: 6 SERVINGS.

- 2 **cups unseasoned dry bread cubes**
- ½ **cup chopped onion**
- ¼ **cup chopped fresh parsley**
- 3 **tablespoons chopped fresh sage or 1 tablespoon rubbed dried sage**
- 1 **egg, beaten**

½ **to ¾ cup chicken broth**
1 **roasting chicken (3 to 4 pounds)**
Melted butter, optional

1. In a large bowl, combine bread cubes, onion, parsley, sage and the egg. Add enough broth until stuffing is moistened and holds together. Stuff loosely into chicken. Fasten with skewers to close.

2. Place with breast side up on a shallow rack in roasting pan. Brush with butter if desired. Bake, uncovered, at 375° for 1¾ to 2¼ hours or until juices run clear. Baste several times with pan juices or butter.

Onion Potato Pancakes

When Grandma prepared potato pancakes, she used an old-fashioned grater, which was great for potatoes but not for knuckles! With homemade applesauce, this side dish complements a meal so well. I made these pancakes for my family and often served them as a main dish for light suppers.

—**JOAN HUTTER** WARWICK, RHODE ISLAND

YIELD: 6-8 SERVINGS (12 PANCAKES).

- 2 **eggs**
- 1 **medium onion, quartered**
- 2 **tablespoons all-purpose flour**
- ¾ **teaspoon salt**
- ¼ **teaspoon pepper**
- ¼ **teaspoon baking powder**
- 4 **medium potatoes, peeled and cubed (about 1½ pounds)**
- 2 **tablespoons chopped fresh parsley**
- 3 **to 4 tablespoons vegetable oil**

1. In a blender or food processor, place the eggs, onion, flour, salt, pepper, baking powder and ½ cup of potatoes. Cover and process on high until smooth. Add parsley and remaining potatoes; cover and pulse 2-4 times until potatoes are chopped.

2. Pour 1 to 2 tablespoons oil onto a hot griddle or skillet. Pour batter by ⅓ cupfuls onto griddle; flatten slightly to a 4-in. to 5-in. diameter. Cook over medium heat until golden on both sides. Add oil as needed until all pancakes are cooked.

Broccoli Bake

This tasty side dish is always a big hit when my son, daughter-in-law and granddaughter come for dinner or when I'm hosting a shower or party. At Easter, it's a great way to use up hard-cooked eggs!

—CAROLYN GRIFFIN MACON, GEORGIA

YIELD: 6 SERVINGS.

- 2 packages (10 ounces each) frozen cut broccoli
- ½ cup chopped onion
- 1 tablespoon butter
- 1 can (10¾ ounces) condensed cream of mushroom soup, undiluted
- ½ teaspoon ground mustard
- ½ teaspoon salt
- 4 hard-cooked eggs, chopped
- 1½ cups (6 ounces) shredded cheddar cheese
- 1 can (2.8 ounces) french-fried onions

1. Cook broccoli according to package directions; drain and set aside. In a skillet or saucepan, saute onion in butter until tender. Stir in soup, mustard and salt; heat until bubbly. In a 1½-qt. baking dish, arrange half of broccoli; top with half the eggs, half the cheese and half the mushroom sauce. Repeat layers. Bake at 350° for 20 minutes. Sprinkle onions on top and bake 5 minutes longer.

Tomato Dumplings

The wonderful fresh tomato taste of the sauce complements these light, savory dumplings. They make a perfect side dish for a meal with beef. My family enjoys them very much.

—LUCILLE TUCKER CLINTON, ILLINOIS

YIELD: 6 SERVINGS.

- ½ cup finely chopped onion
- ¼ cup finely chopped green pepper
- ¼ cup finely chopped celery
- ¼ cup butter
- 1 bay leaf
- 1 can (28 ounces) diced tomatoes, undrained
- 1 tablespoon brown sugar
- ½ teaspoon dried basil
- ½ teaspoon salt
- ¼ teaspoon pepper

DUMPLINGS

- 1 cup all-purpose flour
- 1½ teaspoons baking powder
- ½ teaspoon salt
- 1 tablespoon cold butter
- 1 tablespoon snipped fresh parsley
- ⅔ cup milk

1. In large skillet, saute the onion, green pepper and celery in butter until tender. Add bay leaf, tomatoes, brown sugar, basil, salt and pepper; cover and simmer for 5-10 minutes.

2. Meanwhile, for the dumplings, combine flour, baking powder and salt in a bowl. Cut in butter. Add parsley and milk; stir just until mixed.

3. Drop by tablespoonfuls onto the simmering tomato mixture, making six mounds; cover tightly and simmer for 12-15 minutes or until a toothpick inserted into one of the dumplings comes out clean. Discard the bay leaf. Serve immediately.

Paprika Potatoes

These tasty potatoes are golden and crusty on the outside and tender on the inside. I've served them with many kinds of meat. When a meal needs a homey, comforting touch, I whip up a batch.

—RUTH ANDREWSON
LEAVENWORTH, WASHINGTON

YIELD: 4-6 SERVINGS.

> 4 large potatoes, peeled, cooked and quartered
> 3 tablespoons butter
> ½ teaspoon paprika

1. In a large skillet, slowly saute the potatoes in butter until golden brown, about 10-15 minutes. Sprinkle with the paprika.

As a young girl, I felt privileged when my grandmother asked me to shop for her. I walked to the creamery for some butter and then stopped by the meat market to buy 25 cents worth of German bologna. I'd proudly carry them back to my grandma's house in a little basket.

—HELEN DILLSON
HIXSON, TENNESSEE

Cheese Potato Puff

I enjoy entertaining and always look for recipes I can make ahead of time. I got this satisfying potato recipe from my mother-in-law. It's wonderful because I can prepare it the night before. It also contains basic ingredients that everyone loves, like milk and cheddar cheese.

—BEVERLY TEMPLETON GARNER, IOWA

YIELD: 8-10 SERVINGS.

> 12 medium potatoes, peeled (about 5 pounds)
> 1 teaspoon salt, divided
> ¾ cup butter, cubed
> 2 cups (8 ounces) shredded cheddar cheese
> 1 cup milk
> 2 eggs, beaten
> **Minced chives, optional**

1. Place potatoes in a Dutch oven; cover with water. Add ½ teaspoon salt; cook until tender. Drain; mash potatoes until smooth.

2. In a large saucepan, cook and stir the butter, cheese, milk and remaining salt until smooth. Stir into the potatoes; fold in the eggs. Pour into a greased 3-qt. baking dish.

3. Bake, uncovered, at 350° for 40 minutes or until puffy and golden brown. Sprinkle with chives if desired.

Butternut Squash Bake

If I ask our two girls what to fix for a special meal, they always request this dish. I discovered this slightly sweet, crunchy-topped casserole at a church dinner years ago. Now I take it to potluck dinners and come home with an empty dish!

—JULIE JAHN DECATUR, INDIANA

YIELD: 6-8 SERVINGS.

- ⅓ cup butter, softened
- ¾ cup sugar
- 2 eggs
- 1 can (5 ounces) evaporated milk
- 1 teaspoon vanilla extract
- 2 cups mashed cooked butternut squash

TOPPING
- ½ cup crisp rice cereal
- ¼ cup packed brown sugar
- ¼ cup chopped pecans
- 2 tablespoons butter, melted

1. In a large bowl, cream butter and sugar until fluffy. Beat in the eggs, milk and vanilla. Stir in squash (mixture will be thin).

2. Pour into a greased 11-in. x 7-in. baking dish. Bake, uncovered, at 350° for 45 minutes or until almost set.

3. In a small bowl, combine topping ingredients; sprinkle over casserole. Return to the oven for 5-10 minutes or until bubbly.

Corn and Bacon Casserole

Corn is my three boys' favorite vegetable, so we eat a lot of it. My husband, Bob, and our sons really enjoy it.

—MARCIA HOSTETTER CANTON, NEW YORK

YIELD: 6-8 SERVINGS.

- 6 bacon strips
- ½ cup chopped onion
- 2 tablespoons all-purpose flour
- 2 garlic cloves, minced
- ½ teaspoon salt
- ½ teaspoon pepper
- 1 cup (8 ounces) sour cream
- 3½ cups fresh or frozen whole kernel corn
- 1 tablespoon chopped fresh parsley
- 1 tablespoon minced chives

1. In a large skillet, cook the bacon over medium heat until crisp. Drain, reserving 2 tablespoon of drippings. Crumble bacon; set aside.

2. Saute onion in drippings until tender. Add flour, garlic, salt and pepper. Cook and stir until bubbly; cook and stir 1 minute more. Remove from the heat and stir in sour cream until smooth. Add corn, parsley and half of the bacon; mix well.

3. Pour into a 1-qt. baking dish. Sprinkle with remaining bacon. Bake, uncovered, at 350° for 20-25 minutes or until heated through. Sprinkle with chives.

Delicious Corn Pudding

This old-fashioned dish has been part of our family meals for years, and we've shared it at many gatherings.

—P. MARCHESI ROCKY POINT, NEW YORK

YIELD: 8 SERVINGS.

- 4 eggs, separated
- 2 tablespoons butter, melted and cooled
- 1 tablespoon sugar
- 1 tablespoon brown sugar
- 1 teaspoon salt
- ½ teaspoon vanilla extrsact

Dash each ground cinnamon and nutmeg

- 2 cups fresh or frozen corn
- 1 cup half-and-half cream
- 1 cup milk

1. In a bowl, beat yolks until lemon-colored, 5-8 minutes. Add the butter, sugars, salt, vanilla, cinnamon and nutmeg; mix well. Add corn. Stir in cream and milk. In a small bowl, beat egg whites on high speed until stiff; fold into yolk mixture.

2. Pour into a greased 1½-qt. baking dish. Bake, uncovered, at 350° for 35 minutes or until a knife inserted near the center comes out clean. Cover loosely with foil during the last 10 minutes of baking if top browns too quickly.

Caraway Sauerkraut

Over the years, I've learned that cooking with herbs and spices is fun and rewarding. With sauerkraut, bacon and caraway, this side dish really reflects my German heritage.

—TRUDI JOHNSON HIXSON, TENNESSEE

YIELD: 18-20 SERVINGS.

- 6 bacon strips, chopped
- 1 medium onion, chopped
- 2 bags or jars (32 ounces each) sauerkraut, rinsed and drained
- 1 tablespoon caraway seeds
- 2 cups water
- 1 large potato, peeled and shredded

1. In a 5-qt. Dutch oven, cook bacon and onion over medium heat for 8-9 minutes or until onion is golden brown. Stir in sauerkraut and caraway. Add water; bring to a boil. Reduce heat; cover and simmer for 1½ hours, stirring occasionally. Add potato. Cook for 20 minutes or until potato is tender.

Norwegian Parsley Potatoes

I love to use parsley in many dishes, and it suits the fresh taste of small red potatoes well. Even though these potatoes are easy to prepare, they look fancy and are great with baked ham.

—EUNICE STOEN DECORAH, IOWA

YIELD: 6-8 SERVINGS.

- 2 pounds small red new potatoes
- ½ cup butter, cubed
- ¼ cup chopped fresh parsley
- ¼ teaspoon dried marjoram

1. Cook potatoes in boiling salted water for 15 minutes or until tender. Cool slightly. With a sharp knife, remove one narrow strip of skin around the middle of each potato. In a large skillet, melt butter; add parsley and marjoram. Add the potatoes and stir gently until coated and heated through.

Creamed Peas

I can still taste these wonderful peas in Mama's delicious white sauce. Our food was generally pretty plain during the week, so I thought the sauce made the peas extra fancy and fitting for a Sunday meal.
—**IMOGENE HUTTON** BROWNWOOD, TEXAS

YIELD: 3-4 SERVINGS.

- 1 **package (10 ounces) frozen peas**
- 1 **tablespoon butter**
- 1 **tablespoon all-purpose flour**
- ¼ **teaspoon salt**
- ⅛ **teaspoon pepper**
- ½ **cup milk**
- 1 **teaspoon sugar**

1. Cook peas according to package directions. Meanwhile, in a small saucepan, melt the butter. Stir in the flour, salt and pepper until blended; gradually add milk and sugar. Bring to a boil; cook and stir for 1-2 minutes or until thickened. Drain peas; stir into the sauce and heat through.

Easy Grilled Squash

This is one of my favorite ways to use butternut squash, which I love not just for its flavor but also because it's full of vitamin A. I usually make this when I am grilling steak or chicken.
—**ESTHER HORST** MONTEREY, TENNESSEE

YIELD: 4 SERVINGS.

- 3 **tablespoons olive oil**
- 2 **garlic cloves, minced**
- ¼ **teaspoon salt**
- ¼ **teaspoon pepper**
- 1 **small butternut squash, peeled and cut lengthwise into ½-inch slices**

1. In a small bowl, combine the oil, garlic, salt and pepper. Brush over squash slices.

2. Grill squash, covered, over medium heat or broil 4 in. from the heat for 4-5 minutes on each side or until tender.

Asparagus with Sesame Butter

The first fresh asparagus is a delightful springtime treat. This light butter sauce lets the asparagus flavor come through, and the sprinkling of sesame seeds adds a delicate crunch. It's a simple yet delicious dish.

—EUNICE STOEN DECORAH, IOWA

YIELD: 6-8 SERVINGS.

- 2 **pounds fresh asparagus**
- 1 **cup boiling water**
- ½ **teaspoon salt**
- 1 **tablespoon cornstarch**
- ¼ **cup cold water**
- ¼ **cup butter, cubed**
- 3 **tablespoons sesame seeds, toasted**

1. Place asparagus spears in a large skillet; add boiling water and salt. Cook for 5-7 minutes or until tender. Remove the asparagus and keep warm. Drain cooking liquid, reserving ½ cup in a small saucepan.

2. Combine cornstarch and cold water; stir into liquid. Cook and stir over medium heat until thickened and bubbly; cook and stir 1 minute more. Stir in the butter until melted. Spoon over asparagus; sprinkle with sesame seeds and serve immediately.

Herbed Rice Pilaf

I've relied on this savory side dish for years. We especially enjoy it in summer alongside a grilled entree.

—JERI DOBROWSKI BEACH, NORTH DAKOTA

YIELD: 6 SERVINGS.

- 1 **cup uncooked long grain rice**
- 1 **cup chopped celery**
- ¾ **cup chopped onion**
- ¼ **cup butter**
- 2½ **cups water**
- 1 **package (2 to 2½ ounces) dry chicken noodle soup mix**

- 2 **tablespoons minced fresh parsley**
- ½ **teaspoon dried thyme**
- ¼ **teaspoon rubbed sage**
- ¼ **teaspoon pepper**
- 1 **tablespoon chopped pimientos, optional**

1. In a large skillet, cook the rice, celery and onion in butter, stirring constantly, until rice is browned. Stir in the next six ingredients; bring to a boil.

2. Reduce heat; cover and simmer for 15 minutes. Stir in the pimientos if desired. Remove from the heat and let stand, covered, for 10 minutes.

Creamed Onions

This is my absolute favorite dish of my mom's. The onions have a mild flavor, and there's plenty of the rich creamy sauce. The sweetness makes it a nice complement to beef tenderloin.

—DENISE BITNER REEDSVILLE, PENNSYLVANIA

YIELD: 8-10 SERVINGS.

- 6 **large onions, sliced**
- 1 **cup butter**
- 2 **teaspoons all-purpose flour**
- 2 **teaspoons salt**
- ½ **teaspoon white pepper**
- 2 **cups milk**

1. In a large skillet or Dutch oven, saute onions in butter until tender and golden brown, about 25 minutes. Remove with a slotted spoon. Add flour, salt and pepper to skillet; stir until smooth. Gradually stir in milk until blended.

2. Bring to a boil; cook and stir for 2 minutes or until sauce is thickened. Reduce heat to medium. Return onions to the pan; heat through.

German-Style Spinach

Grandma's Austrian heritage comes through in her spinach dish. It's tasty and always looks so pretty on the plate. We children never had to be told to eat our spinach at Grandma's house!

—JOAN HUTTER WARWICK, RHODE ISLAND

YIELD: 8 SERVINGS.

- 2 **packages (10 ounces each) frozen chopped spinach**
- 1 **large onion, chopped**
- 2 **garlic cloves, minced**
- 2 **tablespoons butter**
- 6 **bacon strips, cooked and crumbled**
- ½ **teaspoon ground nutmeg**
- ½ **teaspoon salt**

Pepper to taste

1. Cook spinach according to package directions. Drain well and set aside. Saute onion and garlic in butter in a large skillet until tender. Stir in the spinach, bacon, nutmeg, salt and pepper; heat through.

Mashed Horseradish Potatoes

Instead of the ordinary garlic mashed potatoes, this unusual—but delicious—recipe calls for prepared horseradish. My family requests it every Thanksgiving, and it is also great with roast beef.

—CYNTHIA GOBELI NORTON, OHIO

YIELD: 6-8 SERVINGS.

- 6 **medium potatoes, peeled and cubed**
- ¼ **cup butter, melted**
- ¾ **teaspoon salt**
- ⅛ **teaspoon pepper**
- ½ **cup sour cream**
- 2 **tablespoons prepared horseradish**

1. Place potatoes in a large saucepan and cover with water. Bring to a boil. Reduce heat and cook for 10 minutes or until tender; drain.

2. Add the butter, salt and pepper. Mash potatoes. Beat in the sour cream and horseradish.

When Mom fried potatoes, she would moisten bread under the faucet, squeeze out the water, then break the bread into the potatoes. It would fry up brown and crunchy. When I got married, I made potatoes the same way. When my daughter got married, so did she.

Not long ago, Mom came for a visit. She decided to fry potatoes. I was stunned when she did not add the bread to the pan. When I asked where the bread was, she said she didn't know what I was talking about. So I explained that when I was a child in the early 1940s, she always fried potatoes that way. She started to laugh. She told me the only reason she did that was because we didn't have enough potatoes!

—JUDIE DUMONT WALTON, INDIANA

Party Potatoes

These creamy potatoes can be prepared the day before and then stored in the refrigerator until you're ready to pop them in the oven. The garlic powder and chives add zip, and the shredded cheese adds color.

—**SHARON MENSING** GREENFIELD, IOWA

YIELD: 10-12 SERVINGS.

    4   cups mashed potatoes (about 8
        to 10 large) or 4 cups prepared
        instant potatoes
    1   cup (8 ounces) sour cream
    1   package (8 ounces) cream cheese,
        softened
    1   teaspoon minced chives
    ¼   teaspoon garlic powder
    ¼   cup dry bread crumbs
    1   tablespoon butter, melted
    ½   cup shredded cheddar cheese

1. In a large bowl, combine potatoes, sour cream, cream cheese, chives and garlic powder. Tranfer to a greased 2-qt. baking dish. Combine the bread crumbs with the butter; sprinkle over the potatoes.

2. Bake at 350° for 50 to 60 minutes. Sprinkle with the cheese and serve immediately.

Hungarian Noodle Side Dish

I first served this rich casserole at a women's meeting at church. Everyone liked it and many of the ladies wanted the recipe. The original recipe was from a friend, but I changed it a bit to suit our tastes.

—**BETTY SUGG** AKRON, NEW YORK

YIELD: 8-10 SERVINGS.

    3   chicken bouillon cubes
    ¼   cup boiling water
    1   can (10¾ ounces) condensed cream of mushroom soup, undiluted
    ½   cup chopped onion
    2   tablespoons Worcestershire sauce
    2   tablespoons poppy seeds
    ⅛   to ¼ teaspoon garlic powder
    ⅛   to ¼ teaspoon hot pepper sauce
    2   cups (16 ounces) 4% cottage cheese
    2   cups (16 ounces) sour cream
    1   package (16 ounces) medium noodles, cooked and drained
    ¼   cup shredded Parmesan cheese
Paprika

1. In a large bowl, dissolve bouillon in water. Add the next six ingredients; mix well. Stir in cottage cheese, sour cream and noodles and mix well.

2. Pour into a greased 2½-qt. baking dish. Sprinkle with the Parmesan cheese and paprika. Cover and bake at 350° for 45 minutes or until heated through.

Continental Zucchini

Zucchini are big and plentiful here, and people often joke about using them up before they multiply! Even with so much zucchini to go around, everyone enjoys it prepared this way.

—MARTHA FEHL BROOKVILLE, INDIANA

YIELD: 6 SERVINGS.

- 1 tablespoon canola oil
- 1 pound zucchini (about 3 small), cubed
- 1 to 2 garlic cloves, minced
- 1 jar (2 ounces) diced pimientos, drained
- 1 can (15¼ ounces) whole kernel corn, drained
- 1 teaspoon salt, optional
- ¼ teaspoon lemon-pepper seasoning
- ½ cup shredded part-skim mozzarella cheese

1. Heat oil in a large skillet. Saute zucchini and garlic for 3 to 4 minutes. Add pimientos, corn, salt if desired and lemon-pepper; cook and stir for 2-3 minutes or until the zucchini is tender. Sprinkle with cheese and heat until the cheese is melted.

Scalloped Pineapple Casserole

My family can't get enough of this sweet and satisfying side dish. The casserole disappears quickly whenever I prepare it.

—JUDY HOWLE COLUMBUS, MISSISSIPPI

YIELD: 6 SERVINGS.

- ¾ cup butter, softened
- 1¼ cups sugar
- 3 eggs
- 1 can (20 ounces) crushed pineapple, well drained
- 1½ teaspoons lemon juice
- 4 cups firmly packed cubed white bread (crusts removed)

1. In a large bowl, cream butter and sugar until light and fluffy. Add eggs, one at a time, beating well after each addition. Stir in the pineapple and lemon juice. Gently fold in bread cubes.

2. Spoon into a greased 2-qt. baking dish. Bake, uncovered, at 350° for 40 to 45 minutes or until the top is lightly golden. Serve warm.

Harvard Beets

My beets are a pretty accompaniment to any meal and have wonderful flavor. Even those who normally shy away from beets will gobble these up.

—JEAN ANN PERKINS NEWBURYPORT, MARYLAND

YIELD: 4-6 SERVINGS.

- 1 can (16 ounces) sliced beets
- ¼ cup sugar
- 1½ teaspoons cornstarch
- 2 tablespoons cider vinegar
- 2 tablespoons orange juice
- 1 tablespoon grated orange peel

1. Drain beets, reserving 2 tablespoons juice; set beets and juice aside. In a saucepan, combine sugar and cornstarch. Add vinegar, orange juice and beet juice; bring to a boil. Reduce heat and simmer for 3-4 minutes or until thickened. Add beets and orange peel; heat through.

Stuffed Baked Potatoes

My whole family, from the smallest grandchild on up, loves these special potatoes. I prepare them up to a week in advance, wrap them well and freeze. The flavorful filling will go nicely with your favorite meat dish.

—**MARGE CLARK** WEST LEBANON, INDIANA

YIELD: 6 SERVINGS.

- 3 **large baking potatoes (1 pound each)**
- 1½ **teaspoons canola oil, optional**
- ½ **cup sliced green onions**
- ½ **cup butter, cubed, divided**
- ½ **cup half-and-half cream**
- ½ **cup sour cream**
- 1 **teaspoon salt**
- ½ **teaspoon white pepper**
- 1 **cup (4 ounces) shredded cheddar cheese**
Paprika

1. Scrub and pierce potatoes. Rub with oil if desired. Bake at 400° for 50-75 minutes or until tender. When cool enough to handle, cut each potato in half lengthwise. Scoop out pulp, leaving a thin shell; set aside.

2. In a small skillet, saute onions in ¼ cup butter until tender. In a large bowl, mash potato pulp. Stir in the onion mixture, cream, sour cream, salt and pepper. Fold in the cheese. Stuff into potato shells.

3. Place on a baking sheet. Melt remaining butter; drizzle over potatoes. Sprinkle with paprika. Bake at 375° for 20 minutes or until heated through.

Editor's Note: *Potatoes may be stuffed ahead of time and refrigerated or frozen. Allow additional time for reheating.*

Ranch Stuffed Baked Potatoes: Stir 1 to 2 tablespoons ranch salad dressing mix into sour cream before adding to mashed potatoes. Fold in 3 crumbled cooked bacon strips along with the cheese.

Tex-Mex Stuffed Baked Potatoes: Omit green onions and ¼ cup butter. Stir in 1 can (4 ounces) chopped green chilies (drained). Substitute pepper Jack cheese for the cheddar. Sprinkle with chili powder instead of paprika.

Herb-Stuffed Baked Potatoes: Add 2 tablespoons each minced chives and fresh parsley with the onions. Susbtitute mozzarella for the cheddar.

Broccoli-Stuffed Baked Potatoes: Omit green onions. Saute 2 cups fresh broccoli florets and ½ cup chopped onion in ¼ cup butter. Stir into mashed potatoes.

Western Beans

I've made these zesty beans many times for picnics and potlucks. They're hearty and zippy with chili pepper and the extra flavor of lentils in the bean mix. I sometimes make them ahead of time and heat right before serving.

—**ARTHUR MORRIS** WASHINGTON, PENNSYLVANIA

YIELD: 8-10 SERVINGS.

- 4 **bacon strips, diced**
- 1 **large onion, chopped**
- 1⅓ **cups water**
- ⅓ **cup dried lentils, rinsed**
- 2 **tablespoons ketchup**
- 1 **teaspoon garlic powder**
- ¾ **teaspoon chili powder**
- ½ **teaspoon ground cumin**
- ¼ **teaspoon dried red pepper flakes**
- 1 **bay leaf**
- 1 **can (14½ ounces) diced tomatoes, undrained**
- 1 **can (15 ounces) pinto beans, drained**
- 1 **can (16 ounces) kidney beans, drained**

1. Lightly fry bacon in a heavy 3-qt. saucepan. Add onion; cook until transparent. Stir in remaining ingredients. Cook over medium heat for 45 minutes or until lentils are tender, stirring once or twice. Remove bay leaf before serving.

Special Garden Medley

My mother used to make this in large batches to can for our family 60 years ago. Now I make it for my freezer.

—NORMA COATS PETERSBURG, TENNESSEE

YIELD: 6 SERVINGS.

- 2 celery ribs, chopped
- 1 large onion, chopped
- 1 medium sweet yellow or green pepper, chopped
- ¼ cup water
- 4 cups chopped seeded peeled tomatoes (about 9 medium)
- 4½ teaspoons sugar
- 1 teaspoon salt

1. In a large saucepan, combine the celery, onion, yellow pepper and water. Bring to a boil. Reduce heat; cover and simmer for 20 minutes or until tender.

2. Stir in the tomatoes, sugar and salt; cook 6-8 minutes longer or until heated through.

Zesty Carrot Bake

For a fun vegetable dish, try tender carrots in a sauce that gets a little extra punch from horseradish. With a crunchy crumb topping and comforting sauce, it will tempt even those who usually don't care for cooked carrots.

—GRACE YASKOVIC
LAKE HIAWATHA, NEW JERSEY

YIELD: 6 SERVINGS.

- 1 pound carrots, cut into ½-inch slices
- 2 tablespoons finely chopped onion
- ¾ cup mayonnaise
- ⅓ cup water
- 1 tablespoon prepared horseradish
- ¼ teaspoon pepper
- ½ cup dry bread crumbs
- 2 tablespoons butter, melted
- ½ cup shredded sharp cheddar cheese

1. On stovetop or microwave, cook the carrots until tender. Transfer to a 1-qt. baking dish; set aside.

2. In a small bowl, combine the next five ingredients. Pour over carrots. Combine bread crumbs and butter; sprinkle over top. Bake, uncovered, at 350° for 25-30 minutes. Sprinkle with cheese. Bake 2-3 minutes longer or until cheese is melted.

Mushroom Rice Medley

We would never hear the end of it if we failed to have my grandmother's mushroom rice dish on the table for any family gathering. It's the dish my dad requests most often.

—SUE MULLIS SHARON, WISCONSIN

YIELD: 6 SERVINGS.

3 cups water
½ cup uncooked brown rice
½ cup uncooked wild rice
1 teaspoon chicken bouillon granules
1 teaspoon dried oregano
½ pound sliced bacon, diced
½ pound sliced fresh mushrooms
1 small onion, chopped
¼ teaspoon salt, optional

1. In a large saucepan, combine the water, brown rice, wild rice, bouillon and oregano. Bring to a boil. Reduce heat; cover and simmer for 50-60 minutes or until rice is tender.

2. In a large skillet, cook bacon over medium heat until crisp. Using a slotted spoon, remove to paper towels. Drain, reserving 2 tablespoons drippings. In the drippings, saute mushrooms and onion until tender. Stir in rice and bacon; heat through. Season with salt if desired.

Finnish Cauliflower

After my Finnish grandmother passed away, I found a large index card in a box of her trinkets. I had the writing translated, and it turned out to be this festive casserole.
—**JUDY BATSON** TAMPA, FLORIDA

YIELD: 8 SERVINGS.

- 2 **cups cubed day-old rye bread**
- 1 **small head cauliflower, cut into florets**
- 2 **tablespoons butter**
- 1 **teaspoon caraway seeds**
- 3 **cups (12 ounces) shredded sharp cheddar cheese**
- 4 **eggs, beaten**
- 1 **cup flat beer or nonalcoholic beer**
- 1 **teaspoon ground mustard**
- ½ **teaspoon ground coriander**
- ¼ **teaspoon pepper**

1. Place bread in a 15-in. x 10-in. x 1-in. baking pan; bake at 300° for 15-20 minutes or until crisp. In a large skillet, saute cauliflower in butter with the caraway seeds until tender. Remove from the heat; stir in bread and cheese. Transfer to a greased 11-in. x 7-in. baking dish.

2. In a small bowl, whisk the eggs, beer, mustard, coriander and pepper. Pour over bread mixture. Bake at 350° for 30-35 minutes or until a knife inserted near the center comes out clean.

Parmesan Noodles

The special blend of flavors in this cheesy side dish makes it a good addition to any meal. It's a nice change of pace from regular pasta and cheese dishes.
—**ELIZABETH EWAN** CLEVELAND, OHIO

YIELD: 8 SERVINGS.

- 2 **packages (3 ounces each) cream cheese, softened**
- ½ **cup butter, softened, divided**
- 2 **tablespoons minced fresh parsley**
- 1 **teaspoon dried basil**
- ½ **teaspoon lemon-pepper seasoning**
- ⅔ **cup boiling water**
- 1 **garlic clove, minced**
- 6 **cups hot cooked thin noodles**
- ⅔ **cup grated Parmesan cheese, divided**

Additional parsley, optional

1. In a small bowl, combine the cream cheese, 2 tablespoons butter, parsley, basil and lemon-pepper. Stir in water; keep warm.

2. In a saucepan, saute the garlic in remaining butter for 1 minute or until golden brown.

3. Place noodles in a serving bowl; top with garlic mixture. Sprinkle with half of the Parmesan cheese; toss lightly. Spoon the cream sauce over noodles and sprinkle with the remaining Parmesan cheese. Garnish with parsley if desired.

Spaetzle Dumplings

It takes only minutes to make my tender homemade noodles. They are a natural accompaniment to chicken. You can enjoy them with chicken gravy or simply eat them buttered and sprinkled with parsley.

—**PAMELA EATON** MONCLOVA, OHIO

YIELD: 6 SERVINGS.

- 2 cups all-purpose flour
- 4 eggs, lightly beaten
- ⅓ cup 2% milk
- 2 teaspoons salt
- 8 cups water
- 1 tablespoon butter

1. In a large bowl, stir the flour, eggs, milk and salt until smooth (dough will be sticky). In a large saucepan, bring water to a boil. Pour dough into a colander or spaetzle maker coated with cooking spray; place over boiling water.

2. With a wooden spoon, press dough until small pieces drop into boiling water. Cook for 2 minutes or until dumplings are tender and float. Remove with a slotted spoon; toss with butter.

Broccoli Rice Casserole

When I was little, serving this dish was the only way my mother could get me to eat broccoli. It's an excellent recipe and very good with poultry.

—**JENNIFER FULLER**
BALLSTON SPA, NEW YORK

YIELD: 8 SERVINGS.

- 1½ cups water
- ½ cup butter, cubed
- 1 tablespoon dried minced onion
- 2 cups uncooked instant rice
- 1 package (16 ounces) frozen chopped broccoli, thawed
- 1 can (10¾ ounces) condensed cream of mushroom soup, undiluted
- 1 jar (8 ounces) process cheese sauce

1. In a large saucepan, bring the water, butter and onion to a boil. Stir in rice. Remove from the heat; cover and let stand for 5 minutes or until water is absorbed.

2. Stir in the broccoli, soup and cheese sauce. Transfer broccoli mixture to a greased 2-qt. baking dish. Bake, uncovered, at 350° for 30-35 minutes or until bubbly.

Potato Gnocchi

My Italian mother remembers her own mother making these dumplings for special occasions. She still has the bowl Grandma mixed the dough in, which will someday be passed down to me.

—TINA REPAK MIRILOVICH JOHNSTOWN, PENNSYLVANIA

YIELD: 6-8 SERVINGS.

- 4 **medium potatoes, peeled and quartered**
- 1 **egg, lightly beaten**
- 1½ **teaspoons salt, divided**
- 1¾ **to 2 cups all-purpose flour**
- 3 **quarts water**
- **Spaghetti sauce, warmed**

1. Place potatoes in a saucepan and cover with water. Bring to a boil. Reduce heat; cover and cook for 15-20 minutes or until tender. Drain and mash.

2. Place 2 cups mashed potatoes in a large bowl (save any remaining mashed potatoes for another use). Stir in egg and 1 teaspoon salt. Gradually beat in flour until blended (dough will be firm and elastic).

3. Turn onto a lightly floured surface; knead 15 times. Roll into ½-in.-wide ropes. Cut ropes into 1-in. pieces. Press down with a lightly floured fork.

4. In a Dutch oven, bring water and remaining salt to a boil. Add gnocchi in small batches; cook for 8-10 minutes or until gnocchi float to the top and are cooked through. Remove with a slotted spoon. Serve immediately with spaghetti sauce.

Zucchini Mozzarella Medley

I love fresh vegetables, especially zucchini, and this recipe of my mother-in-law's is one of my favorite ways to prepare it.

—JENNIFER YODER AMBERG, WISCONSIN

YIELD: 4 SERVINGS.

- 3 **cups sliced zucchini**
- 1 **cup sliced onion**
- ½ **teaspoon dried basil**
- ¼ **teaspoon dried oregano**
- ⅛ **teaspoon salt**
- 3 **tablespoons butter**
- 1 **garlic clove, minced**
- 1 **medium tomato, cut into 12 wedges**
- 1 **cup (4 ounces) shredded part-skim mozzarella cheese**

1. In a large skillet, saute the zucchini, onion and seasonings in butter until crisp-tender. Add garlic; cook 1 minute longer.

2. Gently stir in tomato wedges; sprinkle with cheese. Remove from the heat; cover and let stand for 1-2 minutes or until the cheese is melted.

BREADS

Lemon Blueberry Bread

Of all the quick breads we had growing up, this beautifully glazed berry-studded loaf is the best!

—JULIANNE JOHNSON GROVE CITY, MINNESOTA

YIELD: 1 LOAF (16 SLICES).

⅓ cup butter, melted
1 cup sugar
3 tablespoons lemon juice
2 eggs
1½ cups all-purpose flour
1 teaspoon baking powder
½ teaspoon salt
½ cup milk
1 cup fresh or frozen blueberries
½ cup chopped nuts
2 tablespoons grated lemon peel
GLAZE
2 tablespoons lemon juice
¼ cup sugar

1. In a large bowl, beat the butter, sugar, lemon juice and eggs. Combine the flour, baking powder and salt; stir into the egg mixture alternately with milk, beating well after each addition. Fold in the blueberries, nuts and lemon peel.

2. Transfer to a greased 8-in. x 4-in. loaf pan. Bake at 350° for 60-70 minutes or until a toothpick inserted near the center comes out clean. Cool for 10 minutes before removing from pan to a wire rack.

3. Combine the glaze ingredients; drizzle over warm bread. Cool completely.

Editor's Note: *If using frozen blueberries, use without thawing to avoid discoloring the batter.*

Irish Soda Bread

This bread is prepared much like a biscuit. Mix the dough just until moist to keep it tender.

—GLORIA WARCZAK CEDARBURG, WISCONSIN

YIELD: 6-8 SERVINGS.

2 cups all-purpose flour
2 tablespoons brown sugar
1 teaspoon baking powder
1 teaspoon baking soda
½ teaspoon salt
3 tablespoons butter
2 eggs
¾ cup buttermilk
⅓ cup raisins

1. In a large bowl, combine flour, brown sugar, baking powder, baking soda and salt. Cut in butter until crumbly. In a small bowl, whisk 1 egg and buttermilk. Stir into flour mixture just until moistened. Fold in raisins.

2. Knead on a floured surface for 1 minute. Shape into a round loaf; place on a greased baking sheet. Cut a ¼-in.-deep cross in top of loaf. Beat remaining egg; brush over loaf.

3. Bake at 375° for 30-35 minutes or until golden brown.

Caraway Irish Soda Bread: Add 1 to 2 tablespoons caraway seeds to the dry ingredients.

Pop-Up Rolls

For lightly sweet, biscuit-like rolls that are anything but dry, you can't beat simple Pop-Up Rolls. With just four basic ingredients that are mixed in one bowl, these easy-to-make rolls are great alongside just about everything.

—JUDY BRINEGAR LIBERTY, NORTH CAROLINA

YIELD: 9 ROLLS.

1½ cups self-rising flour
¾ cup milk
3 tablespoons sugar
1½ tablespoons mayonnaise

1. In a large bowl, stir together all ingredients until thoroughly combined. Fill greased muffin cups half full. Bake at 375° for 18-20 minutes or until lightly browned. Serve warm.

Editor's Note: *As a substitute for 1½ cups self-rising flour, place 2¼ teaspoons baking powder and 3/4 teaspoon salt in a measuring cup. Add all-purpose flour to measure 1 cup. Combine with an additional 1/2 cup all-purpose flour.*

Apricot Walnut Bread

Orange juice and oat bran add flavor and texture to this quick bread.

—DIANE HIXON NICEVILLE, FLORIDA

YIELD: 1 LOAF.

4 egg whites
⅔ cup water
½ cup orange juice
¼ cup canola oil
1 teaspoon vanilla extract
¾ cup uncooked oat bran hot cereal
½ cup chopped dried apricots
1¼ cups all-purpose flour
½ cup packed brown sugar
1 teaspoon baking powder
½ teaspoon baking soda
¼ cup chopped walnuts

1. In a bowl, combine the egg whites, water, orange juice, oil and vanilla. Stir in the oat bran and apricots. Combine the flour, brown sugar, baking powder and baking soda; stir into apricot mixture just until moistened. Fold in walnuts.

2. Pour into a greased 8-in. x 4-in. loaf pan. Bake at 350° for 50-55 minutes or a toothpick inserted near the center comes out clean. Cool for 10 minutes before removing from pan to a wire rack.

> My grandmother made a doughnut-shaped bread that she called "pretzel buck." She would deep-fry it like doughnuts and sprinkle cinnamon and sugar on it. You can't buy bread that tastes as good as that old pretzel buck.
>
> **—DAVID KIDD** WATERFORD, MICHIGAN

Cheddar-Dill Bread

With soup and salad, this savory cheese bread makes a terrific meal.

—**KAREN GARDINER** EUTAW, ALABAMA

YIELD: 1 LOAF.

- 2 cups self-rising flour
- 1 tablespoon sugar
- ¼ cup cold butter, cubed
- 1 cup (4 ounces) shredded sharp cheddar cheese
- 2 teaspoons dill weed
- 1 egg
- ¾ cup milk

1. In a large bowl, combine flour and sugar. Cut in butter until crumbly; stir in the cheese and dill. In a small bowl, beat egg and milk; pour into dry ingredients and stir just until moistened. (Batter will be very thick.)

2. Pour into a greased 8-in. x 4-in. loaf pan. Bake at 350° for 35-40 minutes or until a toothpick comes out clean. Cool in pan for 10 minutes before removing to a wire rack.

Editor's Note: *As a substitute for each cup of self-rising flour, place 1½ teaspoons baking powder and 1/2 teaspoon salt in a measuring cup. Add all-purpose flour to measure 1 cup.*

Glazed Cinnamon Biscuits

I often make this easy, delicious variation of glazed cinnamon rolls for our family as a breakfast treat on weekends.

—**SUE GRONHOLZ** BEAVER DAM, WISCONSIN

YIELD: 1 DOZEN.

- 2 cups all-purpose flour
- 4 teaspoons baking powder
- ½ teaspoon salt
- 6 tablespoons butter, divided
- ¾ cup milk
- ¼ cup sugar
- 1 teaspoon ground cinnamon

GLAZE

- 1 cup confectioners' sugar
- 1 tablespoon butter, melted
- 5 to 6 teaspoons milk
- ⅛ teaspoon vanilla extract

1. In a large bowl, combine dry ingredients. Cut in 4 tablespoons of butter until mixture resembles coarse crumbs. Stir in milk just until moistened.

2. Turn onto a lightly floured surface; knead gently 8 to 10 times. Roll into an 11-in. x 8-in. rectangle about ½ in. thick. Melt remaining butter; brush 1 tablespoon over dough. Combine sugar and cinnamon; sprinkle over butter. Roll up jelly-roll style, starting with long edge. Cut into 12 equal slices. Place with cut side down in a greased 8-in. square baking pan. Brush with remaining butter.

3. Bake at 450° for 18 to 20 minutes or until golden brown. Cool for 5 minutes. Combine glaze ingredients; spread over warm biscuits. Serve immediately.

Raspberry Lemon Muffins

These are my all-time favorite muffins, and I have a hard time eating just one. They're pretty, tangy and delectable.

—**SHARON SHINE** BRADFORD, PENNSYLVANIA

YIELD: 18 SERVINGS.

- 2 cups all-purpose flour
- 1 cup sugar
- 1 tablespoon baking powder
- ½ teaspoon salt
- 2 eggs, lightly beaten
- 1 cup half-and-half cream
- ½ cup canola oil
- 1 teaspoon lemon extract
- 1½ cups fresh or frozen raspberries

1. In a large bowl, combine flour, sugar, baking powder and salt. Combine the eggs, cream, oil and lemon extract; stir into dry ingredients just until moistened. Fold in raspberries.

2. Spoon into 18 greased or paper-lined muffin cups. Bake at 400° for 18 to 20 minutes or until a toohpick comes out clean.

Editor's Note: *If using frozen raspberries, use without thawing to avoid discoloring the batter.*

Chocolate Mini Loaves

Rich and moist, these luscious mini breads will remind you of pound cake. Slice them for snacking or to serve as dessert with a cup of coffee or tea.

—ELIZABETH DOWNEY EVART, MICHIGAN

YIELD: 5 MINI LOAVES (6 SLICES EACH).

½ cup butter, softened
⅔ cup packed brown sugar
1 cup (6 ounces) semisweet chocolate chips, melted
2 eggs
2 teaspoons vanilla extract
2½ cups all-purpose flour
1 teaspoon baking powder
1 teaspoon baking soda
1½ cups applesauce
½ cup miniature semisweet chocolate chips

GLAZE
½ cup semisweet chocolate chips
1 tablespoon butter
5 teaspoons water
½ cup confectioners' sugar
¼ teaspoon vanilla extract
Dash salt

1. In a large bowl, cream butter and brown sugar until light and fluffy. Beat in the melted chocolate chips, eggs and vanilla. Combine the flour, baking powder and baking soda; add to creamed mixture alternately with applesauce just until moistened. Fold in miniature chips.

2. Divide batter among five greased 5¾-in. x 3-in. x 2-in. loaf pans, about 1 cup in each. Bake at 350° for 30-40 minutes or until a toothpick inserted near the center comes out clean. Cool for 10 minutes before removing from pans to wire racks to cool completely.

3. For glaze, combine the chocolate chips, butter and water in a saucepan; cook and stir over low heat until chocolate is melted. Remove from the heat; stir in confectioners' sugar, vanilla and salt until smooth. Drizzle over cooled loaves.

Editor's Note: *Two 8-in. x 4-in. x 2-in. loaf pans may be used; bake for 50-55 minutes.*

Blueberry Streusel Muffins

What a joy to set out a basket of these moist blueberry muffins topped with a super streusel on the bake sale table. People rave when they taste them for the first time.

—MARY ANNE MCWHIRTER PEARLAND, TEXAS

YIELD: 1 DOZEN.

   ¼ **cup butter, softened**
   ⅓ **cup sugar**
   1 **egg**
   1 **teaspoon vanilla extract**
   2⅓ **cups all-purpose flour**
   4 **teaspoons baking powder**
   ½ **teaspoon salt**
   1 **cup milk**
   1½ **cups fresh or frozen blueberries**
STREUSEL
   ½ **cup sugar**
   ⅓ **cup all-purpose flour**
   ½ **teaspoon ground cinnamon**
   ¼ **cup cold butter**

1. In a large bowl, cream the butter and sugar. Beat in egg and vanilla; mix well. Combine the flour, baking powder and salt; add to creamed mixture alternately with milk. Fold in the blueberries.

2. Fill 12 greased or paper-lined muffin cups two-thirds full. In a small bowl, combine the sugar, flour and cinnamon; cut in the butter until crumbly. Sprinkle over the muffins. Bake at 375° for 25-30 minutes or until browned. Cool for 5 minutes before removing to a wire rack. Serve warm.

Editor's Note: *If using frozen blueberries, use without thawing to avoid discoloring the batter.*

Pumpkin Bread

You'll love this deliciously spicy, pumpkin-rich quick bread. I keep my freezer stocked with home-baked goodies. This one is always a winner with our harvest crew.

—JOYCE JACKSON BRIDGETOWN, NOVA SCOTIA

YIELD: 1 LOAF (16 SLICES).

   1⅔ **cups all-purpose flour**
   1½ **cups sugar**
   1 **teaspoon baking soda**
   1 **teaspoon ground cinnamon**
   ¾ **teaspoon salt**
   ½ **teaspoon baking powder**
   ½ **teaspoon ground nutmeg**
   ¼ **teaspoon ground cloves**
   2 **eggs**

1 cup canned pumpkin
½ cup canola oil
½ cup water
½ cup chopped walnuts
½ cup raisins, optional

1. In a large small bowl, combine the flour, sugar, baking soda cinnamon, salt, baking powder, nutmeg and cloves. In a small bowl, whisk the eggs, pumpkin, oil, and water. Stir into dry ingredients just until moistened. Fold in walnuts and raisins if desired.

2. Pour into a greased 9-in. x 5-in. loaf pan. Bake at 350° for 65-70 minutes or until a toothpick inserted in the center comes out clean. Cool in pan for 10 minutes before removing to a wire rack.

Poppy Seed Bread

This moist, rich bread is so delicious—it's very popular in our area. It gets golden brown and looks great sliced for a buffet. I also like to make miniature loaves to give as gifts.

—**FAYE HINTZ** SPRINGFIELD, MISSOURI

YIELD: 2 LOAVES.

3 cups all-purpose flour
2¼ cups sugar
1½ tablespoons poppy seeds
3 teaspoons baking powder
1½ teaspoons salt
3 eggs, lightly beaten
1½ cups milk
1 cup canola oil
1½ teaspoons vanilla extract
1½ teaspoons almond extract
1½ teaspoons butter flavoring

GLAZE
¾ cup sugar
¼ cup orange juice
½ teaspoon vanilla extract
½ teaspoon almond extract
½ teaspoon butter flavoring

1. In a large bowl, combine first five ingredients. Add eggs, milk, oil, extracts and flavoring. Pour into two greased 8-in. x 4-in. loaf pans. Bake at 350° for 60-65 minutes or until a toothpick comes out clean. Cool completely in pans.

2. In a saucepan, bring glaze ingredients to a boil. Pour over bread in pans. Cool for 5 minutes before removing from pans to wire racks to cool completely.

Dutch Apple Bread

My fruity streusel-topped bread is delightful for brunch. This is a great make-ahead treat that freezes well, too.

—**JUNE FORMANEK** BELLE PLAINE, IOWA

YIELD: 1 LOAF.

½ cup butter, softened
1 cup sugar
2 eggs
1 teaspoon vanilla extract
2 cups all-purpose flour
1 teaspoon baking soda
½ teaspoon salt
⅓ cup buttermilk
1 cup chopped peeled apple
⅓ cup chopped walnuts

TOPPING
⅓ cup all-purpose flour
2 tablespoons sugar
2 tablespoons brown sugar
½ teaspoon ground cinnamon
3 tablespoons butter

1. In a bowl, cream butter and sugar. Beat in eggs and vanilla. Combine flour, baking soda and salt; stir into the creamed mixture alternately with buttermilk. Fold in apple and nuts.

2. Pour into a greased 9-in. x 5-in. loaf pan. For topping, combine the first four ingredients; cut in butter until crumbly. Sprinkle over batter. Bake at 350° for 55-60 minutes or until a toothpick comes out clean.. Cool in pan for 10 minutes; remove to a wire rack.

Apple Bran Muffins

My mom taught me how to make these moist, tasty muffins. The recipe makes a big batch, so you can freeze the extras or share with co-workers, family or friends.

—**KELLY KIRBY** WESTVILLE, NOVA SCOTIA

YIELD: 2 DOZEN.

- 3 cups all-purpose flour
- 2 teaspoons baking powder
- 2 teaspoons ground cinnamon
- 1 teaspoon salt
- ½ teaspoon baking soda
- ¼ teaspoon ground nutmeg
- 1½ cups 2% milk
- 4 eggs
- ⅔ cup packed brown sugar
- ½ cup canola oil
- 2 teaspoons vanilla extract
- 3 cups All-Bran
- 2 cups shredded peeled tart apples
- 1 cup chopped walnuts
- 1 cup raisins

1. In a large bowl, combine first six ingredients. In another bowl, combine the milk, eggs, brown sugar, oil and vanilla. Stir into dry ingredients just until moistened. Fold in remaining ingredients.

2. Fill greased or paper-lined muffin cups three-fourths full. Bake at 350° for 18-22 minutes or until a toothpick inserted in muffin comes out clean. Cool for 5 minutes before removing from pans to wire racks.

Cranberry Nut Bread

Whenever I serve slices of this favorite treat, someone asks for the recipe. It's a moist, dark holiday bread chock-full of old-fashioned spicy goodness.

—**MAXINE SMITH** OWANKA, SOUTH DAKOTA

YIELD: 2 LOAVES (16 LOAVES EACH).

- 2½ cups halved fresh or frozen cranberries, divided
- ⅔ cup sugar
- 2 teaspoons grated orange peel
- 2¼ cups all-purpose flour
- ¾ cup packed light brown sugar
- 1 tablespoon baking soda
- 2 teaspoons ground cinnamon
- ½ teaspoon salt
- ¼ teaspoon ground cloves
- 2 eggs, lightly beaten
- ¾ cup sour cream
- ¼ cup butter, melted
- 1 cup chopped pecans

1. In a large saucepan, combine 1½ cups cranberries, sugar and orange peel. Bring to a boil; reduce heat and cook for 6-8 minutes or until the cranberries are softened. Remove from the heat; stir in the remaining berries and set aside.

2. In a large bowl, combine the flour, brown sugar, baking soda, cinnamon, salt and cloves. Combine the eggs, sour cream and butter; stir into dry ingredients just until blended. Fold in cranberries and pecans.

3. Pour into two greased 8-in. x 4-in. loaf pans. Bake at 350° for 55-60 minutes or until a toothpick inserted near the center comes out clean. Cool in pan for 10 minutes before removing to a wire rack to cool completely.

Bacon Swiss Bread

I'm a busy mom, so I'm always looking for fast and easy recipes. These savory slices of jazzed-up French bread are great with soup and salad. My daughter and her friends liked to snack on them instead of pizza.

—**SHIRLEY MILLS** TULSA, OKLAHOMA

YIELD: 10 SERVINGS.

- 1 loaf (1 pound) French bread (20 inches)
- 2/3 cup butter, softened
- 1/3 cup chopped green onions
- 4 teaspoons prepared mustard
- 5 slices process Swiss cheese
- 5 bacon strips

1. Cut bread into 1-in.-thick slices, leaving slices attached at bottom. In a bowl, combine the butter, onions and mustard; spread on both sides of each slice of bread. Cut each cheese slice diagonally into four triangles; place between the slices of bread. Cut bacon in half widthwise and then lengthwise; drape a piece over each slice.

2. Place the loaf on a double thickness of heavy-duty foil. Bake at 400° for 20-25 minutes or until bacon is crisp.

Corn Bread Squares

This inexpensive cornbread will disappear as fast as you can make it. It is always fluffy and moist.

—**MARCIA SALISBURY** WAUKESHA, WISCONSIN

YIELD: 9 SERVINGS.

- 1 cup all-purpose flour
- 1 cup yellow cornmeal
- 1/4 cup sugar
- 2 teaspoons baking powder
- 3/4 teaspoon salt
- 2 eggs, lightly beaten
- 1 cup 2% milk
- 1/4 cup canola oil

1. In a bowl, combine flour, cornmeal, sugar, baking powder and salt. Add eggs, milk and oil. Beat just until moistened.

2. Spoon into a greased 8-in. square baking pan. Bake at 400° for 20-25 minutes or until a toothpick inserted near the center comes out clean. Serve warm.

Nutty Apple Muffins

I teach quick-bread making for 4-H, and I'm always on the lookout for good new recipes. My sister-in-law shared this recipe with me for a slightly different kind of muffin. With apples and coconut, each bite is moist, chewy and tasty.

—**GLORIA KAUFMANN** ORRVILLE, OHIO

YIELD: 1½ DOZEN.

- 1½ cups all-purpose flour
- 1½ teaspoons baking powder
- 3/4 teaspoon salt
- 1/2 teaspoon ground nutmeg
- 1/4 teaspoon baking soda
- 2 eggs
- 3/4 cup sugar
- 1/3 cup canola oil
- 3 tablespoons milk
- 1½ cups diced peeled apples
- 1 cup chopped walnuts
- 3/4 cup flaked coconut

1. In a large bowl, combine the flour, baking powder, salt, nutmeg and baking soda. In another bowl, beat the eggs, sugar, oil and milk. Stir in the apples, nuts and coconut. Stir into dry ingredients just until moistened.

2. Fill 18 greased muffin cups three-fourths full. Bake at 350° for 20-25 minutes or until a toothpick comes out clean. Cool in pan for 10 minutes before removing to a wire rack.

My favorite memory of childhood was visiting my great-grandmother. She cooked on a huge, old wood-burning cookstove. She rose every morning at 4 a.m. no matter the weather. After she got that stove going, she'd start baking hot biscuits for breakfast. I don't think anything was ever as wonderful as waking up to the smell of a batch of her fresh hot biscuits.

—**PEGGY NELSON** CAMBRIDGE, MARYLAND

Orange Date Bread

I loved visiting my aunt—she was an excellent baker, and her kitchen always smelled great. With her inspiration, I now bake this moist, yummy bread every holiday season.

—**JOANN WOLFE** SUNLAND, CALIFORNIA

YIELD: 32 SERVINGS.

- 1 cup butter, softened
- 2 cups sugar
- 3 eggs, beaten
- 4 cups all-purpose flour
- 1 teaspoon baking soda
- 1 teaspoon salt
- 1⅓ cups buttermilk
- 1 cup chopped walnuts
- 1 cup chopped dates
- 1 tablespoon grated orange peel

GLAZE
- ¼ cup orange juice
- ½ cup sugar
- 2 tablespoons grated orange peel

1. In a bowl, cream butter and sugar. Add the eggs; mix well. Combine flour, baking soda and salt; add to creamed mixture alternately with buttermilk. Fold in nuts, dates and orange peel.

2. Pour into two greased and floured 8-in. x 4-in. loaf pans. Bake at 350° for 60-65 minutes or until done. Combine glaze ingredients; spoon half over hot bread. Cool for 10 minutes. Remove from pans; spoon remaining glaze over bread.

Mexican Corn Bread

This tasty corn bread is easy to mix up. I serve it often with a meal or hearty bowl of soup as an alternative to rolls. Cheddar cheese makes it especially flavorful, and the diced peppers add nice color.

—**ESTHER SHANK** HARRISONBURG, VIRGINIA

YIELD: 8-10 SERVINGS.

- 1 cup yellow cornmeal
- ⅓ cup all-purpose flour
- 2 tablespoons sugar
- 2 teaspoons baking powder
- 1 teaspoon salt
- ½ teaspoon baking soda
- 2 eggs
- 1 cup buttermilk
- 1 can (8¼ ounces) cream-style corn
- ⅓ cup canola oil
- ⅓ cup chopped onion
- 2 tablespoons chopped green pepper
- ½ cup shredded cheddar cheese

1. In a large bowl, combine the first six ingredients. Whisk together the eggs, buttermilk, corn, oil, onion and green pepper. Stir into dry ingredients just until moistened. Fold in cheese.

2. Pour into a greased 10-in. ovenproof skillet or 9-in. square baking pan. Bake at 350° for 30-35 minutes or until a toothpick inserted near the center comes out clean. Serve warm.

Lemon Bread

You'll often find me baking this sunshiny-sweet bread in the kitchen when company's due. It has a texture like pound cake.

—**KATHY SCOTT** LINGLE, WYOMING

YIELD: 1 LOAF (12 SLICES).

- ½ cup butter, softened
- 1 cup sugar
- 2 eggs
- 2 tablespoons lemon juice
- 1 tablespoon grated lemon peel
- 1½ cups all-purpose flour
- 1 teaspoon baking powder
- ⅛ teaspoon salt
- ½ cup 2% milk

GLAZE
- ½ cup confectioners' sugar
- 2 tablespoons lemon juice

1. In a large bowl, cream butter and sugar until light and fluffy. Beat in the eggs, lemon juice and peel. Combine the flour, baking powder and salt; gradually stir into creamed mixture alternately with milk, beating well after each addition.

2. Pour into a greased 8-in. x 4-in. loaf pan. Bake at 350° for 45 minutes or until a toothpick inserted near the center comes out clean.

3. Combine glaze ingredients. Remove bread from pan; immediately drizzle with glaze. Cool on a wire rack.

Fluffy Whole Wheat Biscuits

This golden biscuit recipe is my favorite. They turn out just scrumptious— light and tasty!

—**RUTH ANN STELFOX** RAYMOND, ALBERTA

YIELD: 1 DOZEN.

- 1 cup all-purpose flour
- 1 cup whole wheat flour
- 4 teaspoons baking powder
- 1 tablespoon sugar
- ¾ teaspoon salt
- ¼ cup cold butter, cubed
- 1 cup milk

1. In a medium bowl, combine flours, baking powder, sugar, and salt; mix well. Cut in the butter until mixture resembles coarse crumbs. Stir in milk just until moistened.

2. Turn out onto a lightly floured surface; knead gently 8 to 10 times. Roll to ¾-in. thickness; cut with a 2½-in. biscuit cutter and place on an ungreased baking sheet. Bake at 450° for 10-12 minutes or until lightly browned. Serve warm.

Sour Cream Yeast Rolls

Tender, soft rolls are the perfect finishing touch for any meal. I think they represent genuine home comfort, especially since they were Mom's recipe.

—CHRISTINE FRAZIER AUBURNDALE, FLORIDA

YIELD: 1 DOZEN.

- 2½ to 3 cups all-purpose flour
- 2 tablespoons sugar
- 1 package (¼ ounce) active dry yeast
- 1 teaspoon salt
- 1 cup (8 ounces) sour cream
- ¼ cup water
- 3 tablespoons butter, divided
- 1 egg

1. In a large bowl, combine 1½ cups flour, sugar, yeast and salt. In a small saucepan, heat sour cream, water and 2 tablespoons butter to 120°-130°; add to dry ingredients. Beat on medium speed for 2 minutes. Add egg and ½ cup flour; beat 2 minutes longer. Stir in enough remaining flour to form a soft dough.

2. Turn onto a floured surface; knead until smooth and elastic, about 6-8 minutes. Place in a greased bowl, turning once to grease the top. Cover and let rise in a warm place until doubled, about 1 hour.

3. Punch dough down. Turn onto a lightly floured surface; divide into 12 pieces. Shape each into a ball. Place in a greased 13-in. x 9-in. baking pan. Cover and let rise until doubled, about 30 minutes.

4. Bake at 375° for 25-30 minutes or until golden brown. Melt the remaining butter; brush over rolls. Remove from pan to a wire rack.

Danish Julekage

Cardamom and lots of fruit enliven this unique holiday bread. The recipe was handed down from my grandmother, who came to the United States from Denmark when she was 16 years old.

—PHYLLIS LEVENDUSKY OSAGE, IOWA

YIELD: 2 LOAVES.

- 2 packages (¼ ounce each) active dry yeast
- ¼ cup warm water (110° to 115°)
- 2 cups warm milk (110° to 115°)
- 1 cup sugar
- ½ cup butter, softened
- 1 tablespoon shortening
- 2 teaspoons salt
- 1 teaspoon ground cardamom
- 3 eggs, beaten
- 8½ to 9 cups all-purpose flour
- 1 cup raisins
- 1 cup chopped candied fruit

FILLING

- 2 tablespoons butter, melted
- ¼ cup sugar

TOPPING

- ¼ cup sugar
- 2 tablespoons all-purpose flour
- ½ teaspoon ground cardamom
- 2 tablespoons cold butter

1. In a bowl, dissolve yeast in warm water. Add milk, sugar, butter, shortening, salt, cardamom, eggs and 4 cups flour; beat until smooth. Stir in raisins, candied fruit and enough remaining flour to form a soft dough.

2. Turn onto a floured surface; knead until smooth and elastic, about 6-8 minutes. Place in a greased bowl, turning once to grease top. Cover and let rise in a warm place until doubled, about 1¼ hours.

3. Punch dough down. Turn onto a lightly floured surface; divide in half. Roll each portion into a 12-in. x 9-in. rectangle. Brush with butter and sprinkle with sugar to within ½-in. of edges. Roll up, jelly-roll style, starting with a long side; pinch seams to seal and tuck ends under. Place, seam side down, in two greased 9-in. x 5-in. loaf pans. Cover and let rise until doubled, about 45 minutes.

4. For topping, combine the sugar, flour and cardamom; cut in butter until mixture resembles coarse crumbs. Sprinkle over loaves. Bake at 350° for 50-60 minutes or until golden brown. Remove from pans to cool on wire racks.

Poteca Nut Roll

You'll need a large surface to roll out the dough for this classic Yugoslavian treat.

—ANTHONY SETTA
SAEGERTOWN, PENNSYLVANIA

YIELD: 1 COFFEE CAKE.

- 1 package (¼ ounce) active dry yeast
- ¼ cup warm water (110° to 115°)
- ¾ cup warm milk (110° to 115°)
- ¼ cup sugar
- 1 teaspoon salt
- 1 egg, lightly beaten
- ¼ cup shortening
- 3 to 3½ cups all-purpose flour

FILLING

- ½ cup butter, softened
- 1 cup packed brown sugar
- 2 eggs, lightly beaten
- 1 teaspoon vanilla extract
- 1 teaspoon lemon extract, optional
- 4 cups ground or finely chopped walnuts

2% milk
Confectioners' sugar icing, optional

1. In a large bowl, dissolve yeast in warm water. Add the milk, sugar, salt, egg, shortening, and 1½ cups flour; beat until smooth. Add enough remaining flour to form a soft dough.

2. Turn onto a floured surface; knead until smooth and elastic, about 6-8 minutes. Place in a greased bowl, turning once to grease top. Cover and let rise in a warm place until doubled, about 1 hour.

3. Punch down. Turn onto a lightly floured surface; roll into a 30-in. x 20-in. rectangle. In a bowl, combine the butter, brown sugar, eggs, vanilla, lemon extract if desired and nuts. Add about ½ cup milk until mixture reaches spreading consistency. Spread over rectangle to within 1 in. of edges.

4. Roll up jelly-roll style, starting with a long side; pinch seams and ends to seal. Place on a greased baking sheet; shape into a tight spiral. Cover and let rise until nearly doubled, about 1 hour.

5. Bake at 350° for 35 minutes or until golden brown. Remove from pan to a wire rack to cool. If desired, combine confectioners' sugar and enough milk to make a thin glaze; brush over roll.

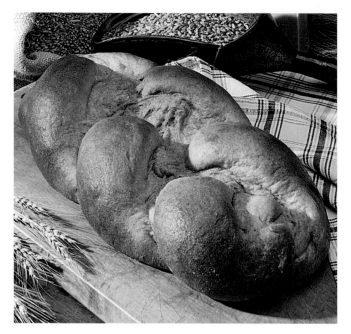

Cheese Twists

These impressive loaves take a little time to prepare, but they're well worth the effort. I've used the recipe for several years. I love making bread—there's no better way to work out life's little frustrations and with such yummy results!

—**MICHELLE BERAN** CLAFLIN, KANSAS

YIELD: 2 LOAVES.

  3¼ **cups all-purpose flour**
   2 **packages (¼ ounce each) active dry yeast**
  1½ **cups buttermilk**
   ¾ **cup butter**
   ½ **cup sugar**
   ½ **teaspoon salt**
   5 **eggs**
  3½ **to 4 cups whole wheat flour, divided**
   2 **cups (8 ounces) shredded cheddar cheese**

1. In a large bowl, combine all-purpose flour and yeast. In a saucepan, heat buttermilk, butter, sugar and salt to 120°-130°; add to flour mixture. Blend on low speed until moistened. Add eggs; beat on low for 30 seconds. Beat on high for 3 minutes. Stir in enough whole wheat flour to make a soft dough.

2. Turn onto a floured surface; knead until smooth and elastic, about 6-8 minutes. Place in a greased bowl, turning once to grease top. Cover and let rise in a warm place until nearly doubled, about 1 hour.

3. Punch dough down; divide in half. On a lightly floured surface, roll each into a 12-in. x 9-in. rectangle. Cut each into three 12-in. x 3-in. strips. Combine cheese with 2 tablespoons of remaining whole wheat flour; sprinkle ⅓ cup down center of each strip. Bring long edges together over cheese and pinch to seal. Place three strips seam side down on greased baking sheets. Braid strips together; secure ends. Cover and let rise until doubled, about 45 minutes.

4. Bake at 375° for 20-25 minutes or until golden. Immediately remove from baking sheets to wire racks; cool.

Apple Raisin Bread

I've been making this bread for many years. It smells so good in the oven and tastes even better. I make bread almost every Saturday, and it doesn't stay around long with our sons home from college in the summer.

—**PERLENE HOEKEMA** LYNDEN, WASHINGTON

YIELD: 3 LOAVES.

   2 **packages (¼ ounce each) active dry yeast**
  1½ **cups warm water (110° to 115°), divided**
   1 **teaspoon sugar**
   3 **eggs, beaten**
   1 **cup applesauce**
   ½ **cup honey**
   ½ **cup canola oil**
   2 **teaspoons salt**
   8 **to 9 cups all-purpose flour**
  1½ **cups diced peeled apples**
  1½ **cups raisins**
   2 **tablespoons lemon juice**
   2 **tablespoons cornmeal**
GLAZE
   1 **egg, beaten**
Sugar

1. In a small bowl, combine yeast, ½ cup water and sugar; set aside. In a large bowl, combine eggs, applesauce, honey, oil, salt and remaining water; mix well. Stir in yeast mixture. Gradually add enough flour to form a soft dough.

2. Knead on a floured surface until smooth and elastic, about 10 minutes. Place dough in a greased bowl; turn once to grease top. Cover and rise in a warm place until doubled, about 1 hour.

3. Punch down; turn over in bowl. Cover and let rise 30 minutes. In a small bowl, combine apples, raisins and lemon juice. Divide dough into three parts; knead a third of the apple mixture into each part. Shape each into round flat balls. Place each in a greased 8-in. round baking pan that has been sprinkled with cornmeal. Cover and let rise until doubled, about 1 hour.

4. Brush each loaf with egg and sprinkle with sugar. Bake at 350° for 30 to 35 minutes or until bread sounds hollow when tapped.

Homemade Egg Bread

People rave about this tender, delicate bread every time I serve it.

—JUNE MULLINS LIVONIA, MISSOURI

YIELD: 2 LOAVES.

 2 packages (¼ ounce each) active dry yeast
 ½ cup warm water (110° to 115°)
 1½ cups warm milk (110° to 115°)
 ¼ cup sugar
 1 tablespoon salt
 3 eggs, beaten
 ¼ cup butter, softened
 7 to 7½ cups all-purpose flour
 1 egg yolk
 2 tablespoons water
Sesame seeds

1. Dissolve yeast in warm water. Add milk, sugar, salt, eggs, butter and 3½ cups flour; mix well. Stir in enough remaining flour to form a soft dough.

2. On a floured surface, knead until smooth and elastic, 6-8 minutes. Place in greased bowl; turn once to grease top. Cover and let rise in warm place until doubled, 1½ to 2 hours.

3. Punch down. Cover and let rise until almost doubled, about 30 minutes. Divide into six portions. On a floured surface, shape each into a 14-in.-long rope. For each loaf, braid three ropes together on greased baking sheet; pinch ends to seal. Cover and let rise until doubled, about 50 minutes.

4. Beat egg yolk and water; brush over loaves. Sprinkle with sesame seeds. Bake at 375° for 30-35 minutes.

Caraway Rye Bread

This pretty round bread's Old World flavor is so comforting and delicious. Just the right amount of caraway flavors the rye.

—CONNIE MOORE MEDWAY, OHIO

YIELD: 1 LOAF.

 2 packages (¼ ounce each) active dry yeast
 1½ cups warm water (110° to 115°), divided
 3 tablespoons molasses
 3 tablespoons butter, melted
 1 tablespoon caraway seeds
 1 teaspoon salt
 1½ to 2 cups all-purpose flour
 1½ cups whole wheat flour
 1 cup rye flour

1. In a large bowl, dissolve yeast in ½ cup warm water. Add molasses, butter, caraway, salt and remaining water; mix well. Combine flours; add 3 cups to batter. Beat until smooth. Add enough remaining flour to form a firm dough.

2. Turn onto a floured surface; knead until smooth and elastic, 6-8 minutes. Place in greased bowl, turning once to grease top. Cover and let rise in a warm place until doubled, about 1 hour.

3. Punch dough down; shape into a round loaf. Place on a greased baking sheet. Cover and let rise until doubled, about 30 minutes.

4. Bake at 375° for 20-25 minutes or until golden brown.

Grandma's Orange Rolls

Our children and grandchildren love these fine-textured sweet rolls. We have our own orange, lime and grapefruit trees, and it's such a pleasure to go out and pick fruit for the rolls right off the tree.

—**NORMA POOLE** AUBURNDALE, FLORIDA

YIELD: 2½ DOZEN.

  1 **package (¼ ounce) active dry yeast**
  ¼ **cup warm water (110° to 115°)**
  1 **cup warm 2% milk (110° to 115°)**
  ¼ **cup shortening**
  ¼ **cup sugar**
  1 **teaspoon salt**
  1 **egg, lightly beaten**
  3½ to 3¾ **cups all-purpose flour**
FILLING
  1 **cup sugar**
  ½ **cup butter, softened**
  2 **tablespoons grated orange peel**
GLAZE
  1 **cup confectioners' sugar**
  4 **teaspoons butter, softened**
  ½ **teaspoon lemon extract**
  4 to 5 **teaspoons 2% milk**

1. In a large bowl, dissolve yeast in water. Add the milk, shortening, sugar, salt, egg and 3 cups flour. Beat until smooth. Stir in enough remaining flour to form a soft dough.

2. Knead on a lightly floured surface until smooth and elastic, about 6-8 minutes. Place in a greased bowl, turning once to grease top. Cover and let rise in a warm place until doubled, about 1 hour. Meanwhile, in a small bowl, combine filling ingredients; set aside.

3. Punch dough down; divide in half. Roll each half into a 15-in. x 10-in. rectangle. Spread half the reserved filling on each rectangle. Roll up, jelly-roll style, starting with a long end. Cut each into 15 rolls.

4. Place in two greased 11-in. x 7-in. baking pans. Cover and let rise until doubled, about 45 minutes.

5. Bake at 375° for 20-25 minutes or until lightly browned. In a small bowl, combine the confectioners' sugar, butter, extract and enough milk to achieve desired consistency; spread over the warm rolls.

Whole Wheat Refrigerator Rolls

This recipe is easy and versatile. I like to mix up the dough beforehand and let it rise in the refrigerator.

—**SHARON MENSING** GREENFIELD, IOWA

YIELD: 2 DOZEN.

  2 **packages (¼ ounce each) active dry yeast**
  2 **cups warm water (110° to 115°)**
  ½ **cup sugar**
  1 **egg**
  ¼ **cup canola oil**
  2 **teaspoons salt**
  4½ to 5 **cups all-purpose flour, divided**
  2 **cups whole wheat flour**

1. In a large bowl, dissolve yeast in warm water. Add the sugar, egg, oil, salt and 3 cups all-purpose flour. Beat on medium speed for 3 minutes. Stir in whole wheat flour and enough remaining all-purpose flour to make a soft dough.

2. Turn out onto a lightly floured surface. Knead until smooth and elastic, about 6-8 minutes. Place in a greased bowl, turning once to grease top. Cover and let rise until doubled or cover and refrigerate overnight.

3. Punch dough down and form into 24 dinner-size rolls. Place on greased baking sheets for plain rolls or knots, or in greased muffin tins for cloverleaf rolls. Cover and let rise until doubled, about 1 hour for dough prepared the same day or 1-2 hours for refrigerated dough.

4. Bake at 375° for 10-12 minutes or until light golden brown. Serve warm. If desired, dough may be kept up to 4 days in the refrigerator. Punch down daily.

Country White Bread

Any time is the right time for a comforting slice of homemade bread. These loaves are especially nice since the crust stays so tender. This recipe is my husband Nick's favorite. He makes most of the bread at our house.

—JOANNE SHEW CHUK ST. BENEDICT, SASKATCHEWAN

YIELD: 2 LOAVES (16 SLICES EACH).

- 2 **packages (¼ ounce each) active dry yeast**
- 2 **cups warm water (110° to 115°)**
- ½ **cup sugar**
- 2 **teaspoons salt**
- 2 **eggs, lightly beaten**
- ¼ **cup canola oil**
- 6½ **to 7 cups all-purpose flour**

1. In a large bowl, dissolve yeast in warm water. Add the sugar, salt, eggs, oil and 3 cups of flour; beat until smooth. Stir in enough remaining flour to form a soft dough.

2. Turn onto a floured surface; knead until smooth and elastic, about 6-8 minutes. Place in a greased bowl, turning once to grease top. Cover and let rise in a warm place until doubled, about 1 hour.

3. Punch dough down. Divide in half and shape into loaves. Place in two greased 9-in. x 5-in. loaf pans. Cover and let rise until doubled, about 1 hour.

4. Bake at 375° for 25-30 minutes or until golden brown. Remove from pans to cool on wire racks.

Herbed Country White Bread: Stir in 2 tablespoons dried parsley flakes, 1 tablespoon dried basil, 1 teaspoon each dried oregano and thyme and ½ teaspoon garlic powder along with the 3 cups of flour.

Angel Biscuits

My biscuit recipe combines both yeast bread and quick bread techniques for fantastic results—a light, airy biscuit.

—FAYE HINTZ SPRINGFIELD, MISSOURI

YIELD: 2½ DOZEN.

- 2 **packages (¼ ounce each) active dry yeast**
- ¼ **cup warm water (110° to 115°)**
- 2 **cups warm buttermilk (110° to 115°)**
- 5 **cups all-purpose flour**
- ⅓ **cup sugar**
- 2 **teaspoons salt**
- 2 **teaspoons baking powder**
- 1 **teaspoon baking soda**
- 1 **cup shortening**
Melted butter

1. Dissolve yeast in warm water. Let stand 5 minutes. Stir in the buttermilk; set aside. In a large bowl, combine the flour, sugar, salt, baking powder and baking soda. Cut in shortening with a pastry blender until mixture resembles coarse meal. Stir in yeast mixture.

2. Turn out onto a lightly floured surface; knead lightly 3-4 times. Roll into a ½-in. thickness. Cut with a 2½-in. biscuit cutter. Place on a lightly greased baking sheet. Cover and let rise in a warm place about 1½ hours.

3. Bake at 450° for 8-10 minutes until golden brown. Lightly brush tops with melted butter. Serve warm.

Grandma Russell's Bread

I remember as a child always smelling fresh homemade bread and rolls whenever I walked into Grandma's house. The warm slices were delicious and melted in my mouth!

—JANET POLITO NAMPA, IDAHO

YIELD: 2 LOAVES OR 2 DOZEN ROLLS.

 1 **package (¼ ounce) active dry yeast**
⅓ **cup warm water (110° to 115°)**
½ **cup sugar, divided**
 1 **cup milk**
½ **cup butter, cubed**
 1 **tablespoon salt**
 1 **cup mashed potatoes**
 2 **eggs, beaten**
5½ **to 6 cups all-purpose flour**
CINNAMON FILLING
¼ **cup butter, melted**
¾ **cup sugar**
 1 **tablespoon ground cinnamon**

1. In a large bowl, combine the yeast, warm water and 1 teaspoon sugar; set aside. In a saucepan, heat milk, butter, salt and remaining sugar until butter is melted. Remove from the heat; stir in potatoes until smooth. Cool to lukewarm; add eggs and mix well.

2. To yeast mixture, add the potato mixture and 5 cups flour. Stir in enough remaining flour to make a soft dough. Turn onto a floured surface and knead until smooth and elastic, about 6-8 minutes. Place in a greased bowl, turning once to grease top. Cover and let rise in a warm place until doubled, about 1½ hours.

3. Punch down and divide in half.

For white bread: Shape two loaves and place in greased 8-in. x 4-in. loaf pans.

For cinnamon bread: Roll each half into a 16-in. x 8-in. rectangle. Brush with melted butter; combine sugar and cinnamon and sprinkle over butter. Starting at the narrow end, roll up into a loaf, sealing the edges and ends. Place in greased 8-in. x 4-in. loaf pans.

For cinnamon rolls: Roll each half into an 18-in. x 12-in. rectangle. Brush with melted butter; sprinkle with cinnamon-sugar. Starting at the narrow end, roll up and seal edges and ends. Cut each into 12 pieces of 1½ in. Place in greased 9-in. round baking pans.

4. Cover and let rise until doubled. Bake loaves at 375° for 20 minutes; bake rolls at 375° for 25-30 minutes. Cover with foil if they brown too quickly.

Cinnamon Twists

These delightful golden twists are perfect as part of a holiday meal. The brown sugar and cinnamon give them a delicate spicy flavor. It's a good thing the recipe makes a big batch because people can rarely eat just one.

—**JANET MOOBERRY** PEORIA, ILLINOIS

YIELD: 4 DOZEN.

- 1 package (¼ ounce) active dry yeast
- ¾ cup warm water (110° to 115°), divided
- 4 to 4½ cups all-purpose flour
- ¼ cup sugar
- 1½ teaspoons salt
- ½ cup warm 2% milk (110° to 115°)
- ¼ cup butter, softened
- 1 egg

FILLING
- ¼ cup butter, melted
- ½ cup packed brown sugar
- 4 teaspoons ground cinnamon

1. In a large bowl, dissolve yeast in ¼ cup warm water. Add 2 cups of flour, sugar, salt, milk, butter, egg and remaining water; beat on medium speed for 3 minutes. Stir in enough remaining flour to form a soft dough.

2. Turn onto a floured surface; knead until smooth and elastic, about 6-8 minutes. Place in a greased bowl, turning once to grease top. Cover and let rise in a warm place until doubled, about 1 hour.

3. Punch down dough. Roll into a 16-in. x 12-in. rectangle. Brush with butter. Combine brown sugar and cinnamon; sprinkle over butter. Let dough rest for 6 minutes. Cut lengthwise into three 16-in. x 4-in. strips. Cut each strip into sixteen 4-in. x 1-in. pieces. Twist and place on greased baking sheets. Cover and let rise until doubled, about 30 minutes.

4. Bake at 350° for 15 minutes or until golden brown.

English Muffin Bread

This recipe is even faster than most batter breads because it has only one rising time. If you can't use both loaves right away, freeze one for later.

—**JANE ZIELINSKI** ROTTERDAM JUNCTION, NEW YORK

YIELD: 2 LOAVES.

- 5 cups all-purpose flour, divided
- 2 packages (¼ ounce each) active dry yeast
- 1 tablespoon sugar
- 2 teaspoons salt
- ¼ teaspoon baking soda
- 2 cups warm milk (120° to 130°)
- ½ cup warm water (120° to 130°)

Cornmeal

1. In a large bowl, combine 2 cups flour, yeast, sugar, salt and baking soda. Add warm milk and water; beat on low speed for 30 seconds, scraping bowl occasionally. Beat on high speed for 3 minutes.

2. Stir in remaining flour (batter will be stiff). Do not knead. Grease two 8-in. x 4-in. loaf pans. Sprinkle pans with cornmeal. Spoon batter into the pans and sprinkle cornmeal on top. Cover and let rise in a warm place until doubled, about 45 minutes.

3. Bake at 375° for 35 minutes or until golden brown. Remove from pans immediately and cool on wire racks. Slice and toast.

BEEF

Peppered Ribeye Steaks

A true Southerner to the core, I love to cook—especially on the grill. This recipe is one of my favorites! The seasoning rub makes a wonderful marinade, and nothing beats the summertime taste of these flavorful grilled steaks.

—SHARON BICKETT CHESTER, SOUTH CAROLINA

YIELD: 8 SERVINGS.

- 4 beef ribeye steaks (1½ inches thick)
- 1 tablespoon olive oil
- 1 tablespoon garlic powder
- 1 tablespoon paprika
- 2 teaspoons dried gound thyme
- 2 teaspoons dried ground oregano
- 1½ teaspoons pepper
- 1 teaspoon salt
- 1 teaspoon lemon-pepper seasoning
- 1 teaspoon cayenne pepper
- 1 teaspoon crushed red pepper flakes

Orange slices, optional
Parsley sprigs, optional

1. Brush steaks lightly with oil. In a small bowl, combine all seasonings. Sprinkle seasonings over steaks and press into both sides. Cover and chill for 1 hour.

2. Grill, covered, over medium heat or broil 4 in. from the heat for 7-8 minutes on each side or until meat reaches desired doneness (for medium-rare, a thermometer should read 145°; medium, 160°; well-done, 170°).

3. Let stand 5 minutes before slicing. Place on a warm serving platter; cut across the grain into thick slices. Garnish with orange slices and parsley if desired.

Baked Stuffed Tomatoes

My family loves these tasty garden "containers" filled with rice and ground beef.

—BERTILLE COOPER CALIFORNIA, MARYLAND

YIELD: 6 SERVINGS.

- 6 medium fresh tomatoes
- ½ pound ground beef
- 1 teaspoon chili powder
- 1 teaspoon sugar
- ½ teaspoon salt
- ½ teaspoon pepper
- ¼ teaspoon dried oregano
- 2 cups uncooked instant rice
- ½ cup dry bread crumbs
- 2 tablespoons butter, melted
- 2 tablespoons water

1. Cut a thin slice off the top of each tomato. Leaving a ½-in.-thick shell, scoop out and reserve pulp. Invert tomatoes onto paper towels to drain.

2. Meanwhile, in a skillet, cook beef over medium heat until no longer pink; drain. Add the tomato pulp, chili powder, sugar, salt, pepper and oregano; bring to a boil. Reduce heat; simmer 45-50 minutes or until slightly thickened, stirring occasionally.

3. Add rice; mix well. Simmer 5-6 minutes longer or until rice is tender. Stuff tomatoes and place in a greased 13-in. x 9-in. baking dish. Combine bread crumbs and butter; sprinkle over tomatoes. Add water to baking dish. Bake, uncovered, at 375° for 20-25 minutes or until crumbs are lightly browned.

Vegetable Beef Casserole

This easy one-dish recipe has been a family favorite ever since my husband's aunt gave it to me more than 35 years ago. Add whatever vegetables you happen to have on hand. A simple salad goes nicely with this dish.

—EVANGELINE REW MANASSAS, VIRGINIA

YIELD: 6-8 SERVINGS.

- 3 medium unpeeled potatoes, sliced
- 3 carrots, sliced
- 3 celery ribs, sliced
- 2 cups cut fresh or frozen cut green beans
- 1 medium onion, chopped
- 1 pound lean ground beef (90% lean)
- 1 teaspoon dried thyme
- 1 teaspoon salt
- 1 teaspoon pepper
- 4 medium tomatoes, peeled, seeded and chopped
- 1 cup (4 ounces) shredded cheddar cheese

1. In a 3-qt. casserole, layer half of the potatoes, carrots, celery, green beans and onion. Crumble half of the uncooked beef over vegetables. Sprinkle with ½ teaspoon each of thyme, salt and pepper. Repeat layers.

2. Top with tomatoes. Cover and bake at 400° for 15 minutes. Reduce heat to 350°; bake about 1 hour longer or until the vegetables are tender and meat is no longer pink. Sprinkle with cheese; cover and let stand until cheese is melted.

Hungarian Goulash

Talk about your heirloom recipes! My grandmother made this for my mother when she was a child, and Mom made it for us to enjoy. Paprika and caraway add wonderful flavor and sour cream gives it a creamy richness. It's simply scrumptious!

—MARCIA DOYLE POMPANO, FLORIDA

YIELD: 12 SERVINGS.

- 3 medium onions, chopped
- 2 medium carrots, chopped
- 2 medium green peppers, chopped
- 3 pounds beef stew meat, cut into 1-inch cubes
- ½ teaspoon plus ¼ teaspoon salt, divided
- ½ teaspoon plus ¼ teaspoon pepper, divided
- 2 tablespoons olive oil
- 1½ cups reduced-sodium beef broth
- ¼ cup all-purpose flour
- 3 tablespoons paprika
- 2 tablespoons tomato paste
- 1 teaspoon caraway seeds
- 1 garlic clove, minced

Dash sugar
- 12 cups uncooked whole wheat egg noodles
- 1 cup (8 ounces) reduced-fat sour cream

1. Place the onions, carrots and green peppers in a 5-qt. slow cooker. Sprinkle meat with ½ teaspoon salt and ½ teaspoon pepper. In a large skillet, brown meat in oil in batches. Transfer to slow cooker.

2. Add broth to skillet, stirring to loosen browned bits from pan. Combine the flour, paprika, tomato paste, caraway seeds, garlic, sugar and remaining salt and pepper; stir into skillet. Bring to a boil; cook and stir for 2 minutes or until thickened. Pour over meat. Cover and cook on low for 7-9 hours or until meat is tender.

3. Meanwhile, cook noodles according to package directions. Stir the sour cream into slow cooker. Drain the noodles; serve with goulash.

Hearty Lasagna

Featuring a cute heart-shaped cutout, this eye-catching dish is perfect to share with friends and family around Valentine's Day. Best of all, you can make the lasagna ahead of time!

—**MARCY CELLA** L'ANSE, MICHIGAN

YIELD: 12 SERVINGS.

- 1½ pounds ground beef
- 1 medium onion, chopped
- 1 garlic clove, minced
- 3 tablespoons olive oil
- 1 can (28 ounces) Italian diced tomatoes, undrained
- 1 can (8 ounces) tomato sauce
- 1 can (6 ounces) tomato paste
- 1 teaspoon dried oregano
- 1 teaspoon sugar
- 1 teaspoon salt
- ¼ teaspoon pepper
- 2 carrots, halved
- 2 celery ribs, halved
- 12 ounces lasagna noodles
- 1 carton (15 ounces) ricotta cheese
- 2 cups (8 ounces) shredded part-skim mozzarella cheese
- ½ cup grated Parmesan cheese

1. In a large skillet, cook beef, onion and garlic in oil until meat is browned and onion is tender; drain. Stir in tomatoes, tomato sauce, tomato paste, oregano, sugar, salt and pepper. Place carrots and celery in sauce. Simmer, uncovered, for 1½ hours, stirring occasionally.

2. Meanwhile, cook lasagna noodles according to package directions. Drain; rinse in cold water. Remove and discard carrots and celery.

3. In a greased 13-in. x 9-in. baking dish, layer one-third of the noodles, one-third of the meat sauce, one-third of the ricotta, one-third of the mozzarella and one-third of the Parmesan. Repeat layers once. Top with remaining noodles and meat sauce.

4. Cut a heart out of aluminum foil and center on top of sauce. Dollop and spread remaining ricotta around heart. Sprinkle with remaining mozzarella and Parmesan. Bake, uncovered, at 350° for 45 minutes. Remove and discard foil heart. Let stand 10-15 minutes before cutting.

Barbecued Beef Sandwiches

You really can't taste the cabbage—which is great for non-cabbage lovers—but it makes these sandwiches hearty and moist.

—**DENISE MARSHALL** BAGLEY, WISCONSIN

YIELD: 10 SERVINGS.

- 2 pounds beef stew meat
- 2 cups water
- 4 cups shredded cabbage
- ½ cup barbecue sauce
- ½ cup ketchup
- ⅓ cup Worcestershire sauce
- 1 tablespoon prepared horseradish
- 1 tablespoon prepared mustard
- 10 hamburger or other sandwich buns, split

1. In a Dutch oven, combine the beef and water. Bring to a boil. Reduce heat; cover and simmer for 1½ hours or until tender. Drain cooking liquid, reserving ¾ cup.

2. Cool beef; shred and return to the Dutch oven. Add the cabbage, barbecue sauce, ketchup, Worcestershire sauce, horseradish, mustard and reserved cooking liquid. Cover and simmer for 1 hour. Serve warm in buns.

Round Steak Italiano

My mom's steak recipe is wonderful. She made this often while I was growing up. I've always enjoyed it and especially like the thick gravy, which is good on both the meat and the potatoes.

—DEANNE STEPHENS MCMINNVILLE, OREGON

YIELD: 8 SERVINGS.

2	pounds beef top round steak
1	can (8 ounces) tomato sauce
2	tablespoons onion soup mix
2	tablespoons canola oil
2	tablespoons red wine vinegar
1	teaspoon ground oregano
½	teaspoon garlic powder
¼	teaspoon pepper
8	medium potatoes (7 to 8 ounces each)
1	tablespoon cornstarch
1	tablespoon cold water

1. Cut steak into serving-size pieces; place in a 5-qt. slow cooker. In a large bowl, combine the tomato sauce, soup mix, oil, vinegar, oregano, garlic powder and pepper; pour over meat. Scrub and pierce potatoes; place over meat. Cover and cook on low for 7 to 7½ hours or until meat and potatoes are tender.

2. Remove meat and potatoes; keep warm. For gravy, pour cooking juices into a small saucepan; skim fat.

3. Combine cornstarch and water until smooth; gradually stir into juices. Bring to a boil; cook and stir for 2 minutes or until thickened. Serve with meat and potatoes.

Steak Potpie

When I hear "meat and potatoes," this is the recipe that comes to mind. I've made it for years and still get compliments on it. Most often, friends comment on how hearty the pie is.

—PATTIE BONNER COCOA, FLORIDA

YIELD: 4-6 SERVINGS.

¾	cup sliced onions
4	tablespoons canola oil, divided
¼	cup all-purpose flour
1	teaspoon salt
½	teaspoon pepper
½	teaspoon paprika
	Pinch ground allspice
	Pinch ground ginger
1	pound beef top round steak, cut into ½-inch pieces
2½	cups boiling water
3	medium potatoes, peeled and diced
	Pastry for single-crust pie

1. In a large skillet, saute the onions in 2 tablespoons oil until golden. Drain and set aside.

2. In a large resealable plastic bag, combine dry ingredients; add meat and shake to coat. Brown meat in remaining oil in the same skillet. Add water; cover and simmer until meat is tender, about 1 hour.

3. Add potatoes; simmer, uncovered, for 15-20 minutes or until the potatoes are tender. Pour into a greased 1½-qt. baking dish. Top with onion slices. Roll pastry to fit baking dish. Place over hot filling; seal to edges of dish. Make slits in the crust.

4. Bake at 450° for 25-30 minutes or until golden brown. If necessary, cover edges of crust with foil to prevent overbrowning.

Mozzarella Meat Loaf

My children were not fond of meat loaf until I dressed up this recipe with pizza flavor. Now the five children are grown and have families of their own, and they still make and serve this hearty, moist meat loaf.

—**DARLIS WILFER** WEST BEND, WISCONSIN

YIELD: 8-10 SERVINGS.

- 2 **pounds lean ground beef (90% lean)**
- 2 **eggs, lightly beaten**
- 1 **cup saltine cracker crumbs**
- 1 **cup milk**
- ½ **cup grated Parmesan cheese**
- ½ **cup chopped onion**
- 1½ **teaspoons salt**
- 1 **teaspoon dried oregano**
- 1 **can (8 ounce) pizza sauce**
- 3 **slices part-skim mozzarella cheese, halved**
Green pepper rings, optional
Sliced mushrooms, optional
- 2 **tablespoons butter, optional**
Chopped fresh parsley, optional

1. Mix beef, eggs, crumbs, milk, Parmesan cheese, onion, salt and oregano. Shape into a loaf and place in a greased 9-in. x 5-in. loaf pan. Bake at 350° for 1¼ hours or until no pink remains; drain.

2. Spoon the pizza sauce over loaf and top with the mozzarella cheese slices. Bake 10 minutes longer or until the cheese is melted.

3. Meanwhile, if desired, saute green pepper and mushrooms in butter; arrange on top of meat loaf. Sprinkle with parsley if desired.

Salisbury Steak Deluxe

This recipe is so good that I truly enjoy sharing it with others. I've always liked Salisbury steak, but I had to search a long time to find a recipe this tasty. It's handy, too, because it can be prepared ahead, kept in the refrigerator and warmed up later.

—**DENISE BARTEET** SHREVEPORT, LOUISIANA

YIELD: 6 SERVINGS.

- 1 **can (10¾ ounces) condensed cream of mushroom soup, undiluted**
- 1 **tablespoon prepared mustard**
- 2 **teaspoons Worcestershire sauce**
- 1 **teaspoon prepared horseradish**
- 1 **egg**
- ¼ **cup dry bread crumbs**
- ¼ **cup finely chopped onion**
- ½ **teaspoon salt**
Dash pepper
- 1½ **pound ground beef**
- 1 **to 2 tablespoons canola oil**
- ½ **cup water**
- 2 **tablespoons chopped fresh parsley**

1. In a small bowl, combine the soup, mustard, Worcestershire sauce and horseradish. Set aside. In another bowl, lightly beat the egg. Add the bread crumbs, onion, salt, pepper and ¼ cup of the soup mixture. Crumble beef over mixture and mix well. Shape into six patties.

2. In a large skillet, brown the patties in oil; drain. Combine remaining soup mixture with water; pour over patties. Cover and cook patties over low heat for 10-15 minutes or until meat is no longer pink and a thermometer reads 160°. Remove patties to a serving platter; serve sauce with meat. Sprinkle with parsley.

Savory Pot Roast

My old-fashioned pot roast and smooth pan gravy evoke memories of dinners at Mom's or Grandma's. My husband and I used to raise cattle, so I prepared a lot of beef, and this recipe is the best.

—LEE LEUSCHNER CALGARY, ALBERTA

YIELD: 14-16 SERVINGS.

- 1 **rolled boneless beef chuck roast (6 pounds)**
- 2 **tablespoons canola oil**

Salt and coarsely ground pepper
- 1 **large onion, coarsely chopped**
- 2 **medium carrots, coarsely chopped**
- 1 **celery rib, coarsely chopped**
- 2 **cups water**
- 1 **can (14½ ounces) beef broth**
- 2 **bay leaves**

GRAVY
- ¼ **cup butter, cubed**
- ¼ **cup all-purpose flour**
- 1 **teaspoon lemon juice**
- 4 **to 5 drops hot pepper sauce**

1. In a large skillet over medium-high heat, brown roast in oil on all sides. Transfer to a large roasting pan; season with salt and pepper. Add the onion, carrots and celery.

2. In a large saucepan, bring the water, broth and bay leaves to a boil. Pour over roast and vegetables. Cover and bake at 350° for 2½ to 3 hours or until meat is tender, turning once.

3. Remove roast to a serving platter and keep warm. For gravy, strain pan juices, reserving 2 cups. Discard vegetables and bay leaves.

4. In a large saucepan over medium heat, melt butter; stir in flour until smooth. Gradually stir in pan juices. Bring to a boil; cook and stir for 2 minutes or until thickened. Stir in lemon juice and hot pepper sauce. Serve with roast.

Editor's Note: *Ask your butcher to tie two 3-pound chuck roasts together to form a rolled chuck roast.*

Classic Beef Stew

Here's a good old-fashioned stew with rich beef gravy that lets the flavor of the potatoes and carrots come through. It's the perfect hearty dish for a blustery winter day. I make it often during the cold-weather months.

—ALBERTA MCKAY BARTLESVILLE, OKLAHOMA

YIELD: 6-8 SERVINGS.

- 2 **pounds beef stew meat, cut into 1-inch cubes**
- 1 **to 2 tablespoons canola oil**
- 1½ **cups chopped onion**
- 1 **can (14½ ounces) diced tomatoes, undrained**
- 1 **can (10½ ounces) condensed beef broth, undiluted**
- 3 **tablespoons quick-cooking tapioca**
- 1 **garlic clove, minced**
- 1 **tablespoon dried parsley flakes**
- 1 **teaspoon salt**
- ¼ **teaspoon pepper**
- 1 **bay leaf**
- 6 **medium carrots, cut into 2-inch pieces**
- 3 **medium potatoes, peeled and cut into 2-inch pieces**
- 1 **cup sliced celery, cut into 1-inch pieces**

1. In a Dutch oven, brown half the beef in oil. Drain. Brown remaining beef; drain. Return all meat to pan. Add onion, tomatoes, beef broth, tapioca, garlic, parsley, salt, pepper and bay leaf. Bring to a boil; remove from the heat.

2. Cover and bake at 350° for 1½ hours. Stir in carrots, potatoes and celery. Bake, covered, 1 hour longer or until meat and vegetables are tender. Discard bay leaf before serving.

Baked Spaghetti

Every time that I make this cheesy dish, I get requests for the recipe. It puts a different spin on spaghetti and is great for any meal. The leftovers, if there are any, also freeze well for a quick meal later on in the week.

—**RUTH KOBERNA** BRECKSVILLE, OHIO

YIELD: 12 SERVINGS.

- 1 **cup chopped onion**
- 1 **cup chopped green pepper**
- 1 **tablespoon butter**
- 1 **can (28 ounces) diced tomatoes, undrained**
- 1 **can (4 ounces) mushroom stems and pieces, drained**
- 1 **can (2¼ ounces) sliced ripe olives, drained**
- 2 **teaspoons dried oregano**
- 1 **pound ground beef, browned and drained, optional**
- 12 **ounces spaghetti, cooked and drained**
- 2 **cups (8 ounces) shredded cheddar cheese**
- 1 **can (10¾ ounces) condensed cream of mushroom soup, undiluted**
- ¼ **cup water**
- ¼ **cup grated Parmesan cheese**

1. In a large skillet, saute onion and green pepper in butter until tender. Add the tomatoes, mushrooms, olives, oregano. Add ground beef if desired. Simmer, uncovered, for 10 minutes.

2. Place half of the spaghetti in a greased 13-in. x 9-in. baking dish. Layer with half of the vegetable mixture and 1 cup of the cheddar cheese. Repeat layers.

3. In a small bowl, combine soup and water until smooth; pour over the casserole. Sprinkle with Parmesan cheese. Bake, uncovered, at 350° for 30-35 minutes or until heated through.

Corned Beef and Mixed Vegetables

For St. Patrick's Day, prepare a traditional corned beef dinner and add a special twist—a colorful medley of cooked fresh vegetables. It's a festive combination to serve family or guests.

—**GLORIA WARCZAK** CEDARBURG, WISCONSIN

YIELD: 6-8 SERVINGS.

- 1 **corned beef brisket with spice packet (3 to 4 pounds), trimmed**
- 6 **to 8 small red potatoes**
- 3 **medium carrots, cut into 2-inch pieces**
- 3 **celery ribs, cut into 2-inch pieces**
- 2 **tablespoons chopped celery leaves**
- 2 **turnips, peeled and cut into wedges**
- 1 **medium head cabbage, cut into 6 to 8 wedges**
- ½ **pound fresh green beans**
- 3 **to 4 ears fresh corn, halved**

1. Place corned beef and enclosed seasoning packet in an 8-qt. Dutch oven. Cover with water and bring to a boil. Reduce heat; cover and simmer for 2 hours or until meat is tender.

2. Add potatoes, carrots, celery, celery leaves and turnips; return to a boil. Reduce heat; cover and simmer for 20 minutes.

3. Add cabbage, beans and corn; return to a boil. Reduce heat; cover and simmer 15-20 minutes or until vegetables are tender.

Cornish Pasties

Years ago, when bakeries in my Midwestern hometown made pasties, people scrambled to get there before they were all gone. Now I make my own. Filled with meat, potatoes and vegetables, they make a complete handheld meal.

—GAYLE LEWIS YUCAIPA, CALIFORNIA

YIELD: 4 SERVINGS.

FILLING
- 1 **pound beef top round steak, cut into ½-inch pieces**
- 2 to 3 **medium potatoes, peeled and cut into ½-inch cubes**
- 1 **cup chopped carrots**
- ½ **cup finely chopped onion**
- 2 **tablespoons minced fresh parsley**
- 1 **teaspoon salt**
- ½ **teaspoon pepper**
- ¼ **cup butter, melted**

PASTRY
- 3 **cups all-purpose flour**
- 1 **teaspoon salt**
- 1 **cup shortening**
- 8 to 9 **tablespoons ice water**
- 1 **egg, lightly beaten, optional**

1. In a large bowl, combine the round steak, potatoes, carrots, onion, parsley, salt and pepper. Add butter and toss to coat; set aside.

2. For pastry, combine flour and salt in a large bowl. Cut in shortening until mixture resembles coarse crumbs. Sprinkle with water, 1 tablespoon at a time. Toss lightly with a fork until dough forms a ball. Do not overmix.

3. Divide dough into fourths. Roll out one portion into a 9-in. circle; transfer to a greased baking sheet. Mound about 1¼ cups of meat filling on half of circle. Moisten edges with water; fold dough over mixture and press edges with fork to seal. Repeat with remaining pastry and filling.

4. Cut slits in top of each pasty. Brush with beaten egg if desired. Bake at 375° for 50-60 minutes or until golden brown.

All-American Barbecue Sandwiches

I came up with this delicious recipe on my own. It's my husband's favorite and is a big hit with family and friends who enjoyed it at our Fourth of July picnic.

—SUE GRONHOLZ
BEAVER DAM, WISCONSIN

YIELD: 18 SERVINGS.

- 4½ **pounds ground beef**
- 1½ **cups chopped onion**
- 2¼ **cups ketchup**
- 3 **tablespoons prepared mustard**
- 3 **tablespoons Worcestershire sauce**
- 2 **tablespoons vinegar**
- 2 **tablespoons sugar**
- 1 **tablespoon salt**
- 1 **tablespoon pepper**
- 18 **hamburger buns, split**

1. In a Dutch oven, cook beef and onion over medium heat until meat is no longer pink and onion is tender; drain. Combine ketchup, mustard, Worcestershire, vinegar, sugar, salt and pepper; stir into beef mixture. Heat though. Serve on buns.

> When I was in grade school, I often went to see my granny and granddad at lunchtime. Granny, who thought a cold sandwich wasn't "fitting for a growing child," always served me a hot meal with a glass of cold buttermilk from the old wooden icebox.
>
> **—DALE SMITH** WEST WORTHINGTON, OHIO

Standing Rib Roast

Treat your family to tender slices of standing rib roast or use the seasoning blend on a different beef roast for a hearty, delicious main dish.

—LUCY MEYRING WALDEN, COLORADO

YIELD: 10 SERVINGS.

- 1 tablespoon lemon-pepper seasoning
- 1 tablespoon paprika
- 1½ teaspoons garlic salt
- 1 teaspoon dried rosemary, crushed
- ½ teaspoon cayenne pepper
- 1 bone-in beef rib roast (6 to 7 pounds)
- 2 cups water
- 1 teaspoon beef bouillon granules

1. In a small bowl, mix the first five ingredients; rub over roast. Place roast in a large roasting pan, fat side up. Roast at 325° for 2¼ to 2¾ hours or until meat reaches desired doneness (for medium-rare, a thermometer should read 145°; medium, 160°; well-done, 170°).

2. Remove roast from oven; tent with foil. Let stand for 15 minutes before slicing.

3. Meanwhile, pour drippings and loosened browned bits into a small saucepan; skim fat. Stir in water and bouillon; bring to a boil; serve with the roast.

Savory Spaghetti Sauce

My fresh-tasting spaghetti sauce is a real crowd-pleaser. With a husband and 12 kids to feed every day, I rely on this flavorful recipe often. It tastes especially good in the summer, when I can make it with fresh garden herbs.

—ANNE HEINONEN HOWELL, MICHIGAN

YIELD: 4-6 SERVINGS (ABOUT 1 QUART).

- 1 pound ground beef
- 1 large onion, chopped
- 2 cans (15 ounces each) tomato sauce
- 1 garlic clove, minced
- 1 bay leaf
- 1 tablespoon minced fresh basil or 1 teaspoon dried basil
- 2 teaspoons minced fresh oregano or ¾ teaspoon dried oregano
- 2 teaspoon sugar
- ½ to 1 teaspoon salt
- ½ teaspoon pepper
Hot cooked spaghetti
Fresh oregano, optional

1. In a Dutch oven, cook ground beef and onion until meat is no longer pink and onion is tender; drain. Add the next eight ingredients; bring to a boil.

2. Reduce heat; cover and simmer for 1 hour, stirring occasionally. Discard the bay leaf. Serve with spaghetti. Garnish with oregano if desired.

Spicy Tomato Steak

My family loves this spicy tomato dish. I came up with the recipe years ago after eating a similar dish on vacation in New Mexico. I came home and tried to duplicate it from memory. The results were delicious!

—**ANNE LANDERS** LOUISVILLE, KENTUCKY

YIELD: 6 SERVINGS.

2 tablespoons cider vinegar
1 teaspoon salt
1 teaspoon pepper
1 pound beef round steak, trimmed and cut into ¼-inch strips
¼ cup all-purpose flour
2 tablespoons olive oil
3 medium tomatoes, peeled, seeded and cut into wedges
2 medium potatoes, peeled and thinly sliced
2 cans (4 ounces each) chopped green chilies
1 garlic clove, minced
1 teaspoon dried basil

1. In a large resealable bag, combine the vinegar, salt and pepper. Add the beef; seal bag and turn to coat. Refrigerate for 30 minutes.

2. Drain marinade. Place flour in another large resealable bag; add beef and toss to coat. In a large skillet, cook beef in oil over medium heat for 15-20 minutes or until tender.

3. Add the remaining ingredients. Cover and simmer for 20-30 minutes or until the potatoes are tender, stirring occasionally.

Barbecued Brisket

For a mouthwatering main dish to star in a summer meal, this brisket can't be beat. Baked slowly, the meat gets nice and tender and picks up the sweet and tangy flavor of the barbecue sauce.

—**PAGE ALEXANDER** BALDWIN CITY, KANSAS

YIELD: 6-8 SERVINGS.

1 fresh beef brisket (3 to 4 pounds)
1¼ cups water, divided
½ cup chopped onion
3 garlic cloves, minced
1 tablespoon canola oil
1 cup ketchup
3 tablespoons red wine vinegar
2 tablespoons lemon juice
2 tablespoons brown sugar
1 tablespoon Worcestershire sauce
2 teaspoons cornstarch
1 teaspoon paprika
1 teaspoon chili powder
¼ teaspoon salt
¼ teaspoon pepper
¼ teaspoon Liquid Smoke, optional

1. Place brisket in a large Dutch oven. Add ½ cup water. Cover and bake at 325° for 2 hours.

2. Meanwhile, in a small saucepan, saute onion and garlic in oil until tender. Add the ketchup, vinegar, lemon juice, brown sugar, Worcestershire sauce, cornstarch, paprika, chili powder, salt, pepper and remaining water. Simmer, uncovered, for 1 hour, stirring occasionally.

3. Add Liquid Smoke; mix well. Drain drippings from Dutch oven. Pour sauce over meat. Cover and bake 1 hour longer or until meat is tender.

Editor's Note: *This is a fresh beef brisket, not corned beef.*

Grilled Asian Flank Steak

I created this variation of the marinated ginger-sake flank steak my mother used to make. My version is lighter, but the tender meat, and the wonderful flavor and aroma, are equally as good. You'll want to try this one!

—SHAWN SOLLEY MORGANTOWN, WEST VIRGINIA

YIELD: 6 SERVINGS.

¼ cup Worcestershire sauce
¼ cup reduced-sodium soy sauce
3 tablespoons honey
1 tablespoon sesame oil
1 teaspoon Chinese five-spice powder
1 teaspoon minced garlic
½ teaspoon minced fresh gingerroot
1 beef flank steak (1½ pounds)
2 tablespoons hoisin sauce, warmed
3 green onions, thinly sliced
1 tablespoon sesame seeds, toasted, optional

1. In a large resealable plastic bag, combine the first seven ingredients; add steak. Seal bag and turn to coat; refrigerate overnight.

2. Drain and discard marinade. Grill steak, covered, over medium heat for 6-7 minutes on each side or until meat reaches desired doneness (for medium-rare, a thermometer should read 145°; medium, 160°; well-done, 170°). Let stand for 5 minutes.

3. Thinly slice steak across the grain. Drizzle with hoisin sauce; garnish with onions. Sprinkle with sesame seeds if desired.

Spaghetti 'n' Meatballs

One evening, we had unexpected company. Since I had some of these meatballs left over in the freezer, I warmed them up as appetizers. Everyone raved! This classic recipe makes a big batch and is perfect for entertaining.

—MARY LOU KOSKELLA PRESCOTT, ARIZONA

YIELD: 12-16 SERVINGS.

- 1½ cups chopped onion
- 2 tablespoons olive oil
- 3 garlic cloves, minced
- 3 cups water
- 1 can (29 ounces) tomato sauce
- 2 cans (12 ounces each) tomato paste
- ⅓ cup minced fresh parsley
- 1 tablespoon dried basil
- 1 tablespoon salt
- ½ teaspoon pepper

MEATBALLS

- 4 eggs, lightly beaten
- 2 cups soft bread cubes (¼-inch pieces)
- 1½ cups milk
- 1 cup grated Parmesan cheese
- 3 garlic cloves, minced
- 1 tablespoon salt
- ½ teaspoon pepper
- 3 pounds ground beef
- 2 tablespoons canola oil

Hot cooked spaghetti

1. In a Dutch oven over medium heat, saute onion in oil. Add garlic; cook 1 minute longer. Add the water, tomato sauce and paste, parsley, basil, salt and pepper; bring to a boil. Reduce heat; cover and simmer for 50 minutes.

2. In a large bowl, combine the first seven meatball ingredients. Crumble beef over mixture and mix well. Shape into 1½-in. balls.

3. In a large skillet over medium heat, brown meatballs in oil until no longer pink; drain. Add to sauce; bring to a boil. Reduce heat; cover and simmer for 1 hour or until flavors are blended, stirring occasionally. Serve with spaghetti.

Tex-Mex Beef Barbecues

I recently took this dish to a potluck and guests loved it! The recipe came from my mom and it is so easy to make.

—LYNDA ZUNIGA CRYSTAL CITY, TEXAS

YIELD: 14 SERVINGS.

- 1 fresh beef brisket (3½ pounds)
- 1 jar (18 ounces) hickory smoke-flavored barbecue sauce
- ½ cup finely chopped onion
- 1 envelope chili seasoning
- 1 tablespoon Worcestershire sauce
- 1 teaspoon minced garlic
- 1 teaspoon lemon juice
- 14 hamburger buns, split

1. Cut the brisket in half; place in a 5-qt. slow cooker.

2. In a small bowl, combine the barbecue sauce, onion, chili seasoning, Worcestershire sauce, garlic and lemon juice. Pour over the beef. Cover and cook on high for 5-6 hours or until the meat is tender.

3. Remove beef; cool slightly. Shred and return to the slow cooker; heat through. Serve on buns.

Editor's Note: *This is a fresh beef brisket, not corned beef.*

POULTRY

Italian Christmas Turkey

We never had stuffing without sausage, and my mom's Italian stuffing is my favorite. I rarely buy the sausage, preferring to make my own instead, the way my relatives do.

—LINDA HARRINGTON WINDHAM, NEW HAMPSHIRE

YIELD: 16 SERVINGS (12 CUPS STUFFING).

- ½ cup butter, cubed
- 1 pound bulk Italian sausage
- 2 celery ribs, chopped
- 1 medium onion, chopped
- 1 package (14 ounces) seasoned stuffing cubes
- ¼ cup egg substitute
- 2 to 3 cups hot water
- 1 turkey (16 pounds)

Salt and pepper to taste

1. In a large skillet over medium heat, melt butter. Add the sausage, celery and onion; cook and stir until meat is no longer pink. Transfer to a large bowl; stir in the stuffing cubes, egg substitute and enough water to reach desired moistness.

2. Just before baking, loosely stuff turkey with stuffing. Place remaining stuffing in a greased 2-qt. baking dish; cover and refrigerate. Remove from the refrigerator 30 minutes before baking.

3. Skewer turkey openings; tie drumsticks together. Place breast side up in a roasting pan. Rub with salt and pepper.

4. Bake, uncovered, at 325° for 3¾ to 4¼ hours or until a meat thermometer reads 180° for turkey thigh and 165° for stuffing, basting occasionally with pan drippings. (Cover loosely with foil if turkey browns too quickly.)

5. Bake additional stuffing, covered, for 25-30 minutes. Uncover; bake 10 minutes longer or until a thermometer reads 160°.

6. Cover turkey and let stand for 20 minutes before removing stuffing and carving turkey. If desired, thicken pan drippings for gravy.

Down-Home Chicken

A thick, tangy sauce coats tender chicken for a heavenly dinner. Use the sauce as a gravy over rice or mashed potatoes.

—**DONNA SASSER HINDS** MILWAUKIE, OREGON

YIELD: 6 SERVINGS.

- ½ **cup all-purpose flour**
- 1 **teaspoon salt**
- ½ **teaspoon pepper**
- 1 **broiler/fryer chicken (3 to 4 pounds), cut up**
- ¼ **cup canola oil**

SAUCE

- ⅔ **cup lemon juice**
- ⅔ **cup ketchup**
- ⅔ **cup molasses**
- ⅓ **cup canola oil**
- ¼ **cup Worcestershire sauce**
- 1 **teaspoon ground cloves**
- ½ **teaspoon salt**
- ¼ **teaspoon pepper**

Hot cooked rice

1. In a large resealable plastic bag, combine the flour, salt and pepper. Add chicken, a few pieces at a time, and shake to coat.

2. In a large skillet, heat oil. Brown chicken in oil on all sides; remove to paper towels. Drain drippings and return chicken to the pan.

3. In a bowl, combine the lemon juice, ketchup, molasses, oil, Worcestershire sauce, cloves, salt and pepper. Pour over chicken. Bring to a boil. Reduce heat; simmer, uncovered, for 35-40 minutes or until chicken juices run clear. Serve with rice.

Hungarian Chicken Paprikash

My mom volunteered to help prepare the dinners served at her church. As the volunteers cooked and served up a variety of dishes, she learned several new recipes, like chicken paprikash. It's my favorite main dish, and the gravy, made with paprika, sour cream and onions, is the best.

—**PAMELA EATON** MONCLOVA, OHIO

YIELD: 6 SERVINGS.

- 1 **large onion, chopped**
- ¼ **cup butter, cubed**
- 4 **to 5 pounds broiler/fryer chicken pieces**
- 2 **tablespoons paprika**
- 1 **teaspoon salt**
- ½ **teaspoon pepper**
- 1½ **cups hot water**
- 2 **tablespoons cornstarch**
- 2 **tablespoons cold water**
- 1 **cup (8 ounces) sour cream**

1. In a large skillet, saute onion in butter until tender. Sprinkle chicken with paprika, salt and pepper; place in an ungreased roasting pan. Spoon onion mixture over chicken. Add hot water. Cover and bake at 350° for 1½ hours or until chicken juices run clear.

2. Remove the chicken and keep warm. In a small bowl, combine the cornstarch and cold water until smooth. Gradually add to the pan juices with onion. Bring to a boil over medium heat; cook and stir for 2 minutes or until thickened. Remove from the heat. Stir in the sour cream. Serve with chicken.

Chicken Cheese Lasagna

I like to make a double batch of this lasagna and freeze one for another day. The filling can also be stuffed in manicotti shells.

—MARY ANN KOSMAS MINNEAPOLIS, MINNESOTA

YIELD: 12 SERVINGS.

1   **medium onion, chopped**
½   **cup butter, cubed**
1   **garlic clove, minced**
½   **cup all-purpose flour**
1   **teaspoon salt**
2   **cups chicken broth**
1½ **cups 2% milk**
4   **cups (16 ounces) shredded part-skim mozzarella cheese, divided**
1   **cup grated Parmesan cheese, divided**
1   **teaspoon dried basil**
1   **teaspoon dried oregano**
½   **teaspoon white pepper**
2   **cups (15 to 16 ounces) ricotta cheese**
1   **tablespoon minced fresh parsley**
9   **lasagna noodles, cooked and drained**
2   **packages (10 ounces each) frozen spinach, thawed and well drained**
2   **cups cubed cooked chicken**

1. In a large saucepan, saute onion in butter until tender. Add garlic; cook 1 minute longer. Stir in flour and salt until blended; cook until bubbly. Gradually stir in broth and milk. Bring to a boil; cook and stir for 1 minute or until thickened. Stir in 2 cups mozzarella, ½ cup Parmesan cheese, basil, oregano and pepper; set aside.

2. In a large bowl, combine the ricotta cheese, parsley and remaining mozzarella; set aside. Spread one-quarter of the cheese sauce into a greased 13-in. x 9-in. baking dish; cover with one-third of the noodles. Layer with half of the ricotta mixture, half of the spinach and half of the chicken.

3. Cover with one-quarter of the cheese sauce and one-third of the noodles. Repeat layers of ricotta mixture, spinach, chicken and one-quarter cheese sauce. Cover with remaining noodles and cheese sauce.

4. Sprinkle with remaining Parmesan cheese. Bake at 350°, uncovered, for 35-40 minutes. Let stand 15 minutes.

Editor's Note: *For a change, substitute cooked bulk Italian sausage for the chicken. Using 1% milk and reduced-fat cheeses will help keep the calories down. You can also use no-cook lasagna noodles without making any adjustments to the liquid or cooking time.*

Honey-Glazed Chicken

My family raves over this nicely browned chicken. The rich honey glaze gives each luscious piece a spicy tang. This dish is simple enough to prepare for a family dinner and delightful enough to serve to guests.

—RUTH ANDREWSON LEAVENWORTH, WASHINGTON

YIELD: 4-6 SERVINGS.

- ¼ cup all-purpose flour
- 1 teaspoon salt
- ½ teaspoon cayenne pepper
- 1 broiler/fryer chicken (about 3 pounds), cut up
- ½ cup butter, melted, divided
- ¼ cup packed brown sugar
- ¼ cup honey
- ¼ cup lemon juice
- 1 tablespoon reduced-sodium soy sauce
- 1½ teaspoons curry powder

1. In a large resealable plastic bag, combine the flour, salt and cayenne pepper; add the chicken pieces, a few at a time, and shake to coat. Pour 4 tablespoons butter into a 13-in. x 9-in. baking pan; place chicken in pan, turning pieces once to coat.

2. Bake, uncovered at 350° for 30 minutes. Combine brown sugar, honey, lemon juice, soy sauce, curry powder and remaining butter; pour over the chicken. Bake 45 minutes longer or until the chicken is tender, basting several times with pan drippings.

Chicken Rice Dinner

Everyone enjoys the country-style combination of chicken, rice and mushrooms. Using chicken bouillon adds to this entree's wonderful flavor.

—JUDITH ANGLEN RIVERTON, WYOMING

YIELD: 5 SERVINGS.

- ½ cup all-purpose flour
- 1 teaspoon salt
- ½ teaspoon pepper

- 10 bone-in chicken thighs (about 3¾ pounds)
- 3 tablespoons canola oil
- 1 cup uncooked long grain rice
- ¼ cup chopped onion
- 2 garlic cloves, minced
- 1 can (4 ounces) mushroom stems and pieces, undrained
- 2 teaspoons chicken bouillon granules
- 2 cups boiling water

Minced fresh parsley, optional

1. In a large resealable plastic bag, combine the flour, salt and pepper. Add chicken thighs, one at a time, and shake to coat. In a large skillet over medium heat, brown chicken in oil.

2. Place rice in an ungreased 13-in. x 9-in. baking dish. Sprinkle with onion and garlic; top with mushrooms. Dissolve bouillon in boiling water; pour over all. Place chicken on top.

3. Cover and bake at 350° for 1 hour or until a thermometer reads 180° and rice is tender. Sprinkle with parsley if desired.

Roasted Duck with Apple-Raisin Dressing

As a boy growing up on the farm, my husband had duck every Sunday. I tried to maintain that tradition after we married more than 50 years ago!

—FRAN KIRCHHOFF HARVARD, ILLINOIS

YIELD: 4 SERVINGS.

- 2 domestic ducks (4 to 5 pounds each)

Salt

DRESSING

- 1 tube (12 ounces) bulk pork sausage
- ½ cup chopped onion
- ½ cup chopped celery
- 1 cup chopped peeled apple
- 1 cup golden raisins
- ½ cup water
- 1½ teaspoons salt
- 1 teaspoon rubbed sage
- ¼ teaspoon pepper
- 2 tablespoons chopped fresh parsley
- 8 cups cubed crustless day-old white bread
- 3 eggs, lightly beaten
- ½ cup chicken broth

1. Sprinkle the inside of ducklings with salt; prick skin well all over and set aside.

2. In a large skillet, cook sausage with onion and celery until sausage is no longer pink and vegetables are tender. Add apple and simmer for 3 minutes, stirring occasionally; drain.

3. Meanwhile, simmer raisins in water for 8 minutes; do not drain. In a large bowl, combine sausage mixture, raisins, salt, sage, pepper and parsley; mix well. Add the bread cubes, eggs and broth; mix lightly. Divide and spoon into ducklings.

4. Place duck breast side up on a rack in a large shallow roasting pan. Bake, uncovered, at 375° for 1¾ to 1¼ hours or until the thermometer reads 185°. Drain fat from pan as it accumulates. Remove all dressing.

Wild Goose with Giblet Stuffing

This recipe is one of our favorite ways to prepare goose, and it's especially nice for the holidays. My husband does a lot of hunting, so I'm always looking for new ways to fix game.

—LOUISE LAGINESS
EAST JORDAN, MICHIGAN

YIELD: 6-8 SERVINGS.

- 1 **wild goose (6 to 8 pounds)**
- **Lemon wedges**
- **Salt**
- **STUFFING**
- **Goose giblets**
- 2 **cups water**
- 10 **cups crumbled corn bread**
- 2 **large Granny Smith apples, chopped**
- 1 **large onion, chopped**
- ⅓ **cup minced fresh parsley**
- 1 **to 2 tablespoons rubbed sage**
- 1 **teaspoon salt**
- ¼ **teaspoon pepper**
- ¼ **teaspoon garlic powder**
- **Butter, softened**

1. Rub inside goose cavity with lemon and salt; set aside. In a saucepan, cook giblets in water until tender, about 20-30 minutes.

2. Remove giblets with a slotted spoon and reserve liquid. Chop giblets and place in a large bowl with the corn bread, apples, onion, parsley, sage, salt, pepper and garlic powder. Add enough of the reserved cooking liquid to make a moist stuffing; toss gently. Stuff the body and neck cavity; truss openings. Place goose, breast side up, on a rack in a shallow roasting pan. Spread with softened butter.

3. Bake, uncovered, at 325° for 25 minutes per pound or until fully cooked and tender. If goose is an older bird, add 1 cup of water to pan and cover for the last hour of baking.

Oven Barbecued Chicken

Chicken and Sunday dinner go together in my mind. During my 20 years of married life on a dairy farm, I'd often brown the chicken and mix up the sauce while my husband milked, then pop it in the oven when we left for church.

—ESTHER SHANK HARRISONBURG, VIRGINIA

YIELD: 6-8 SERVINGS.

- 1 **broiler/fryer chicken, cut up (3 to 4 pounds)**
- 2 **tablespoons canola oil**
- ⅓ **cup chopped onion**
- 3 **tablespoons butter**
- ¾ **cup ketchup**
- ½ **cup hot water**
- ⅓ **cup cider vinegar**
- 3 **tablespoons brown sugar**
- 1 **tablespoon Worcestershire sauce**
- 2 **teaspoons prepared mustard**
- ¼ **teaspoon salt**
- ⅛ **teaspoon pepper**

1. In a large skillet, brown chicken in oil in batches. Drain chicken on paper towels.

2. Meanwhile, in a small saucepan, saute onion in butter until tender; stir in the remaining ingredients. Simmer, uncovered, for 15 minutes.

3. Place chicken in an ungreased 13-in. x 9-in. baking dish. Pour barbecue sauce over chicken. Bake, uncovered, at 350° for 45-60 minutes or until chicken juices run clear, basting occasionally.

Roasted Chicken with Rosemary

Herbs, garlic and butter give this hearty meal-in-one a classic flavor. It's a lot like pot roast, only it uses chicken instead of beef.
—**ISABEL ZIENKOSKY** SALT LAKE CITY, UTAH

YIELD: 9 SERVINGS.

½ cup butter, cubed
4 tablespoons minced fresh
   rosemary or 2 tablespoons dried
   rosemary, crushed
2 tablespoons minced fresh parsley
3 garlic cloves, minced
1 teaspoon salt
½ teaspoon pepper
1 whole roasting chicken (5 to 6
   pounds)
6 small red potatoes, halved
6 medium carrots, halved lengthwise
   and cut into 2-inch pieces
2 medium onions, quartered

1. In a small saucepan, melt butter; stir in the seasonings. Place chicken breast side up on a rack in a shallow roasting pan; tie drumsticks together with kitchen string. Spoon half of the butter mixture over chicken. Place the potatoes, carrots and onions around chicken. Drizzle remaining butter mixture over vegetables.

2. Cover and bake at 350° for 1½ hours, basting every 30 minutes. Uncover; bake 30-60 minutes longer or until a thermometer reads 180° in chicken thigh, basting occasionally.

3. Cover chicken with foil and let stand for 10-15 minutes before carving. Serve with the vegetables.

Turkey Mushroom Casserole

My mother first cooked up her fabulous casserole years ago. The flavor, cheese and splash of sherry make it elegant enough to serve at a dinner party.

—PEGGY KROUPA LEAWOOD, KANSAS

YIELD: 2 CASSEROLES (4 SERVINGS EACH).

- 1 **pound uncooked spaghetti**
- ½ **pound sliced fresh mushrooms**
- 1 **cup chopped onion**
- 2 **tablespoons olive oil**
- ½ **teaspoon minced garlic**
- 3 **cans (10¾ ounces each) condensed cream of mushroom soup, undiluted**
- 3 **cups cubed cooked turkey**
- 1 **cup chicken broth**
- ⅓ **cup sherry or additional chicken broth**
- 1 **teaspoon Italian seasoning**
- ¾ **teaspoon pepper**
- 2 **cups grated Parmesan cheese, divided**

1. Cook spaghetti according to package directions.

2. Meanwhile, in a Dutch oven, saute the mushrooms and onion in oil until tender. Add the garlic; cook 1 minute longer. Stir in the soup, turkey, broth, sherry, Italian seasoning, pepper and 1 cup cheese. Drain spaghetti; stir into turkey mixture.

3. Transfer to two greased 8-in. square baking dishes. Sprinkle with remaining cheese. Cover and freeze one casserole for up to 3 months. Cover and bake the remaining casserole at 350° for 30-40 minutes or until heated through.

To use frozen casserole: Thaw in the refrigerator overnight. Remove from the refrigerator 30 minutes before baking. Cover and bake at 350° for 45 minutes. Uncover; bake 5-10 minutes longer or until bubbly.

Savory Lemonade Chicken

I don't know where it originally came from, but my mother used to prepare this chicken for our family when I was little. Now I love to make it! A sweet and tangy sauce nicely glazes the chicken.

—JENNY COOK EAU CLAIRE, WISCONSIN

YIELD: 6 SERVINGS.

- 6 **boneless skinless chicken breast halves (4 ounces each)**
- ¾ **cup thawed lemonade concentrate**
- 3 **tablespoons ketchup**
- 2 **tablespoons brown sugar**
- 1 **tablespoon cider vinegar**
- 2 **tablespoons cornstarch**
- 2 **tablespoons cold water**

1. Place chicken in a 5-qt. slow cooker. In a small bowl, combine the lemonade concentrate, ketchup, brown sugar and vinegar; pour over chicken. Cover and cook on low for 2½ hours or until chicken is tender.

2. Remove chicken and keep warm. For gravy, combine the cornstarch and water until smooth; gradually stir into the cooking juices. Cover and cook on high for 30 minutes or until thickened. Return chicken to the slow cooker; heat through.

Fried Chicken Strips

I recently made this recipe of Mom's for my in-laws and they said it was the best fried chicken ever. Slicing the chicken breasts into strips cuts down on cooking time and ensures that every piece is crunchy and evenly coated.

—GENNY MONCHAMP REDDING, CALIFORNIA

YIELD: 6 SERVINGS.

- 2⅔ cups crushed saltines (about 80 crackers)
- 1 teaspoon garlic salt
- ½ teaspoon dried basil
- ½ teaspoon paprika
- ⅛ teaspoon pepper
- 1 egg
- 1 cup milk
- 1½ pounds boneless skinless chicken breasts, cut into ½-inch strips

Oil for frying

1. In a shallow bowl, combine the first five ingredients. In another shallow bowl, beat egg and milk. Dip chicken into egg mixture, then cracker mixture.

2. In an electric skillet or deep-fat fryer, heat oil to 375°. Fry chicken, a few strips at a time, for 2-3 minutes on each side or until golden brown. Drain on paper towels.

Duck with Cherry Sauce

My mom prepared this tender roast duck often for Sunday dinner when I was growing up. It was one of my dad's favorite meals. The cherry sauce stirs up easily and makes this duck simply delightful.

—SANDY JENKINS ELKHORN, WISCONSIN

YIELD: 4-5 SERVINGS.

- 1 domestic duckling (4 to 5 pounds)
- 1 jar (12 ounces) cherry preserves
- 1 to 2 tablespoons red wine vinegar

Bing cherries, star fruit and kale, optional

1. Prick skin of duckling well and place breast side up on a rack in a shallow roasting pan. Tie drumsticks together. Bake, uncovered, at 350° for 2 to 2½ hours or until juices run clear and a thermometer reads 180°. (Drain fat from pan as it accumulates.) Cover and let stand 20 minutes before carving.

2. Meanwhile, for sauce, combine preserves and vinegar in a small saucepan. Cook and stir over medium heat until heated through. Serve with duck. Garnish platter with fruit and kale if desired.

PORK, HAM & SAUSAGE

Oktoberfest Pork Roast

My favorite fall flavors, such as apples, pork roast, sauerkraut and potatoes, are combined in one sensational dish. I took my mom's dish and changed it for the slow cooker. I often coat the slow cooker insert with cooking spray to prevent the potatoes and meat from sticking.

—TONYA SWAIN SEVILLE, OHIO

YIELD: 8 SERVINGS.

- 16 **small red potatoes**
- 1 **can (14 ounces) sauerkraut, rinsed and well drained**
- 2 **large tart apples, peeled and cut into wedges**
- 1 **pound smoked kielbasa or Polish sausage, cut into 16 slices**
- 2 **tablespoons brown sugar**
- 1 **teaspoon caraway seeds**
- 1 **teaspoon salt, divided**
- 1 **teaspoon pepper, divided**
- 1 **boneless pork loin roast (3 pounds)**
- 3 **tablespoons canola oil**

1. Place potatoes in a greased 6-qt. slow cooker. Top with sauerkraut, apples and kielbasa. Sprinkle with brown sugar, caraway seeds, ½ teaspoon salt and ½ teaspoon pepper.

2. Cut roast in half. Combine remaining salt and pepper; rub over meat. In a large skillet, brown meat in oil on all sides. Transfer to slow cooker. Cover and cook on low for 8-10 hours or until a thermometer reads 160° and vegetables are tender. Skim fat and thicken pan juices if desired.

Smoked Sausage Potato Bake

This delicious bake came from my mom's recipes files. I often fix it for company because it's pleasing to the eye as well as the appetite. I rarely have leftovers, as second helpings are a given.

—JOANNE WERNER LA PORTE, INDIANA

YIELD: 4-6 SERVINGS.

  1¾ cups water
  ⅔ cup milk
  5 tablespoons butter, divided
  ½ teaspoon salt
  2⅔ cups mashed potato flakes
  1 cup (8 ounces) sour cream
  1 cup (4 ounces) shredded cheddar cheese
  1 pound smoked sausage links, halved lengthwise and cut into ½-inch slices
  1 cup (4 ounces) shredded Monterey Jack cheese
  2 tablespoons dry bread crumbs

1. In a large saucepan, bring the water, milk, 4 tablespoons butter and salt to a boil. Remove from the heat; stir in potato flakes. Let stand for 30 seconds or until liquid is absorbed. Whip with a fork until fluffy. Stir in the sour cream and cheddar cheese.

2. Spoon half into a greased 2-qt. baking dish. Top with sausage and remaining potatoes. Sprinkle with Monterey Jack cheese.

3. Melt the remaining butter and toss with bread crumbs; sprinkle over the top. Bake, uncovered, at 350° for 30-35 minutes or until heated through and edges are golden brown.

Grandma Edna's Cajun Pork

My grandma used to make this every year as part of our Christmas dinner. She's been gone for a few years, but we still carry on the delicious tradition of serving Grandma's Cajun pork.

—TONYA CLINE GREENVILLE, OHIO

YIELD: 12 SERVINGS (2¼ CUPS SAUCE).

  1 small onion
  1 celery rib
  1 small green pepper
  3 tablespoons butter
  3 garlic cloves, minced
  2 teaspoons dried thyme
  1 teaspoon paprika
  ½ teaspoon each salt, white pepper and pepper
  ½ teaspoon ground mustard
  ½ teaspoon hot pepper sauce
  1 boneless whole pork loin roast (4 pounds)
  2 tablespoons cornstarch
  2 tablespoons cold water

1. Finely chop vegetables. In a large skillet, saute vegetables in butter until tender. Add garlic; cook 1 minute longer. Stir in seasonings and pepper sauce.

2. Cut roast in half. Cut several slits in roast to within ½ in. of bottom. Place in a 4-qt. slow cooker. Spoon onion mixture between slits and over the top of meat. Cover and cook on low for 6-8 hours or until pork is tender.

3. Transfer the roast to a serving platter; keep warm. Let stand for 10 minutes before slicing. Pour cooking juices into a small saucepan. Combine cornstarch and water until smooth; stir into the pan. Bring to a boil; cook and stir for 2 minutes or until thickened. Serve with roast.

Sauerkraut 'n' Sausage

I've fixed this satisfying stovetop supper for dozens of group gatherings, and everyone seems to enjoy the wonderful blend of flavors. Sweet and tart ingredients balance nicely, complemented with bacon and spices.

—EDNA HOFFMAN HEBRON, INDIANA

YIELD: 10-12 SERVINGS.

- 1 small onion, chopped
- 1 tablespoon butter
- 1 jar (32 ounces) sauerkraut, rinsed and drained
- 1 pound fully cooked Polish sausage, cut into ½-inch chunks
- 3½ cups diced cooked peeled potatoes
- 1 cup apple juice
- 2 medium unpeeled apple, diced
- 2 tablespoons brown sugar
- 2 tablespoons all-purpose flour
- 1 tablespoon caraway seeds
- 3 bacon strips, cooked and crumbled

1. In a large saucepan, saute the onion in butter until tender. Add the sauerkraut, sausage, potatoes, apple juice and apple. In a small bowl, combine the brown sugar, flour and caraway; stir into saucepan. Simmer for 35 minutes, stirring occasionally. Garnish with bacon.

Kielbasa Skillet Stew

I grew up on a Montana ranch, and this dish reminds me of the type of stew we used to prepare for the hay and harvest crews. The bacon and sausage provide rich flavor in this comforting meal.

—MACHELLE LEWIS HENDERSON, NEVADA

YIELD: 6-8 SERVINGS.

- 5 bacon strips
- 1 to 1½ pounds smoked kielbasa or Polish sausage, thinly sliced
- 1 medium onion, chopped
- 2 cans (15½ ounces each) great northern beans, undrained
- 2 cans (8 ounces each) tomato sauce
- 1 can (4 ounces) chopped green chilies
- 2 medium carrots, thinly sliced
- ½ medium green pepper, chopped
- ½ teaspoon Italian seasoning
- ½ teaspoon dried thyme
- ⅛ teaspoon pepper

1. In a 12-in. skillet, cook bacon until crisp; remove to paper towel to drain. Cook sausage and onions in drippings over medium heat until onion is tender; drain.

2. Stir in remaining ingredients; bring to a boil. Reduce heat; cover and simmer for 45 minutes or until vegetables are tender, stirring occasionally. Crumble bacon; sprinkle over stew.

Sweet-and-Sour Pork

My children asked for this tangy pork dish whenever they came home from school for the weekend. Today, they still appreciate the stir-fry's comforting flavor.

—**DORIS SOKOLOTOSKY** SMOKY LAKE, ALBERTA

YIELD: 4 SERVINGS.

- 1   can (20 ounces) pineapple chunks
- 2   tablespoons cornstarch
- ¼   cup soy sauce
- 1   tablespoon honey
- ½   teaspoon chicken bouillon granules
- 1   garlic clove, minced
- ⅛   teaspoon pepper
- 2   tablespoons canola oil
- ¾   pound pork tenderloin, cut into bite-size pieces
- 1   medium green pepper, thinly sliced

Hot cooked rice

1. Drain pineapple, reserving the juice; set pineapple aside. Add enough water to juice to measure ¾ cup. Combine the cornstarch, soy sauce, honey, bouillon, garlic, pepper and pineapple juice mixture until smooth; set aside.

2. Heat oil in a large skillet; cook and stir pork and green pepper for 6-8 minutes or until pork is no longer pink and green pepper is crisp-tender.

3. Stir the pineapple juice mixture; add to the skillet with pineapple. Bring to a boil. Cook and stir for 1-2 minutes or until thickened and bubbly. Serve with rice.

Ham-Stuffed Manicotti

Here's a fun and different use for ham. It's unexpected combined with the manicotti, yet delicious. The creamy cheese sauce makes this casserole perfect for chilly days. I'm always asked for the recipe whenever I serve it.

—**DOROTHY ANDERSON** OTTAWA, KANSAS

YIELD: 8 SERVINGS.

- 8   manicotti shells
- ½   cup chopped onion
- 1   tablespoon canola oil
- 3   cups (1 pound) ground fully cooked ham
- 1   can (4 ounces) sliced mushrooms, drained
- 1   cup (4 ounces) shredded Swiss cheese, divided
- 3   tablespoons grated Parmesan cheese
- ¼   to ½ cup chopped green pepper
- 3   tablespoons butter
- 3   tablespoons all-purpose flour
- 2   cups 2% milk

Paprika
Chopped fresh parsley

1. Cook manicotti according to package directions; set aside. In a large skillet, saute onion in oil until tender. Remove from the heat. Add the ham, mushrooms, half of Swiss and Parmesan cheeses; set aside.

2. In a small saucepan, saute green pepper in butter until tender. Stir in flour until combined. Add milk; cook and stir for 2 minutes or until thickened. Stir a quarter of the sauce into ham mixture.

3. Stuff each shell with about ⅓ cup of filling. Place in a greased 11-in. x 7-in. baking dish. Top with remaining sauce; sprinkle with paprika.

4. Cover and bake at 350° for 30 minutes or until heated through. Sprinkle with parsley and remaining Swiss cheese before serving.

Editor's Note: *Recipe can easily be doubled for a larger group.*

Pork Chops with Caraway Cabbage

Pork and cabbage naturally bring out the best flavors in each other. Each fall, my family requests this hearty skillet supper.

—DAVID FRAME WAXAHACHIE, TEXAS

YIELD: 4 SERVINGS.

- 4 pork loin chops (¾ inch thick)
- 2 tablespoons canola oil
- ½ teaspoon pepper
- 1½ cups finely chopped onion
- 3 tablespoons butter
- 6 cups shredded cabbage
- 2 garlic cloves, minced
- 3 tablespoons red wine vinegar
- 1 teaspoon caraway seeds
- ½ teaspoon salt

1. In a large skillet over medium heat, brown the pork chops in oil; drain. Sprinkle with pepper; remove and keep warm.

2. In same skillet, saute onion in butter for 1-2 minutes or until tender. Add the cabbage, garlic, vinegar, caraway and salt; cook, stirring occasionally, until the cabbage wilts. Add chops to the skillet. Cover and simmer for 15-17 minutes or until meat is tender. Serve immediately.

Broccoli-Ham Hot Dish

One of my best friends shared this recipe with me. My family loves it because it includes one of our favorite vegetables—broccoli. It's a delicious and colorful way to use up leftover ham.

—MARGARET ALLEN ABINGDON, VIRGINIA

YIELD: 8 SERVINGS.

- 2 packages (10 ounces each) frozen cut broccoli
- 2 cups cooked rice
- 6 tablespoons butter, cubed
- 2 cups fresh bread crumbs (about 2½ slices)
- 1 medium onion, chopped
- 3 tablespoons all-purpose flour
- 1 teaspoon salt
- ¼ teaspoon pepper
- 3 cups milk
- 1½ pounds fully cooked ham, cubed

Shredded cheddar or Swiss cheese

1. Cook broccoli according to package directions; drain. Spoon rice into a 13-in. x 9-in. baking pan. Place broccoli over rice.

2. Melt butter in a large skillet. Sprinkle 2 tablespoons of melted butter over the bread crumbs and set aside. In remaining butter, saute the onion until soft. Add the flour, salt and pepper, stirring constantly until blended; stir in milk. Bring to a boil; cook and stir for 2 minutes or until thickened. Add the ham.

3. Pour over rice and broccoli. Sprinkle with the crumbs. Bake at 350° for 30 minutes or until heated through. Sprinkle with the cheese; let stand for 5 minutes before serving.

Pork and Spinach Salad

I serve this hearty main dish salad at family gatherings throughout the year. You just can't beat a salad that tastes great and is good for you, too.

—**MARIAN PRATT** SEQUIM, WASHINGTON

YIELD: 4 SERVINGS.

    1 package (10 ounces) fresh spinach, torn
    1 can (15½ ounces) black-eyed peas, rinsed and drained
    ½ cup sliced fresh mushrooms
    ⅓ cup Italian or low-fat Italian dressing
    2 green onions, thinly sliced
    ¼ cup sliced celery
    1 jar (2 ounces) sliced pimientos, drained
    2 to 3 tablespoons sliced ripe olives
    ½ pound pork tenderloin, cut into thin strips
    1 tablespoon olive oil
    2 garlic cloves, minced

1. Line four plates with spinach leaves; set aside. In a large bowl, combine the black-eyed peas, mushrooms, dressing, onions, celery, pimientos and olives; set aside.

2. In a small skillet, saute the pork in oil for 1 minute. Add the garlic; saute 1-2 minutes longer or until no longer pink. Remove from the heat; add to black-eyed pea mixture and mix well.

3. Spoon mixture onto spinach-lined plates. Serve immediately.

Cranberry-Glazed Pork Roast

My family loves this festive treatment for pork. I think you'll be just as proud as we are to serve this succulent roast with its ruby glaze at the holidays year after year.

—**THERESA PEARSON** OGILVIE, MINNESOTA

YIELD: 12-14 SERVINGS.

    1 boneless pork shoulder butt roast (3½ to 4 pounds)
   12 small whole onions
    2 teaspoons cornstarch
    ¼ cup orange juice
    1 can (14 ounces) whole-berry cranberry sauce
    ½ to 1 teaspoon grated orange peel
    ¼ teaspoon ground cinnamon
    ⅛ teaspoon salt

1. Place the roast, fat side up, in a greased roasting pan. Bake, uncovered, at 325° for 45 minutes. Place onions around roast, cover and bake for 30 minutes.

2. Meanwhile, in a saucepan, combine cornstarch and orange juice until smooth. Stir in the cranberry sauce, orange peel, cinnamon and salt. Bring to a boil over medium heat; cook and stir for 2 minutes or until thickened. Spoon ¾ cup over roast and onions; set remaining sauce aside.

3. Bake, basting occasionally, 30-45 minutes longer or until a thermometer reads 145°-160° and onions are tender. Let stand for 15 minutes before slicing. Heat reserved sauce; serve with roast and onions.

Ham a la King

My mom and I used to have a catering business, and this dish was a popular choice from our menu. It looks elegant on the plate and people always enjoy it. Being able to make the sauce a day ahead is a big plus.

—JEAN GRUBB BASTROP, TEXAS

YIELD: 6 SERVINGS.

- 1 package (10 ounces) frozen puff pastry shells
- ¼ cup butter, cubed
- ¼ cup all-purpose flour
- 1 teaspoon chicken bouillon granules
- ½ cup hot water
- 1½ cups milk
- 3 slices process American cheese
- 1 teaspoon Worcestershire sauce
- 1 teaspoon prepared mustard
- 2 cups cubed fully cooked ham
- ½ cup frozen peas, thawed, optional
- 1 can (2¼ ounces) sliced ripe olives, drained
- 2 tablespoons diced pimientos
- 2 tablespoons minced fresh parsley

1. Bake pastry shells according to the package directions. Meanwhile, in a large saucepan, melt butter; stir in flour until smooth. Dissolve bouillon in water. Gradually add the milk and bouillon to the saucepan. Bring to a boil; cook and stir for 2 minutes or until thickened.

2. Reduce heat; add the cheese, Worcestershire sauce and mustard. Stir until cheese is melted. Add the ham, peas if desired, olives, pimientos and parsley; heat through. Serve in pastry shells.

Ham 'n' Cheese Pasta

Whenever we had leftover ham, we could look forward to my mother preparing her yummy, comforting pasta. Horseradish gives it a nice zip. I quickened the preparation by using process cheese instead of making a cheese sauce from scratch. Now my kids love it.

—KAREN KOPP INDIANAPOLIS, INDIANA

YIELD: 4 SERVINGS.

- 8 ounces uncooked medium pasta shells
- 1 pound process cheese (Velveeta), cubed
- ½ cup milk
- 2 tablespoons ketchup
- 1 tablespoon prepared horseradish
- 2 cups cubed fully cooked ham
- 1 package (8 ounces) frozen peas, thawed

1. Cook pasta according to package directions. Meanwhile, in a microwave-safe bowl, combine cheese and milk. Cover and microwave on high for 2 minutes; stir. Heat 1-2 minutes longer or until smooth, stirring twice. Stir in ketchup and horseradish until blended.

2. Drain pasta and place in a large bowl. Stir in the ham, peas and cheese sauce.

3. Transfer to a greased 2-qt. baking dish. Cover and bake at 350° for 30-35 minutes or until heated through.

Sweet-Sour Franks

When I married my husband more than 30 years ago, I asked my mother-in-law for some of his favorite dishes. Knowing money was tight, she sent a budget-friendly hot dog dish along. It's so good that I still make it today.

—DIANE HENDRIXSON WAPAKONETA, OHIO

YIELD: 3 SERVINGS.

1 **can (20 ounces) pineapple tidbits**
1 **teaspoon beef bouillon granules**
⅓ **cup boiling water**
1 **tablespoon cornstarch**
1 **tablespoon brown sugar**
2 **tablespoons cider vinegar**
1 **tablespoon reduced-sodium soy sauce**
1 **medium onion, chopped**
1 **medium green pepper, julienned**
2 **tablespoons butter**
5 **hot dogs, halved lengthwise and cut into ½-inch slices**
3 **cups hot cooked rice**

1. Drain pineapple, reserving juice. Set aside 1 cup pineapple and 6 tablespoons juice; refrigerate remaining pineapple and juice for another use. Dissolve bouillon in water. In a small bowl, combine the cornstarch, brown sugar, vinegar, soy sauce, bouillon and reserved juice until smooth; set aside.

2. In a large skillet, saute the onion and green pepper in butter. Stir cornstarch mixture; stir into skillet. Bring to a boil; cook and stir for 2 minutes or until thickened. Add the hot dogs and reserved pineapple; cook until heated through. Serve over rice.

SEAFOOD & MEATLESS MAIN DISHES

Broiled Fish

Mother's secret in preparing this recipe was to butter the fish before dusting it with flour. That seals in the moisture, making it succulent and absolutely delicious.

—ANN BERG CHESAPEAKE, VIRGINIA

YIELD: 4 SERVINGS.

    4   orange roughy, red snapper, catfish or trout fillets
        (1½ to 2 pounds)
    6   tablespoons butter, melted, divided
    1   tablespoon all-purpose flour
Paprika
Juice of 1 lemon
    1   tablespoon minced fresh parsley
    2   teaspoons Worcestershire sauce

1. Place fish on a broiler rack that has been coated with cooking spray. Drizzle 3 tablespoons butter over fillets; dust with flour and sprinkle with paprika.

2. Broil 5-6 in. from the heat for 5 minutes or until the fish just begins to brown. Combine the lemon juice, parsley, Worcestershire sauce and remaining butter; pour over fish. Broil 5 minutes longer or until fish flakes easily with a fork.

Budget Macaroni and Cheese

You can't beat this comforting recipe for pleasing the family and going easy on the budget. It's a classic, satisfying meatless entree.

—DEBBIE CARLSON SAN DIEGO, CALIFORNIA

YIELD: 4 SERVINGS.

    1   package (7 ounces) elbow macaroni
    3   tablespoons butter
    3   tablespoons all-purpose flour
    ¼   teaspoon salt
Dash pepper
    1   cup milk
    1   cup (4 ounces) shredded cheddar cheese

1. Cook the macaroni according to the package directions. Meanwhile, in a large saucepan, melt butter over medium-low heat. Add the flour, salt and pepper; stir until smooth; gradually add milk. Bring to a boil; cook and stir for 2 minutes or until thickened. Remove from the heat; stir in cheese until melted.

2. Drain macaroni. Add to the cheese mixture; toss to coat.

Red Beans and Rice

This recipe originated with my sister-in-law, but I changed it around a bit to suit the tastes of my family.

—MARCIA SALISBURY WAUKESHA, WISCONSIN

YIELD: 12 SERVINGS.

    ½   pound dried kidney beans, rinsed
    ½   pound dried pinto beans, rinsed
    4   cups water
    4   cups chicken broth
    2   garlic cloves, minced
    2   bay leaves
    1   can (14½ ounces) diced tomatoes, undrained
    1   jar (4 ounces) chopped pimientos, drained
    1   large green pepper, chopped
    1   large sweet red pepper, chopped
    1   large onion, chopped
    1   cup chopped celery
    1   can (4 ounces) diced green chilies
    ¼   cup snipped fresh parsley
    1   tablespoon vinegar
    1   teaspoon salt
    1   teaspoon paprika
    ¼ to ½ teaspoon ground cumin
    ¼ to ½ teaspoon crushed red pepper flakes
    ¼ to ½ teaspoon hot pepper sauce
Hot cooked rice

1. Place beans in a Dutch oven with water. Bring to a boil; boil for 2 minutes. Remove from the heat; cover and let soak for 1-4 hours or until softened. Drain and rinse beans; discard liquid.

2. Return beans to Dutch oven; add the broth, garlic and bay leaves. Bring to a boil. Reduce heat; cover and simmer for 1¼ hours. Stir in remaining ingredients except rice. Cover and simmer 1 hour longer or until beans and vegetables are tender and sauce is thickened. Remove bay leaves. Serve over rice.

Lime Broiled Catfish

To serve a reduced-calorie dish that is ready in about 15 minutes, I came up with this fast recipe. I think the lime juice adds fresh flavor to the mild taste of the fish.

—NICK NICHOLSON CLARKSDALE, MISSISSIPPI

YIELD: 2 SERVINGS.

1 tablespoon butter
2 tablespoons lime juice
½ teaspoon salt, optional
¼ teaspoon pepper
¼ teaspoon garlic powder
2 catfish fillets (6 ounces each)
Lime slices or wedges, optional
Fresh parsley, optional

1. Melt butter in a small saucepan. Stir in the lime juice, salt if desired, pepper and garlic powder. Remove from the heat and set aside.

2. Place fillets in a shallow baking pan. Brush each fillet generously with lime-butter sauce. Broil for 5-8 minutes or until fish flakes easily with a fork.

3. Remove to a warm serving dish; spoon pan juices over each fillet. Garnish with lime slices and parsley if desired.

Mushroom Crab Melts

I received this recipe from my grandmother. The rich open-faced treats are great with a green salad, but I've also cut them into quarters to serve as hors d'oeuvres. To save time, make the crab-mushroom topping early in the day and store it in the refrigerator.

—JEAN BEVILACQUA RHODODENDRON, OREGON

YIELD: 6 SERVINGS.

3 **bacon strips, diced**
1 **cup sliced fresh mushrooms**
¼ **cup chopped onion**
1 **can (6 ounces) crabmeat, drained, flaked and cartilage removed or 1 cup chopped imitation crabmeat**
1 **cup (4 ounces) shredded Swiss cheese**
½ **cup mayonnaise**
⅓ **cup grated Parmesan cheese**
2 **tablespoons butter, softened**
6 **English muffins, split**
Dash each cayenne pepper and paprika

1. In a large skillet, cook bacon over medium heat until crisp; remove to paper towels. Drain, reserving 2 tablespoons drippings. Saute mushrooms and onion in drippings until tender.

2. In a large bowl, combine the crab, Swiss cheese, mayonnaise, mushroom mixture, Parmesan cheese and bacon.

3. Spread butter over muffin halves. Top with crab mixture; sprinkle with cayenne and paprika. Place on an ungreased baking sheet.

4. Bake at 400° for 10-15 minutes or until lightly browned.

Eggplant Parmigiana

This delicious eggplant casserole—from my mom—makes a wonderful meatless meal. It's a resourceful way to use up the eggplant in your garden, and the homemade marinara sauce tastes really good.

—VALERIE BELLEY ST. LOUIS, MISSOURI

YIELD: 10-12 SERVINGS.

- 2 medium eggplant, peeled and cut into ½-inch slices
- 2 teaspoons salt
- 2 large onions, chopped
- 2 tablespoons minced fresh basil or 2 teaspoons dried basil
- 2 bay leaves
- 1 tablespoon minced fresh oregano or 1 teaspoon dried oregano
- 1 tablespoon minced fresh thyme or 1 teaspoon dried thyme
- 3 tablespoons olive oil
- 1 can (14½ ounces) diced tomatoes, undrained
- 1 can (12 ounces) tomato paste
- 1 tablespoon honey
- 1½ teaspoons lemon-pepper seasoning
- 4 garlic cloves, minced
- 2 eggs, lightly beaten
- ½ teaspoon pepper
- 1½ cups dry bread crumbs
- ¼ cup butter, divided
- 8 cups (32 ounces) shredded part-skim mozzarella cheese
- 1 cup grated Parmesan cheese

1. Place the eggplant in a colander; sprinkle with salt. Let stand for 30 minutes. Meanwhile, in a large skillet, saute the onions, basil, bay leaves, oregano and thyme in oil until the onions are tender.

2. Add the tomatoes, tomato paste, honey and lemon-pepper. Bring to a boil. Reduce heat; cover and simmer for 30 minutes. Add garlic; simmer 10 minutes longer. Discard bay leaves.

3. Rinse eggplant slices; pat dry with paper towels. In a shallow bowl, combine eggs and pepper; place bread crumbs in another shallow bowl. Dip eggplant into eggs, then coat with crumbs. Let stand for 5 minutes.

4. In a large skillet, cook half of the eggplant in 2 tablespoons butter for 3 minutes on each side or until lightly browned. Repeat with remaining eggplant and butter.

5. In each of two greased 11-in. x 7-in. baking dishes, layer a fourth of each of the eggplant, tomato sauce and mozzarella cheese. Repeat layers. Sprinkle with the Parmesan cheese. Bake, uncovered, at 375° for 35 minutes or until a thermometer reads 160°.

Grandma's French Tuna Salad Wraps

My French-Canadian grandmother always made tuna salad with chopped egg in it. I tried a version of it, added veggies for complete nutrition and turned it into a wrap. It's fun to eat, and we are reminded of my grandmother with each bite.

—JENNIFER MAGREY STERLING, CONNECTICUT

YIELD: 2 SERVINGS.

- 1 can (5 ounces) light water-packed tuna, drained and flaked
- 1 celery rib, finely chopped
- ¼ cup fat-free mayonnaise
- ¼ teaspoon pepper
- 2 whole wheat tortillas (8 inches), room temperature
- ½ cup shredded lettuce
- 1 small carrot, shredded
- 4 slices tomato
- 2 slices red onion, separated into rings
- 1 hard-cooked egg, sliced

1. In a small bowl, combine the tuna, celery, mayonnaise and pepper. Spoon tuna mixture down the center of each tortilla. Top with lettuce, carrot, tomato, onion and egg. Roll up tightly; secure with toothpicks.

The partial text on the left edge:

Fl...

We...
out...
and...
And...
—LU...

YIEI...

⅓
¼
¼
½
½
1
1
2
1
1
1
2
1
1
1

1. I...
unti...
for 2...
crab...

2. T...
or u...

Stuffed Sole

Seafood was a staple for my large family when I was growing up. Inspired by my mother's delicious meals, I developed this recipe. The fish is moist and flavorful, and the sauce is so good over rice. I predict you'll get many compliments and recipe requests when you serve this dish, just as I do.

—WINNIE HIGGINS SALISBURY, MARYLAND

YIELD: 8 SERVINGS.

- 1 cup chopped onion
- 2 cans (6 ounces each) small shrimp, rinsed and drained
- 1 jar (4½ ounces) sliced mushrooms, drained
- 2 tablespoons butter
- ½ pound fresh cooked or canned crabmeat, drained and cartilage removed
- 8 sole or flounder fillets (2 to 2½ pounds)
- ½ teaspoon salt
- ¼ teaspoon pepper
- ¼ teaspoon paprika
- 2 cans (10¾ ounces each) condensed cream of mushroom soup, undiluted
- ⅓ cup chicken broth
- 2 tablespoons water
- ⅔ cup shredded cheddar cheese
- 2 tablespoons minced fresh parsley

Cooked wild, brown or white rice or a mixture, optional

1. In a large saucepan, saute onion, shrimp and mushrooms in butter until onion is tender. Add the crabmeat; heat through. Sprinkle fillets with salt, pepper and paprika. Spoon crabmeat mixture on fillets; roll up and fasten with a toothpick.

2. Place in a greased 13-in. x 9-in. baking dish. Combine the soup, broth and water; blend until smooth. Pour over fillets. Sprinkle with cheese.

3. Cover and bake at 400° for 30 minutes. Sprinkle with parsley; return to the oven, uncovered, for 5 minutes or until the fish flakes easily with a fork. Serve with rice if desired.

Tomato Pizza

My children liked to eat pizza with a lot of toppings, so I came up with this recipe for them. With fresh tomatoes available year-round here, we still make it often, even though the kids are now grown. It's a delightful change from the usual meat-topped pizza.

—LOIS MCATEE OCEANSIDE, CALIFORNIA

YIELD: 8 SERVINGS.

- 6 medium firm tomatoes, thinly sliced
- 1 prebaked 12-inch pizza crust
- 2 tablespoons olive oil
- 1 teaspoon salt
- 1 teaspoon pepper
- 1 can (2¼ ounces) sliced ripe olives, drained, optional
- ½ cup diced green pepper
- ½ cup diced onion
- 1 tablespoon minced fresh basil
- 1 cup (4 ounces) shredded mozzarella cheese
- 1 cup (4 ounces) shredded cheddar cheese

1. Place tomato slices in a circle on crust, overlapping slightly until crust is completely covered. Drizzle with olive oil. Season with salt and pepper. Cover with olives if desired, green pepper and onion. Sprinkle with basil.

2. Cover with mozzarella and cheddar cheeses. Bake at 400° for 15 minutes or until cheese is melted. Serve immediately.

Homemade Pasta Sauce

When my tomatoes ripen, the first things I make are BLT's and this from-scratch spaghetti sauce.

—SONDRA BERGY LOWELL, MICHIGAN

YIELD: 2 QUARTS.

- 4 medium onions, chopped
- ½ cup canola oil
- 12 cups chopped peeled fresh tomatoes
- 4 garlic cloves, minced
- 3 bay leaves
- 4 teaspoons salt
- 2 teaspoons dried oregano
- 1¼ teaspoons pepper
- ½ teaspoon dried basil
- 2 cans (6 ounces each) tomato paste
- ⅓ cup packed brown sugar
- Hot cooked spaghetti

1. In a Dutch oven, saute onions in oil until tender. Add the tomatoes, garlic, bay leaves, salt, oregano, pepper and basil. Bring to a boil. Reduce heat; cover and simmer for 2 hours, stirring occasionally.

2. Add tomato paste and brown sugar; simmer, uncovered, for 1 hour. Discard bay leaves. Serve with spaghetti.

Editor's Note: *Browned ground beef or Italian sausage can be added to the cooked sauce if desired. The sauce also freezes well.*

Mock Lobster

When I want a quick fish dinner, this is the mouthwatering recipe I turn to. My husband and I like the flavor so much that I serve it a couple of times a month.

—GLORIA JARRETT LOVELAND, OHIO

YIELD: 4-6 SERVINGS.

- 1½ to 2 pounds cod or haddock
- 1½ teaspoons salt
- 2 teaspoons seafood seasoning or paprika
- 3 tablespoons white vinegar
- Melted butter
- Lemon wedges

1. Cut fillets into 2-in. x 2-in. pieces; place in a large skillet. Cover with water. Add salt and seafood seasoning; bring to a boil. Reduce heat; simmer, uncovered, for 10 minutes. Drain.

2. Cover with cold water. Add vinegar and bring to a boil. Reduce heat; simmer, uncovered, for 10 minutes or until fish flakes easily with a fork. Drain. Serve with melted butter and lemon.

Catch-of-the-Day Casserole

My dear mother-in-law is one of the best cooks I know and one of the best mothers—a real gem. This casserole was one of her recipes.

—**CATHY CLUGSTON**
CLOVERDALE, INDIANA

YIELD: 4 SERVINGS.

- 4 ounces uncooked small shell pasta
- 1 can (10¾ ounces) condensed cream of celery soup, undiluted
- ½ cup mayonnaise
- ¼ cup milk
- ¼ cup shredded cheddar cheese
- 1 package (10 ounces) frozen peas, thawed
- 1 can (7½ ounces) salmon, drained, bones and skin removed
- 1 tablespoon finely chopped onion

1. Cook pasta according to package directions. Meanwhile, in a large bowl, combine the soup, mayonnaise, milk and cheese until blended. Stir in peas, salmon and onion.

2. Drain pasta; add to salmon mixture. Transfer to a greased 2-qt. baking dish. Bake, uncovered, at 350° for 30-35 minutes or until bubbly.

Catfish Cakes

These cakes are crispy on the outside and moist and flavorful on the inside—a real treat! I like to serve them with hush puppies and coleslaw. I use this recipe to make the most of all the catfish we catch at our lake cabin.

—**JAN CAMPBELL** HATTIESBURG, MISSISSIPPI

YIELD: 8 SERVINGS.

- 1½ pounds catfish fillets
- 2 eggs, lightly beaten
- 1 large potato, peeled, cooked and mashed
- 1 large onion, finely chopped
- 1 to 2 tablespoons minced fresh parsley
- 2 to 3 drops hot pepper sauce
- 1 garlic clove, minced
- 1 teaspoon salt
- ½ teaspoon pepper
- ½ teaspoon dried basil
- 2 cups finely crushed butter-flavored crackers

Canola oil
Tartar sauce, optional

1. Poach or bake catfish fillets until fish flakes easily with a fork. Drain and refrigerate. Flake cooled fish into a large bowl. Add the eggs, potato, onion, parsley, pepper sauce, garlic, salt, pepper and basil; mix well. Shape into eight patties.

2. Place cracker crumbs in a shallow bowl. Coat patties in cracker crumbs. In a large skillet over medium heat, cook catfish cakes in oil in batches on each side or until golden brown. Serve with tartar sauce if desired.

Grilled Salmon

We love to cook on the grill at our house. I've used this flavorful salmon recipe several times and we always enjoy it. The parsley, rosemary and green onions help make the tender fillets a tempting main dish that looks impressive.

—**MONELL NUCKOLS** CARPINTERIA, CALIFORNIA

YIELD: 4 SERVINGS.

2 **salmon fillets (about 1 pound each)**
½ **cup canola oil**
¼ **cup lemon juice**
4 **green onions, thinly sliced**
3 **tablespoons minced fresh parsley**
1½ **teaspoons minced fresh rosemary or ½ teaspoon dried rosemary, crushed**
½ **teaspoon salt**
⅛ **teaspoon pepper**

1. Place salmon in shallow dish. Combine the remaining ingredients. Set aside ¼ cup for basting; pour the remaining marinade over salmon. Cover and refrigerate for 30 minutes.

2. Drain, discarding marinade. Grill salmon over medium heat, skin side down, for 15-20 minutes or until fish flakes easily with a fork. Baste occasionally with reserved marinade.

Baked Lemon Haddock

Fish products are abundant here on the East Coast, so I'm always in search of new and fun ways to prepare it. Our family never tires of this simple but superb baked fish. As a matter of fact, it's my husband's favorite.

—**JEAN ANN PERKINS** NEWBURYPORT, MARYLAND

YIELD: 6 SERVINGS.

2 **pounds haddock fillets**
1 **cup seasoned dry bread crumbs**
¼ **cup butter, melted**
2 **tablespoons dried parsley flakes**
2 **teaspoons grated lemon peel**
½ **teaspoon garlic powder**

1. Cut the fish into serving-size pieces. Place in a greased 11-in. x 7-in. baking dish. Combine remaining ingredients; sprinkle over fish. Bake at 350° for 25 minutes or until fish flakes easily with a fork.

> To me, nothing tasted as good as the cool water that came from the well on my grandparents' farm. We lowered a wooden bucket with a rope on a pulley, and when we pulled that bucket back up, we'd drink from a tin dipper.
>
> —**DOROTHY ELLIOTT** ORANGE, TEXAS

Shrimp Scampi

Served over pasta, this main dish is pretty enough for company, yet is a snap to prepare. You'll love the fresh flavor the lemon and herbs add to the dish.

—LORI PACKER OMAHA, NEBRASKA

YIELD: 4 SERVINGS.

  3 **to 4 garlic cloves, minced**
  ¼ **cup butter, cubed**
  ¼ **cup olive oil**
  1 **pound uncooked medium shrimp, peeled and deveined**
  ¼ **cup lemon juice**
  ½ **teaspoon pepper**
  ¼ **teaspoon dried oregano**
  ½ **cup grated Parmesan cheese**
  ¼ **cup dry bread crumbs**
  ¼ **cup minced fresh parsley**
Hot cooked angel hair pasta

1. In a 10-in. ovenproof skillet, saute garlic in butter and oil for 1 minute or until tender. Stir in the shrimp, lemon juice, pepper and oregano; cook and stir for 2-3 minutes or until shrimp turn pink. Sprinkle with the cheese, bread crumbs and parsley.

2. Broil 6 in. from the heat for 2-3 minutes or until topping is golden brown. Serve with pasta.

Crispy Cajun Panfish

My mother was happiest with a fishing rod in her hands, and her method of frying her catch was always a hit. Whenever someone gives us fresh fish or if I buy some, I use this wonderful recipe of hers.

—GAYLE COOK MINOT, NORTH DAKOTA

YIELD: 8 SERVINGS.

- 2 **cups all-purpose flour**
- 2 **teaspoons salt**
- 2 **teaspoons Cajun seasoning**
- 1½ **teaspoons pepper**
- ⅛ **teaspoon ground cinnamon**
- 2 **pounds bass or perch fillets**
- 2 **eggs**
- ¼ **cup water**
- 2 **cups mashed potato flakes**
- 6 **tablespoons canola oil**

1. In a large resealable plastic bag, combine the first five ingredients. Add fish, one piece at a time; shake to coat. Whisk eggs and water in a shallow dish. Place potato flakes in another shallow dish. Dip each fillet in eggs, then coat with potato flakes. Dip fish again in eggs and potato flakes.

2. In a large skillet, heat 3 tablespoons oil over medium-high heat. Cook fish in batches for 3-4 minutes on each side or until fish flakes easily with a fork, adding oil as needed.

Sole in Herbed Butter

I often rely on seafood recipes for quick meals. This flavorful fish is easy to make and is ready in just a few minutes. I know your family will request this often throughout the year!

—MARILYN PARADIS
WOODBURN, OREGON

YIELD: 6 SERVINGS.

- 4 **tablespoons butter, softened**
- 1 **teaspoon dill weed**
- ½ **teaspoon onion powder**
- ½ **teaspoon garlic powder**
- ½ **teaspoon salt, optional**
- ¼ **teaspoon white pepper**
- 2 **pounds sole fillets**
- **Fresh dill and lemon wedges, optional**

1. In a small bowl, combine the butter, dill, onion powder, garlic powder, salt if desired and pepper.

2. Transfer to a large skillet; heat on medium heat until melted. Add the sole and saute several minutes on each side or until fish flakes easily with a fork. Garnish with dill and lemon if desired.

CAKES & CHEESECAKES

Butter Pecan Cheesecake

Fall always makes me yearn for this pecan cheesecake, but it's delicious any time of year. You'll want to put it on your list of favorite holiday desserts.

—LAURA SYLVESTER MECHANICSVILLE, VIRGINIA

YIELD: 16 SERVINGS.

- 1½ cups graham cracker crumbs
- ½ cup finely chopped pecans
- ⅓ cup sugar
- ⅓ cup butter, melted

FILLING

- 3 packages (8 ounces each) cream cheese, softened
- 1½ cups sugar
- 2 cups (16 ounces) sour cream
- 1 teaspoon vanilla extract
- ½ teaspoon butter flavoring
- 3 eggs, lightly beaten
- 1 cup finely chopped pecans

1. In a large bowl, combine the cracker crumbs, pecans, sugar and butter; set aside ⅓ cup for topping. Press remaining crumb mixture onto the bottom and 1 in. up the sides of a greased 9-in. springform pan.

2. Place springform pan on a double thickness of heavy-duty foil (about 18 in. square). Securely wrap foil around pan.

3. In a large bowl, beat cream cheese and sugar until smooth. Beat in the sour cream, vanilla and butter flavoring. Add eggs; beat on low speed just until combined. Fold in pecans. Pour into crust; sprinkle with reserved crumb mixture. Place springform pan in a large baking pan; add 1 in. of hot water to larger pan.

4. Bake at 325° for 70-80 minutes or until center is almost set. Remove springform pan from water bath. Cool on a wire rack for 10 minutes. Carefully run a knife around the edge of pan to loosen; cool 1 hour longer. Refrigerate overnight. Remove the sides of pan.

Banana Cupcakes

I've been making these scrumptious cupcakes for more than 40 years. My husband's mother passed along the recipe for them. They taste as good today as they did back then!

—**ARLOIA LUTZ** SEBEWAING, MICHIGAN

YIELD: 1 DOZEN.

⅓ cup shortening
⅔ cup sugar
1 egg
1 teaspoon vanilla extract
¾ cup mashed ripe bananas (about 2 small bananas)
1⅓ cups cake flour
1 teaspoon baking powder
½ teaspoon salt
½ teaspoon baking soda
½ teaspoon ground cinnamon
½ teaspoon ground cloves
¼ teaspoon ground nutmeg
1 tablespoon confectioners' sugar

1. In a large bowl, cream shortening and sugar until light and fluffy. Beat in the egg, vanilla and bananas. Combine the flour, baking powder, salt, baking soda, cinnamon, cloves and nutmeg; add to the creamed mixture just until combined.

2. Fill paper-lined muffin cups two-thirds full. Bake at 375° for 18-20 minutes or until a toothpick comes out clean. Cool for 10 minutes before removing from pan to a wire rack to cool completely. Dust with confectioners' sugar.

Toffee Poke Cake

My family and friends have declared my poke cake one of their favorite treats. I enjoy making it because it is so simple. The oozing caramel tastes wonderful with the smooth chocolate cake.

—**JEANETTE HOFFMAN** OSHKOSH, WISCONSIN

YIELD: 15 SERVINGS.

1 package (18¼ ounces) chocolate cake mix
1 jar (17 ounces) butterscotch-caramel ice cream topping
1 carton (12 ounces) frozen whipped topping, thawed
3 Heath candy bars (1.4 ounces each), chopped

1. Prepare and bake cake according to package directions, using a greased 13-in. x 9-in. baking pan. Cool on a wire rack.

2. Using the handle of a wooden spoon, poke holes in the cake. Pour ¾ cup caramel topping into holes. Spoon remaining caramel over cake. Top with whipped topping. Sprinkle with the candy. Refrigerate for at least 2 hours before serving.

Luscious Almond Cheesecake

Almonds and almond extract give a traditional sour cream-topped cheesecake a tasty twist.

—**BRENDA CLIFFORD** OVERLAND PARK, KANSAS

YIELD: 14-16 SERVINGS.

1¼ cups crushed vanilla wafers (about 40 wafers)
¾ cup finely chopped almonds
¼ cup sugar
⅓ cup butter, melted

FILLING

4 packages (8 ounces each) cream cheese, softened
1¼ cups sugar
4 eggs, lightly beaten
1½ teaspoons almond extract
1 teaspoon vanilla extract

TOPPING

2 cups (16 ounces) sour cream
¼ cup sugar
1 teaspoon vanilla extract
⅛ cup toasted sliced almonds

1. In a bowl, combine the wafer crumbs, almonds and sugar; stir in the butter and mix well. Press into the bottom of a greased 10-in. springform pan; set aside.

2. In a large bowl, beat cream cheese and sugar until smooth. Add eggs; beat on low speed just until combined. Stir in extracts. Pour into crust. Place on a baking sheet.

3. Bake at 350° for 50-55 minutes or until center is almost set. Remove from the oven; let stand for 5 minutes (leave oven on). Combine the sour cream, sugar and vanilla. Spoon topping around the edge of cheesecake; carefully spread over filling. Bake 5 minutes longer. Cool on a wire rack for 10 minutes. Carefully run a knife around edge of pan to loosen; cool 1 hour longer. Refrigerate overnight.

4. Just before serving, sprinkle with almonds and remove sides of pan. Refrigerate leftovers.

Pineapple Bundt Cake

I write a recipe column for my local newspaper, so I try lots of new recipes. This one's a keeper. Fruity and firm-textured, this beautiful cake makes a delicious dessert or a nice afternoon treat.

—**FAYNE LUTZ** TAOS, NEW MEXICO

YIELD: 12-16 SERVINGS.

1 cup butter, softened
1½ cups sugar

2 eggs, lightly beaten
2 egg whites
2 teaspoons lemon extract
2⅔ cups all-purpose flour
1 teaspoon baking powder
1 can (8 ounces) crushed pineapple, undrained

GLAZE
1 cup confectioners' sugar
1 to 2 tablespoons milk
½ teaspoon lemon extract

1. In a large bowl, cream butter and sugar until light and fluffy. Beat in the eggs, egg whites and extract until well blended. Combine flour and baking powder; gradually add to creamed mixture, beating well after each addition. Stir in pineapple.

2. Pour into a greased 10-in. fluted tube pan. Bake at 350° for 55-60 minutes. Cool for 10 minutes before removing from pan to a wire rack to cool completely. In a small bowl, combine glaze ingredients. Drizzle over cake.

White Texas Sheet Cake

This cake gets better the longer it sits, so make it a day ahead.
—**JOANIE WARD** BROWNSBURG, INDIANA

YIELD: 20 SERVINGS.

1 cup butter, cubed
1 cup water
2 cups all-purpose flour
2 cups sugar
2 eggs, beaten
½ cup sour cream
1 teaspoon salt
1 teaspoon baking powder
1 teaspoon almond extract
¼ teaspoon baking soda

FROSTING
½ cup butter, cubed
¼ cup milk
4½ cups confectioners' sugar
½ teaspoon almond extract
1 cup chopped walnuts

1. In a large saucepan, bring the butter and water just to a boil. Immediately remove from the heat; stir in the flour, sugar, eggs, sour cream, salt, baking powder, extract and baking soda until smooth.

2. Pour into a greased 15-in. x 10-in. x 1-in. baking pan. Bake at 375° for 18-22 minutes or until golden brown and a toothpick inserted near the center comes out clean. Cool on a wire rack for 20 minutes.

3. For frosting, in a large saucepan, bring the butter and milk just to a boil. Immediately remove from the heat; stir in the confectioners' sugar and extract. Stir in walnuts; spread over warm cake. Cool completely.

Great-Grandma's Ginger Cake

I received this recipe from my great-grandmother and it remains one of my favorite cakes to make during the holidays. It is so tasty.
—**TERESA PELKEY** CHERRY VALLEY, MASSACHUSETTS

YIELD: 9 SERVINGS.

½ cup shortening
½ cup sugar
⅔ cup molasses
1 egg
2¼ cups all-purpose flour
1 teaspoon baking soda
1 teaspoon ground ginger
1 teaspoon ground cinnamon
½ teaspoon salt
Dash ground cloves
¾ cup water
Whipped topping

1. In a small bowl, cream shortening and sugar until light and fluffy. Add molasses and egg; mix well. Combine the flour, baking soda, ginger, cinnamon, salt and cloves. Add to the creamed mixture alternately with water, beating well after each addition.

2. Pour into a greased 9-in. square baking pan. Bake at 350° for 35-40 minutes or until a toothpick inserted near the center comes out clean. Cool on a wire rack. Garnish with the whipped topping.

Fresh Citrus Cheesecake

Here's the perfect cheesecake for spring. The rich cookie-like crust and creamy filling make the zesty citrus taste a wonderful surprise.

—MARCY CELLA L'ANSE, MICHIGAN

YIELD: 12-14 SERVINGS.

½ cup butter, softened
⅓ cup sugar
1 egg yolk
½ teaspoon vanilla extract
1¼ cups all-purpose flour
1 teaspoon grated lemon peel

FILLING

5 packages (8 ounces each) cream cheese, softened
1¾ cups sugar
3 tablespoons all-purpose flour
1½ teaspoons grated lemon peel
1½ teaspoons grated orange peel
¼ teaspoon vanilla extract
5 eggs, lightly beaten
2 egg yolks, lightly beaten
¼ cup heavy whipping cream

TOPPING

1½ cups (about 12 ounces) sour cream
3 tablespoons sugar
1 teaspoon vanilla extract

1. In a large bowl, cream butter and sugar until light and fluffy. Beat in egg yolk and vanilla. Combine flour and lemon peel; gradually add to creamed mixture. Mix until dough forms a ball and pulls away from the sides of the bowl. Divide dough in half; cover and refrigerate for 1 hour or until easy to handle.

2. Remove sides of a 9-in. springform pan. Grease bottom. Between waxed paper, roll half the dough to fit bottom of pan. Peel off top paper; invert dough onto bottom of pan. Remove paper; trim dough to fit pan.

3. Place on a baking sheet. Bake at 400° for 6-8 minutes or until light browned. Cool completely on a wire rack.

4. Attach sides of the pan and grease sides. Pat remaining dough 1½ in. up sides of pan, pressing dough to bottom crust to seal.

5. For filling, in another large bowl, beat the cream cheese, sugar, flour, peels and vanilla until smooth. Add eggs and yolks; beat on low speed just until combined. Stir in cream just until combined. Pour into crust. Return pan to baking sheet.

6. Bake at 400° for 10 minutes. Reduce heat to 325°; bake 55-65 minutes or until center is almost set. Cool on a wire rack for 10 minutes.

7. Carefully run a knife around edge of pan to loosen; cool 1 hour longer. Combine topping ingredients; spread over cheesecake. Refrigerate overnight.

Heavenly Surprise Mini Cupcakes

My grandmother was an accomplished baker, and this was one of the many special treats she liked to make. It's fun to bite into these dense chocolate cupcakes and discover a surprise inside.

—JORUN MEIERDING MANKATO, MINNESOTA

YIELD: 6 DOZEN.

FILLING
- 1 package (8 ounces) cream cheese, softened
- ⅓ cup sugar
- 1 egg
- ⅛ teaspoon salt
- 1 cup flaked coconut
- 1 cup finely chopped walnuts
- 1 cup (6 ounces) miniature semisweet chocolate chips

BATTER
- 2 cups sugar
- 1½ cups water
- ¾ cup canola oil
- 2 eggs
- 2 teaspoons vanilla extract
- 1 teaspoon white vinegar
- 3 cups all-purpose flour
- ½ cup baking cocoa
- 1 teaspoon baking soda
- 1 teaspoon salt

FROSTING
- 1⅓ cups semisweet chocolate chips
- ½ cup heavy whipping cream

1. For filling, in a small bowl, beat cream cheese and sugar until light and fluffy. Add egg and salt; mix well. Stir in the coconut, walnuts and chocolate chips. Set aside.

2. For batter, in a large bowl, beat the sugar, water, oil, eggs, vanilla and vinegar until well blended. Combine the flour, cocoa, baking soda and salt; gradually beat into oil mixture until blended.

3. Fill paper-lined miniature muffin cups one-third full with batter. Drop filling by teaspoonfuls into center of each. Top with additional batter, filling muffin cups three-fourths full.

4. Bake at 350° for 12-15 minutes or until a toothpick inserted in the cake portion of a cupcake comes out clean. Cool in pans for 10 minutes before removing to wire racks to cool completely.

5. For frosting, in a small saucepan, melt chocolate with cream over low heat; stir until blended. Remove from the heat. Cool to room temperature. Frost cupcakes. Refrigerate leftovers.

Editor's Note: *Cupcakes may also be baked in 30 paper-lined standard-size muffin cups for 20-25 minutes.*

Ladyfinger Cheesecake

My mom's friend made this cheesecake. After one taste, we knew we had to have the recipe. It's so good that we've promised to never make cheesecake any other way.

—MARCIA SAVERY NEW BEDFORD, MASSACHUSETTS

YIELD: 14 SERVINGS.

- 4½ cups sliced fresh strawberries (about 2 pounds)
- 2 tablespoons plus 2 cups sugar, divided
- 3 packages (3 ounces each) ladyfingers, split
- 4 packages (8 ounces each) cream cheese, softened
- 2 cups heavy whipping cream

1. In a large bowl, combine strawberries and 2 tablespoons sugar. Cover; refrigerate for at least 1 hour. Meanwhile, arrange 25 split ladyfingers around the edges of a lightly greased 10-in. springform pan. Place 25 more on the bottom; set aside.

2. In a large bowl, beat cream cheese and remaining sugar until smooth. In another large bowl, beat cream until stiff peaks form. Gradually fold into cream cheese mixture.

3. Spoon half of the cream cheese mixture into prepared pan. Spread with half of strawberry mixture to within 1 in. of edges. Cover; refrigerate remaining strawberry mixture.

4. Arrange remaining ladyfingers over top. Spoon remaining cream cheese mixture over ladyfingers. Cover and refrigerate overnight. Serve with reserved strawberry mixture.

Chocolate Almond Bundt

Folks will be pleasantly surprised to see a rich chocolate cake beneath the white frosting. Sliced toasted almonds on top add a little crunch.

—SHERRI GENTRY DALLAS, OREGON

YIELD: 12-16 SERVINGS.

- ¾ cup butter, softened
- 1⅔ cups sugar
- 2 eggs
- ¾ cup sour cream
- 1 teaspoon vanilla extract
- 1 teaspoon almond extract
- 2 cups all-purpose flour
- ⅔ cup baking cocoa
- 2 teaspoons baking soda
- ½ teaspoon salt
- 1 cup buttermilk

FROSTING

- 5 tablespoons butter, softened
- 2½ cups confectioners' sugar
- 1 teaspoon vanilla extract
- ½ teaspoon almond extract
- 3 to 4 tablespoons milk
- Sliced almonds, toasted

1. In a large bowl, cream butter and sugar. Add eggs, one at a time, beating well after each addition. Add sour cream and extracts; mix well. Combine flour, cocoa, baking soda and salt; add to the creamed mixture alternately with buttermilk, beating well after each addition.

2. Pour into a greased 10-in. fluted tube pan. Bake at 350° for 50-55 minutes or until a toothpick inserted near the center comes out clean. Cool for 10 minutes before removing from pan to a wire rack to cool completely.

3. For frosting, cream butter, sugar and extracts in a small bowl until smooth. Add milk until the frosting achieves desired spreading consistency. Spread over cake. Sprinkle with almonds.

Spiced Pudding Cake

I came across this recipe years ago and made a few changes. It's very popular. My mom's church group serves it for dessert regularly.

—KELLY KIRBY WESTVILLE, NOVA SCOTIA

YIELD: 15 SERVINGS.

- ½ cup butter, softened
- ½ cup sugar
- 1 egg
- 1 cup molasses
- 2½ cups all-purpose flour
- 1½ teaspoons baking soda
- 1½ teaspoons ground cinnamon
- 1¼ teaspoons ground ginger
- ½ teaspoon ground allspice
- ¼ teaspoon ground nutmeg
- ¼ teaspoon salt
- 1 cup water
- ⅔ cup packed brown sugar
- 1½ cups water
- ¼ cup butter, cubed
- Whipped cream and ground cinnamon, optional

1. In a large bowl, cream butter and sugar until light and fluffy. Add egg; beat well. Beat in molasses. Combine the flour, baking soda, spices and salt; add to the creamed mixture alternately with water, beating well after each addition.

2. Transfer to an ungreased 13-in. x 9-in. baking pan; sprinkle with brown sugar. In a microwave, heat water and butter until butter is melted; carefully pour mixture over batter.

3. Bake at 350° for 35-40 minutes or until a toothpick inserted near the center comes out clean. Serve warm. Garnish with whipped cream and cinnamon if desired.

My most vivid childhood memory is of my grandmother cracking walnuts and hickory nuts. I'd sit patiently beside Grandmother, waiting for her to pick the meat out of the nuts with a large horse-blanket safety pin. Then she'd feed me the goodies!

—**CAROL BEATTLE** BARRETT, PENNSYLVANIA

Grandma's Red Velvet Cake

No one thinks it's Christmas in our family without this cake. I baked the first one for Christmas in 1963 when I found the recipe in the newspaper. It's different than other versions I've tasted over the years, since it has a mild chocolate taste, and the icing is as light as snow.

—**KATHRYN DAVISON** CHARLOTTE, NORTH CAROLINA

YIELD: 14 SERVINGS.

- ½ cup butter, softened
- 1½ cups sugar
- 2 eggs
- 2 bottles (1 ounce each) red food coloring
- 1 tablespoon white vinegar
- 1 teaspoon vanilla extract
- 2¼ cups cake flour
- 2 tablespoons baking cocoa
- 1 teaspoon baking soda
- 1 teaspoon salt
- 1 cup buttermilk

FROSTING
- 1 tablespoon cornstarch
- ½ cup water
- 2 cups butter, softened
- 2 teaspoons vanilla extract
- 3½ cups confectioners' sugar

1. In a large bowl, cream butter and sugar until light and fluffy. Add eggs, one at a time, beating well after each addition. Beat in the food coloring, vinegar and vanilla. Combine the flour, cocoa, baking soda and salt; add to creamed mixture alternately with buttermilk, beating well after each addition.

2. Pour into two greased and floured 9-in. round baking pans. Bake at 350° for 20-25 minutes or until a toothpick inserted near the center comes out clean. Cool for 10 minutes before removing from pans to wire racks to cool completely.

3. For frosting, in a small saucepan, combine cornstarch and water until smooth. Cook and stir over medium heat for 2-3 minutes or until thickened and opaque. Cool to room temperature.

4. In a large bowl, beat butter and vanilla until light and fluffy. Beat in cornstarch mixture. Gradually add confectioners' sugar; beat until frosting is light and fluffy. Spread frosting between layers and over top and sides of cake.

Chocolate Caramel Cheesecake

Our guests love this rich, delicious dessert, and I like being able to make it the day before. I garnish it just before serving.

—**JO GROTH** PLAINFIELD, IOWA

YIELD: 16 SERVINGS.

- 2 cups vanilla wafer crumbs
- ½ cup butter, melted
- 1 package (14 ounces) caramels
- 1 can (5 ounces) evaporated milk
- 2 cups chopped pecans, toasted, divided
- 4 packages (8 ounces each) cream cheese, softened
- 1 cup sugar
- 2 teaspoons vanilla extract
- 4 eggs, lightly beaten
- 1 cup (6 ounces) semisweet chocolate chips, melted and slightly cooled

Whipped cream, optional

1. In a bowl, combine the wafer crumbs and butter. Press into the bottom and 2 in. up the sides of a 10-in. springform pan. Place pan on a baking sheet. Bake at 350° for 8-10 minutes or until set. Cool on a wire rack.

2. In a microwave melt caramels with milk; stir until smooth. Cool for 5 minutes. Pour into crust; top with 1 ½ cups of pecans.

3. In a bowl, beat cream cheese until smooth. Add sugar and vanilla; mix well. Add eggs; beat on low speed just until combined. Add chocolate; mix just until blended. Carefully spread over pecans. Return to baking sheet.

4. Bake at 350° for 55-65 minutes or until center is almost set. Cool on a wire rack for 10 minutes. Carefully run a knife around the edge of pan to loosen; cool 1 hour longer. Refrigerate overnight.

5. Remove sides of pan. Garnish with remaining pecans and whipped cream if desired. Refrigerate leftovers.

Texas Chocolate Cupcakes

My husband remembers his mother making "little black cupcakes with caramel icing," so she passed down this recipe to me. I never thought about putting caramel icing on chocolate cupcakes, but boy, was I wrong. It's to die for!

—CATHY BODKINS DAYTON, VIRGINIA

YIELD: 2 DOZEN.

- 2 cups all-purpose flour
- 2 cups sugar
- 1 teaspoon salt
- ½ teaspoon baking soda
- ¼ cup baking cocoa
- 1 cup water
- 1 cup canola oil
- ½ cup butter, cubed
- 2 eggs
- ⅓ cup buttermilk
- 1 teaspoon vanilla extract

CARAMEL ICING
- 1 cup packed brown sugar
- ½ cup butter, cubed
- ¼ cup milk
- 2 to 2¼ cups confectioners' sugar

1. In a large bowl, combine the flour, sugar, salt and baking soda. In a large saucepan over medium heat, bring the cocoa, water, oil and butter to a boil. Gradually add to dry ingredients and mix well. Combine the eggs, buttermilk and vanilla; gradually add to batter and mix well (batter will be very thin).

2. Fill paper-lined muffin cups three-fourths full. Bake at 350° for 15-20 minutes or until a toothpick inserted near the center comes out clean. Cool for 10 minutes before removing from pans to wire racks to cool completely.

3. For icing, in a heavy saucepan, combine the brown sugar, butter and milk. Cook and stir over low heat until sugar is dissolved. Increase heat to medium. Do not stir. Cook mixture for 3-6 minutes or until bubbles form in the center and syrup turns amber. Remove from the heat; transfer to a small bowl. Cool to room temperature. Gradually beat in confectioners' sugar until smooth. Frost cupcakes.

Cupcake Cones

I experimented with these cupcakes when my girls were young. Now I'm a grandmother of nine, and these are still our favorites. They're a great treat for kids to take to school.

—BETTY ANDERSON STURGEON BAY, WISCONSIN

YIELD: ABOUT 3 DOZEN.

- 1 package (18¼ ounces) chocolate cake mix
- 1 package (8 ounces) cream cheese, softened
- ⅓ cup sugar
- 1 egg
- ½ teaspoon vanilla extract
- 1 cup miniature semisweet chocolate chips
- 36 ice-cream cake cones (about 3 inches tall)

FROSTING
- ½ cup shortening
- 3¾ cups confectioners' sugar
- 1 teaspoon vanilla extract
- 4 to 5 tablespoons milk

Sprinkles

1. Prepare cake mix according to package directions; set aside. In a large bowl, beat the cream cheese, sugar, egg and vanilla until smooth; stir in chocolate chips.

2. Place ice cream cones in muffin cups. Spoon about 1 tablespoon of cake batter into each cone; top with a rounded teaspoon of cream cheese mixture. Fill with remaining batter to within ¾ in. of top.

3. Bake at 350° for 25-30 minutes or until a toothpick inserted near the center comes out clean.

4. In a small bowl, beat the shortening, confectioners' sugar and vanilla until smooth. Add enough milk to achieve spreading consistency. Frost tops of cooled cones and top with sprinkles.

Editor's Note: *These cupcakes are best served the day they are made.*

Brittle Torte

For special occasions, my mom wanted no treat but this torte. When I was in high school, she often asked me to make it for her. The brittle gives it a satisfying crunch.

—PHYLLIS MURPHEY LOWER LAKE, CALIFORNIA

YIELD: 12 SERVINGS.

8 **eggs, separated**
1½ **cups all-purpose flour**
1½ **cups sugar**
1 **teaspoon salt**
¼ **cup water**
1 **teaspoon lemon juice**
1 **teaspoon vanilla extract**
1 **teaspoon cream of tartar**
TOPPING
1½ **cups sugar**
¼ **cup light corn syrup**
¼ **cup water**
¼ **teaspoon instant coffee granules**
1 **teaspoon baking soda**
WHIPPED CREAM
2 **cups heavy whipping cream**
2 **tablespoons sugar**
2 **teaspoons vanilla extract**

1. Let eggs stand at room temperature 30 minutes. Combine flour, sugar and salt. Whisk egg yolks, water, lemon juice and vanilla; add to flour mixture. Beat until blended.

2. Beat egg whites and cream of tartar until soft peaks form; fold into batter. Spoon into an ungreased 10-in. tube pan. Cut through batter with a knife to remove air pockets. Bake on lowest oven rack at 325° for 50-60 minutes or until top springs back when touched. Immediately invert pan; cool completely.

3. For topping, grease a 15-in. x 10-in. x 1-in. pan. In a heavy saucepan, combine the sugar, corn syrup, water and coffee granules. Bring to a boil; stir constantly. Cook, without stirring, until a candy thermometer reads 300° (hard-crack stage).

4. Remove from heat; stir in baking soda. Immediately pour into prepared pan. Stretch brittle in pan with two forks; cool. Break into pieces. In a large bowl, beat cream until it begins to thicken. Add sugar and vanilla; beat until stiff peaks form.

5. Unmold cake; cut horizontally into four layers. Place bottom layer on a serving plate; top with ½ cup whipped cream. Repeat layers twice; top with remaining layer. Frost top and sides of cake with remaining cream. Sprinkle with brittle.

Editor's Note: *We recommend testing your candy thermometer before using by placing it in boiling water; it should read 212°. Adjust recipe temperature up or down based on this test.*

Rhubarb Upside-Down Cake

I've baked this cake every spring for many years, and my family loves it! At potluck dinners it disappears quickly, drawing compliments even from those who normally don't care for rhubarb. Use your own rhubarb or find a neighbor who'll trade stalks for the recipe!

—HELEN BREMAN MATTYDALE, NEW YORK

YIELD: 8-10 SERVINGS.

TOPPING
- 3 cups sliced fresh or frozen rhubarb
- 1 cup sugar
- 2 tablespoons all-purpose flour
- ¼ teaspoon ground nutmeg
- ¼ cup butter, melted

BATTER
- ¼ cup butter, melted
- ¾ cup sugar
- 1 egg
- 1½ cups all-purpose flour
- 2 teaspoons baking powder
- ½ teaspoon ground nutmeg
- ¼ teaspoon salt
- ⅔ cup milk
- Sweetened whipped cream, optional

1. Place rhubarb in a greased 10-in. heavy ovenproof skillet. Combine sugar, flour and nutmeg; sprinkle over rhubarb. Drizzle with butter; set aside. For batter, in a large bowl, beat the butter and sugar until blended. Beat in the egg. Combine the flour, baking powder, nutmeg and salt. Gradually add to egg mixture alternately with milk, beating well after each addition.

2. Spread over rhubarb mixture. Bake at 350° for 35 minutes or until a toothpick inserted near the center comes out clean. Loosen edges immediately and invert onto a serving dish. Serve warm. Serve with whipped cream if desired.

Snowflake Cake

This beautiful dessert with coconut frosting is an elegant ending for any special meal.

—LYNNE PETERSON SALT LAKE CITY, UTAH

YIELD: 12-16 SERVINGS.

- 2 eggs plus 4 egg yolks
- 1½ cups sugar
- 1 cup milk
- ½ cup butter, cubed
- 2½ cups all-purpose flour
- 1 tablespoon baking powder
- 1 teaspoon vanilla extract
- ½ cup chopped nuts, optional

FROSTING
- 1¾ cups sugar
- ½ cup water
- 4 egg whites
- ½ teaspoon cream of tartar
- 1 teaspoon vanilla extract
- 2 cups flaked coconut

1. In a bowl, beat eggs, egg yolks and sugar until light and fluffy, about 5 minutes. In a saucepan, heat the milk and butter until butter melts. Combine flour and baking powder; add to the egg mixture alternately with milk mixture. Beat until well mixed. Add vanilla. Fold in nuts if desired. Pour into three greased 9-in. round baking pans. Bake at 350° for 15-18 minutes or until toothpick inserted in center comes out clean. Cool in pans 10 minutes before removing to wire racks to cool completely.

2. For frosting, in a saucepan, combine sugar and water. Bring to a boil; cook over medium-high heat until a thermometer reads 244° (firm-ball stage). Meanwhile, beat egg whites and cream of tartar in a bowl on high speed until foamy. Slowly pour the hot sugar syrup over the egg whites while beating continuously. Continue beating on high until stiff glossy peaks form, about 7 minutes. Add vanilla; beat until frosting cools slightly and reaches desired consistency.

3. Place one cake layer on a serving plate; spread with ½ cup frosting. Sprinkle with ¼ cup coconut. Repeat layers. Top with remaining cake layer. Frost top and sides of cakes; sprinkle with remaining coconut. Refrigerate until serving.

Editor's Note: *We recommend testing your candy thermometer before using it. In boiling water, it should read 212°. Adjust recipe temperature up or down based on this test.*

Decadent Fudge Cake

Everyone I serve this to seems to love the rich flavor. Four types of chocolate make it so wonderfully decadent.

—ANNA HOGGE YORKTOWN, VIRGINIA

YIELD: 16-20 SERVINGS.

- 1 cup butter, softened
- 1½ cups sugar
- 4 eggs
- 2½ cups all-purpose flour
- ½ teaspoon baking soda
- 1 cup buttermilk
- 8 ounces German sweet chocolate, melted
- 1 cup chocolate syrup
- 2 teaspoons vanilla extract
- 1¼ cups miniature semisweet chocolate chips, divided
- 4 ounces white baking chocolate, chopped
- 2 tablespoons plus 1 teaspoon shortening, divided

1. In a large bowl, cream butter and sugar until light and fluffy. Add eggs, one at a time, beating well after each addition. Combine flour and baking soda; add to creamed mixture alternately with buttermilk, beginning and ending with flour. Add melted chocolate, chocolate syrup and vanilla. Stir in 1 cup miniature chocolate chips. Pour into a greased and floured 10-in. fluted tube pan. Bake at 325° for 1¼ hours or until a toothpick inserted near the center comes out clean. Immediately invert cake onto a serving plate; cool completely.

2. Meanwhile, in a microwave, melt white chocolate and 2 tablespoons shortening; stir until smooth. Cool slightly; drizzle over cake. Melt remaining chips and shortening in a small saucepan over low heat, stirring until smooth. Remove from the heat; cool slightly. Drizzle over white chocolate.

Golden Chocolate Cake

At our Wisconsin farm, dessert was just as important as the main course. This idea has followed us to California, where I'm still on the lookout for good dessert recipes. This moist cake is a favorite since it's full of fun ingredients like chocolate candy bar pieces, coconut and pecans.

—KAY HANSEN ESCONDIDO, CALIFORNIA

YIELD: 12 SERVINGS.

- 1 package (18¼ ounces) yellow cake mix
- 1 package (3.4 ounces) instant vanilla pudding mix
- 4 eggs
- 1 cup (8 ounces) sour cream
- ½ cup canola oil
- ½ cup water
- 3 milk chocolate candy bars (1.55 ounces each), chopped
- 1 cup (6 ounces) semisweet chocolate chips
- 1 cup chopped pecans
- 1 cup flaked coconut
  Confectioners' sugar, optional

1. In a large bowl, combine the cake mix, pudding mix, eggs, sour cream, oil and water; beat on low speed for 30 seconds. Beat on medium for 2 minutes. Stir in candy bars, chocolate chips, nuts and coconut.

2. Pour into a greased and floured 10-in. fluted tube pan. Bake at 350° for 60-65 minutes or until a toothpick inserted near the center comes out clean.

3. Cool in pan 15 minutes before removing to a wire rack to cool completely. Chill before slicing. Dust with confectioners' sugar if desired.

Viennese Plum Cake

This is one of my husband's all-time favorite desserts. His mother gave me the recipe. She was usually pretty hesitant to share recipes, but knew how much he loved this one.

—LORRAINE DYDA RANCHO PALOS VERDES, CALIFORNIA

YIELD: 9 SERVINGS.

- ½ cup butter, softened
- ½ cup plus 1 tablespoon sugar, divided
- 2 eggs
- 1 teaspoon vanilla extract
- 1 cup all-purpose flour
- 1 teaspoon baking powder
- ¼ teaspoon salt
- 3 cups sliced fresh plums (about 1¾ pounds)
- ¼ teaspoon ground cinnamon

TOPPING
- ½ cup all-purpose flour
- ¼ cup sugar
- ¼ cup cold butter, cubed
- 3 tablespoons chopped walnuts, optional

1. In a large bowl, cream butter and ½ cup sugar until light and fluffy. Add eggs, one at a time, beating well after each addition. Beat in vanilla. Combine the flour, baking powder and salt; add to creamed mixture and mix well.

2. Transfer to a greased 9-in. square baking dish. Top with plums. Combine cinnamon and remaining sugar; sprinkle over plums.

3. For topping, in a small bowl, combine flour and sugar; cut in butter until mixture resembles coarse crumbs. Stir in walnuts if desired. Sprinkle over top.

4. Bake at 350° for 50-55 minutes or until topping is golden brown and plums are tender. Cool on a wire rack.

Banana Nut Layer Cake

On family birthdays, the "birthday child" always wants this cake!

—PATSY HOWARD BAKERSFIELD, CALIFORNIA

YIELD: 10-12 SERVINGS.

- ½ cup shortening
- 2 cups sugar
- 1 egg plus 1 egg white
- 1 cup buttermilk
- 1 cup mashed ripe bananas
- 1 teaspoon vanilla extract
- 2 cups all-purpose flour
- 1 teaspoon baking soda
- 1 teaspoon salt
- ½ cup chopped walnuts

FILLING
- ¼ cup butter, cubed
- ½ cup packed brown sugar
- ¼ cup all-purpose flour
- Pinch salt
- ¾ cup milk

1 egg yolk
1 teaspoon vanilla extract
½ cup chopped walnuts
Confectioners' sugar

1. In a large bowl, cream shortening and sugar until light and fluffy. Beat in egg and egg white. Add the buttermilk, bananas and vanilla. Combine flour, baking soda and salt; stir into the creamed mixture. Stir in walnuts.

2. Pour into two greased and floured 9-in. round baking pans. Bake at 350° for 35 minutes or until a toothpick inserted near the center comes out clean. Cool in pans 10 minutes before removing to a wire rack.

3. For filling, in a small saucepan, melt butter and brown sugar over medium heat. In a small bowl, combine flour and salt with a small amount of milk until smooth. Gradually add the remaining milk. Stir in egg yolk. Add to brown sugar mixture. Cook and stir mixture over medium heat for about 10 minutes or until thickened.

4. Remove from the heat; add vanilla and nuts. Cool. Spread between cake layers. Dust with confectioners' sugar. Chill. Store in refrigerator.

Mocha Cupcakes

A bit of Instant coffee adds depth of flavor to this luscious cake's chocolate frosting.

—LORNA SMITH NEW HAZELTON, BRITISH COLUMBIA

YIELD: ABOUT 1½ DOZEN.

1 cup boiling water
1 cup mayonnaise
1 teaspoon vanilla extract
2 cups all-purpose flour
1 cup sugar
½ cup baking cocoa

2 teaspoons baking soda
MOCHA FROSTING
¾ cup confectioners' sugar
¼ cup baking cocoa
½ to 1 teaspoon instant coffee granules
Pinch salt
1½ cups heavy whipping cream

1. In a large bowl, combine the water, mayonnaise and vanilla. Combine the flour, sugar, cocoa and baking soda; add to the mayonnaise mixture and beat until well mixed.

2. Fill greased or paper-lined muffins cups two-thirds full. Bake at 350° for 20-25 minutes or until a toothpick comes out clean. Cool for 10 minutes before removing to wire racks to cool completely.

3. For frosting, combine the, confectioners' sugar, cocoa, coffee granules and salt in a large bowl. Stir in cream. Place mixer beaters in bowl; cover and chill for 30 minutes. Beat frosting until stiff peaks form. Frost the cupcakes. Refrigerate leftovers.

Carrot Cake

You'll love the texture this pretty, moist cake gets from pineapple, coconut and, of course, carrots. Its traditional cream cheese frosting adds just the right amount of sweetness.

—DEBBIE JONES CALIFORNIA, MARYLAND

YIELD: 12-16 SERVINGS.

2 cups all-purpose flour
2 cups sugar
2 teaspoons ground cinnamon
1 teaspoon baking soda
½ teaspoon salt
3 eggs
1½ cups canola oil
2 cups finely grated carrots
1 teaspoon vanilla extract
1 cup well-drained crushed pineapple
1 cup flaked coconut
1 cup chopped nuts
CREAM CHEESE FROSTING
2 packages (3 ounces each) cream cheese, softened
6 tablespoons butter, softened
3 cups confectioners' sugar
1 teaspoon vanilla extract
Additional nuts

1. In a large bowl, combine the flour, sugar, cinnamon, baking soda and salt. Add the eggs, oil, carrots and vanilla; beat until combined. Stir in pineapple, coconut and nuts.

2. Pour into a greased 13-in. x 9-in. baking pan. Bake at 350° for 50-60 minutes or until a toothpick inserted near the center comes out clean. Cool on a wire rack.

3. For frosting, beat the cream cheese and butter in a small bowl until fluffy. Add the confectioners' sugar and vanilla; beat until smooth. Frost cake. Sprinkle with remaining nuts. Store in the refrigerator.

Orange Chiffon Cake

The delicate orange flavor of this simply delicious cake is perfect for rounding out a rich meal. If you don't have time to bake, just use the orange glaze to dress up a store-bought angel food cake.

—MARJORIE EBERT CONEWANGO VALLEY, NEW YORK

YIELD: 16 SERVINGS.

- 6 eggs, separated
- 2 cups all-purpose flour
- 1½ cups sugar
- 1 teaspoon salt
- ½ teaspoon baking soda
- ¾ cup fresh orange juice
- ½ cup canola oil
- 2 tablespoons grated orange peel
- ½ teaspoon cream of tartar

ORANGE GLAZE

- ½ cup butter
- 2 cups confectioners' sugar
- 2 to 4 tablespoons fresh orange juice
- ½ teaspoon grated orange peel

1. Let eggs stand at room temperature for 30 minutes. In a large bowl, combine the flour, sugar, salt and baking soda. In a bowl, whisk the egg yolks, orange juice, oil and orange peel; add to dry ingredients. Beat until well blended.

2. In another large bowl and with clean beaters, beat egg whites and cream of tartar on high speed until stiff peaks form. Fold into orange mixture.

3. Gently spoon batter into an ungreased 10-in. tube pan. Cut through the batter with a knife to remove air pockets. Bake on the lowest rack at 350° for 45-50 minutes or until top springs back when lightly touched. Immediately invert pan; cool completely. Run a knife around sides and center tube of pan. Invert cake onto a serving plate.

4. For glaze, melt butter in a small saucepan; add remaining glaze ingredients. Stir until smooth. Pour over top of cake, allowing it to drizzle down sides.

Cherry Spice Cake

At least four generations of women in my family have baked this cake. It's always my mom's pick for her birthday. I like to use cream cheese frosting, but when my mother was growing up, my grandma frosted the cake with buttercream.

—LAURIE SANDERS MANCHESTER, MICHIGAN

YIELD: 16 SERVINGS.

- ½ cup butter, softened
- 1½ cups sugar
- 2 eggs
- 2 cups all-purpose flour
- 1 teaspoon ground cinnamon
- 1 teaspoon ground cloves
- ½ teaspoon baking soda
- ¼ teaspoon baking powder
- ¼ teaspoon salt
- 1 cup buttermilk
- 1 can (14½ ounces) pitted tart cherries, drained
- ½ cup chopped pecans or walnuts

FROSTING

- 1 package (8 ounces) cream cheese, softened
- 3¾ cups confectioners' sugar
- 1 to 2 teaspoons water
- 2 to 3 drops red food coloring, optional

Additional chopped pecans, optional

1. Line two 9-in. round baking pans with waxed paper. Grease and flour the pans and paper; set aside.

2. In a large bowl, cream butter and sugar until light and fluffy. Add eggs, one at a time, beating well after each addition. Combine the flour, cinnamon, cloves, baking soda, baking powder and salt. Add to the creamed mixture alternately with buttermilk, beating well after each addition. Fold in cherries and pecans.

3. Pour the batter into prepared pans. Bake at 350° for 25-30 minutes or until a toothpick inserted near the center comes out clean. Cool for 10 minutes before removing from pans to wire racks to cool completely.

4. For frosting, in a large bowl, beat the cream cheese until fluffy. Add the confectioners' sugar and enough water to achieve spreading consistency. Tint with food coloring if desired. Spread frosting between layers and over top and sides of cake. Garnish with additional pecans. Store in the refrigerator.

Streusel-Topped Apple Cheesecake

I just love cheesecake and apple pie so what could be better than to combine the two! It has everything that makes an apple pie delicious—apples, cinnamon, and a nice crumble topping plus the creamy goodness of a cheesecake.

—SARAH GILBERT BEAVERTON, OREGON

YIELD: 16 SERVINGS.

1¼ cups crushed gingersnap cookies (about 25 cookies)
3 tablespoons butter, melted

FILLING

2 packages (8 ounces each) reduced-fat cream cheese
1 package (8 ounces) fat-free cream cheese
1 cup sugar
¼ cup fat-free milk
2 tablespoons all-purpose flour
1 teaspoon vanilla extract
3 eggs, lightly beaten
2 medium tart apples, peeled and thinly sliced
2 tablespoons brown sugar
1 teaspoon ground cinnamon

TOPPING

¼ cup all-purpose flour
¼ cup packed brown sugar
2 tablespoons butter, melted

1. In a small bowl, combine crushed cookies and butter. Press onto the bottom of a 9-in. springform pan coated with cooking spray. Place pan on a baking sheet. Bake at 325° for 10 minutes. Cool on a wire rack.

2. In a large bowl, beat cream cheeses and sugar until smooth. Beat in the milk, flour and vanilla. Add eggs; beat on low speed just until combined. Pour 2 cups filling over crust. In a large bowl, toss the apples, brown sugar and cinnamon until well coated; arrange over filling to within 1 in. of edges. Pour remaining filling over apple mixture. Bake at 325° for 30 minutes.

3. In a small bowl, combine topping ingredients. Sprinkle over cheesecake. Bake 15-20 minutes longer or until center is almost set. Cool on a wire rack for 10 minutes.

4. Carefully run a knife around edge of pan to loosen; cool 1 hour longer. Refrigerate overnight. Remove sides of pan.

Spicy Applesauce Cake

My moist cake cake travels and slices exceptionally well, making it perfect to pack and take along for a picnic or other outing.

—MARIAN PLATT SEQUIM, WASHINGTON

YIELD: 20-24 SERVINGS.

2 cups applesauce
1½ cups sugar
½ cup shortening
2 eggs, lightly beaten
2 cups all-purpose flour
1 tablespoon baking cocoa
1½ teaspoons baking soda
1 teaspoon salt
1 teaspoon each ground cinnamon, nutmeg, allspice and cloves
1 cup raisins
½ cup semisweet chocolate chips
½ cup chopped walnuts

TOPPING

½ cup semisweet chocolate chips
½ cup chopped walnuts
2 tablespoons brown sugar

1. In a large bowl, beat the applesauce, sugar, shortening and eggs. Combine the flour, cocoa, baking soda, salt, cinnamon, nutmeg, allspice and cloves; gradually beat into applesauce mixture until blended. Stir in the raisins, chocolate chips and walnuts.

2. Pour into a greased 13-in. x 9-in. baking pan. Combine topping ingredients and sprinkle over batter. Bake at 350° for 35-40 minutes or until a toothpick inserted near the center comes out clean. Cool on a wire rack.

Cherry Cheesecake Dessert

My grown sons consider this my signature dessert, but it really is my mother's creation. Sometimes I bake and freeze the cheesecake ahead. On the day I serve it, I thaw it, then add the fruit.

—**CHRISTINE EILERTS** TULSA, OKLAHOMA

YIELD: 9 SERVINGS.

  1¼ cups graham cracker crumbs
    2 tablespoons sugar
  ⅓ cup butter, melted
FILLING
    2 packages (one 8 ounces, one
       3 ounces) cream cheese, softened
  ½ cup sugar
    1 teaspoon vanilla extract
    2 eggs, lightly beaten
    1 can (21 ounces) cherry pie filling

1. In small bowl, combine the cracker crumbs and sugar; stir in the butter. Press into a greased 8-in. square baking dish; set aside.

2. In a large bowl, beat cream cheese, sugar and vanilla until smooth. Add the eggs; beat on low speed just until combined. Pour into crust.

3. Bake at 350° for 15-20 minutes or until almost set. Cool for 1 hour on a wire rack. Refrigerate for 8 hours or overnight. Spoon pie filling over top.

Almond Pear Torte

We had fruit trees in our garden when I was growing up. My mother spiced up the pears in her torte with nutmeg, so I do, too. I serve this in the fall, when pears are abundant at the farmers market and crisp evenings call for a traditional dessert.

—**TRISHA KRUSE** EAGLE, IDAHO

YIELD: 14 SERVINGS.

  1⅓ cups all-purpose flour
  ¾ cup butter, softened
  ½ cup sugar
  ½ cup ground almonds, toasted
  ¼ teaspoon ground nutmeg
FILLING
    2 packages (8 ounces each) cream cheese, softened
  ¼ cup packed brown sugar
  ¼ teaspoon almond extract
    2 eggs, lightly beaten
TOPPING
  ½ cup packed brown sugar
  ¼ teaspoon ground nutmeg
    3 cups thinly sliced peeled fresh pears
  ½ cup slivered almonds

1. In a small bowl, combine the flour, butter, sugar, almonds and nutmeg. Press onto the bottom of a greased 9-in. springform pan; set aside.

2. In a large bowl, beat the cream cheese, brown sugar and extract until smooth. Add eggs; beat on low speed just until combined. Pour over crust.

3. For topping, combine brown sugar and nutmeg. Add pears; toss to coat. Arrange over top. Sprinkle with almonds.

4. Bake at 350° for 50-60 minutes or until center is almost set. Cool on a wire rack for 10 minutes. Carefully run a knife around edge of pan to loosen; cool 1 hour longer. Refrigerate leftovers.

Lemon Chiffon Cake

This moist, airy cake was my dad's favorite. Mom revamped the original recipe to include lemons. I'm not much of a baker, so I don't make it very often. But when I do, my family is thrilled!

—TRISHA KAMMERS CLARKSTON, WASHINGTON

YIELD: 12-16 SERVINGS.

7   **eggs, separated**
2   **cups all-purpose flour**
1½ **cups sugar**
3   **teaspoons baking powder**
1   **teaspoon salt**
¾   **cup water**
½   **cup canola oil**
4   **teaspoons grated lemon peel**
2   **teaspoons vanilla extract**
½   **teaspoon cream of tartar**

LEMON FROSTING
⅓   **cup butter, softened**
3   **cups confectioners' sugar**
¼   **cup lemon juice**
4½ **teaspoons grated lemon peel**
Dash salt

1. Place egg whites in a large bowl; let stand at room temperature for 30 minutes.

2. In a large bowl, combine the flour, sugar, baking powder and salt. In another bowl, whisk the egg yolks, water, oil, lemon peel and vanilla; add to dry ingredients and beat until well blended. Add cream of tartar to egg whites; with clean beaters, beat on medium speed until soft peaks form. Fold into batter.

3. Gently spoon into an ungreased 10-in. tube pan. Cut through batter with a knife to remove air pockets. Bake on the lowest oven rack at 325° for 50-55 minutes or until cake springs back when lightly touched. Immediately invert pan; cool completely, about 1 hour.

4. Run a knife around sides and center tube of pan. Remove cake to a serving plate. In a small bowl, combine frosting ingredients; beat until smooth. Frost top of cake.

PIES

Club Pie

During the '30s, my mother made this pie for the ladies in her club. I'd hurry home from school so I could help her and then try a piece myself! It became such a family favorite that Mother made it part of our Christmas meals.

—MELVIN WELSHHAUS
BARBERTON, OHIO

YIELD: 6-8 SERVINGS.

  ⅓ **cup butter, softened**
  1 **cup sugar**
  2 **eggs, separated**
  ¼ **cup milk**
  ½ **cup chopped walnuts**
  1 **cup raisins**
  1 **unbaked pie pastry (9 inches)**
Whipped cream, optional

1. In a bowl, cream butter and sugar. Add the egg yolks; beat well. Blend in milk. Stir in nuts and raisins; set aside. Using clean beaters, beat egg whites until stiff peaks form; fold into the raisin mixture. Pour into pie shell.

2. Bake the pie at 350° for 15 minutes. Reduce the temperature to 300°; bake 40 minutes longer or until lightly browned. Cool. Refrigerate. Serve pie chilled with whipped cream if desired.

Peanut Butter Pie

Who can resist a tempting chocolate crumb crust and a creamy filling with big peanut butter taste? Be prepared to take an empty plate home when you serve this pie at your next potluck.

—DORIS DOHERTY ALBANY, OREGON

YIELD: 8-10 SERVINGS.

  1¼ **cup chocolate cookie crumbs (20 cookies)**
  ¼ **cup sugar**
  ¼ **cup butter, melted**
FILLING
  1 **package (8 ounces) cream cheese, softened**
  1 **cup creamy peanut butter**
  1 **cup sugar**
  1 **tablespoon butter, softened**
  1 **teaspoon vanilla extract**
  1 **cup heavy whipping cream, whipped**
Grated chocolate or chocolate cookie crumbs, optional

1. In a small bowl, combine cookie crumbs and sugar; stir in butter. Press onto the bottom and up the sides of a 9-in. pie plate. Bake at 375° for 10 minutes. Cool on a wire rack.

2. For filling, in a large bowl, beat the cream cheese, peanut butter, sugar, butter and vanilla until smooth. Fold in whipped cream. Gently spoon into crust. Garnish with chocolate or cookie crumbs if desired. Store in refrigerator.

Grandma's Berry Tart

With seven children and 12 grandchildren, our household is always busy. But everyone makes time for a slice of this fruity pie from my grandma.
—LORRAINE NUZZO STATEN ISLAND, NEW YORK

YIELD: 6-8 SERVINGS.

1¼ cups all-purpose flour
¼ teaspoon salt
¼ cup cold butter, cubed
¼ cup shortening
5 to 6 tablespoons cold water
FILLING
1 cup each fresh blueberries, raspberries, blackberries and sliced strawberries
½ cup sugar
2 tablespoons cornstarch
2 teaspoons grated lemon peel
1 teaspoon vanilla extract
½ teaspoon ground ginger
¼ teaspoon ground allspice
Milk
Additional sugar

TOPPING
¼ cup sugar
3 tablespoons all-purpose flour
2 tablespoons cold butter

1. In a small bowl, combine flour and salt; cut in butter and shortening until crumbly. Gradually add water, tossing with a fork until dough forms a ball. On a lightly floured surface, roll out dough into a 13-in. circle. Transfer to a 9-in. deep-dish pie plate.

2. Place the berries in a large bowl. Combine the sugar, cornstarch, lemon peel, vanilla, ginger and allspice; add to berries and toss gently to coat. Pour into crust. Fold edges of pastry over filling. Brush folded pastry with milk; sprinkle with sugar.

3. For topping, combine the sugar and flour in a small bowl; cut in butter until crumbly. Sprinkle over filling.

4. Bake at 400° for 50-55 minutes or until pastry is golden brown. Cool on a wire rack.

Mom's Peach Pie

A delightful summertime pie, this dessert is overflowing with fresh peach flavor. Each sweet slice is pack with old-fashioned appeal. The streusel topping makes it a little different than the ordinary fruit pie and adds homemade flair.

—**SALLY HOLBROOK** PASADENA, CALIFORNIA

YIELD: 6-8 SERVINGS.

- 1 **refrigerated pie pastry**
- 1 **egg white, lightly beaten**
- ¾ **cup all-purpose flour**
- ½ **cup packed brown sugar**
- ⅓ **cup sugar**
- ¼ **cup cold butter, cubed**
- 6 **cups sliced peeled fresh peaches**

1. Unroll pastry into a 9-in. pie plate; flute edges. Brush egg white over the bottom and sides of the pastry.

2. In a small bowl, combine flour and sugars; cut in butter until mixture resembles fine crumbs. Sprinkle two-thirds into pastry; top with peaches. Sprinkle with remaining crumb mixture.

3. Bake at 375° for 40-45 minutes or until filling is bubbly and peaches are tender.

Freezer Pumpkin Pie

Here's a cool twist on tradition with this wonderful do-ahead dessert. Gingersnaps and pecans form the delicious baked crust for this pie's pumpkin and ice cream filling.

—**VERA REID** LARAMIE, WYOMING

YIELD: 6-8 SERVINGS.

- 1 **cup ground pecans**
- ½ **cup finely crushed gingersnaps**

- ¼ cup sugar
- ¼ cup butter, softened

FILLING
- 1 cup canned pumpkin
- ½ cup packed brown sugar
- ½ teaspoon salt
- ½ teaspoon ground cinnamon
- ½ teaspoon ground ginger
- ¼ teaspoon ground nutmeg
- 1 quart vanilla ice cream, slightly softened

1. In a bowl, combine pecans, gingersnaps, sugar and butter; mix well. Press into a 9-in. pie pan; bake at 450° for 5 minutes. Cool completely.

2. In a bowl, beat first six filling ingredients. Stir in ice cream and mix until well blended. Spoon into crust. Freeze until firm, at least 2-3 hours. Store in freezer.

Citrus Cranberry Pie

This lattice-topped pie showcases abundant fall cranberries. A dollop of orange cream complements the slightly tart flavor.

—TASTE OF HOME TEST KITCHEN

YIELD: 6-8 SERVINGS.

Pastry for double-crust pie (9 inches)
- 3½ cups fresh or frozen cranberries
- 1 small navel orange, peeled, sectioned and chopped
- 1 cup sugar
- 2 tablespoons butter, melted
- 4½ teaspoons all-purpose flour
- 2 teaspoons grated lemon peel
- 1 teaspoon grated orange peel

- ¼ teaspoon salt
- 1 egg, lightly beaten
Additional sugar

ORANGE CREAM
- 1 cup heavy whipping cream
- 1 tablespoon sugar
- 2 teaspoons grated orange peel
- 1 teaspoon orange extract

1. Line a 9-in. pie plate with bottom pastry; trim pastry even with edge of plate. In a large bowl, combine the cranberries, orange, sugar, butter, flour, lemon and orange peel and salt. Pour into pastry shell.

2. Roll out remaining pastry; make a lattice crust. Trim, seal and flute edges. Brush lattice crust with egg. Sprinkle with additional sugar. Cover edges loosely with foil.

3. Bake at 450° for 10 minutes. Reduce heat to 350° and remove foil. Bake 40-45 minutes longer or until golden brown.

4. Meanwhile, in a large bowl, beat cream until it begins to thicken. Add the sugar, orange peel and extract; beat until stiff peaks form. Cover and refrigerate. Serve with warm pie.

Cookie Sheet Apple Pie

This dessert is a real time-saver when you have a large crowd to feed. It serves more than a traditional pie with about the same amount of effort.

—BERTHA JEFFRIES GREAT FALLS, MONTANA

YIELD: 16-20 SERVINGS.

- 6 cups all-purpose flour
- 1½ teaspoons salt
- 1½ teaspoons baking powder
- 1½ cups shortening
- 6 egg yolks
- ¾ cup plus 4½ teaspoons water
- 3 tablespoons lemon juice
- 8 cups sliced peeled tart apples
- 1½ cups sugar
- 1 cup crushed cornflakes
- 1 teaspoon ground cinnamon
- ½ teaspoon ground nutmeg
- 1 egg white, lightly beaten

1. In a large bowl, combine the flour, salt and baking powder. Cut in shortening until mixture resembles coarse crumbs. Whisk the egg yolks, water and lemon juice; gradually add to flour mixture, tossing with a fork until dough forms a ball. Cover and refrigerate for 30 minutes.

2. Divide dough in half so that one portion is slightly larger than the other. On a lightly floured surface, roll out larger portion to fit the bottom and sides of a greased 15-in. x 10-in. x 1-in. baking pan. Arrange apples over crust. Combine the sugar, cornflakes, cinnamon and nutmeg; sprinkle over apples.

3. Roll out remaining dough to fit top of pie; place over apples. Seal edges; cut slits in top. Brush with egg white. Bake at 400° for 15 minutes. Reduce heat to 350°; bake 20-25 minutes longer or until golden brown.

Lemon Blueberry Pie

When blueberries are ripe, I find every way possible to enjoy them. My tart, delicious pie proves the point!

—PATRICIA KILE
ELIZABETHTOWN, PENNSYLVANIA

YIELD: 8 SERVINGS.

- 6 eggs, lightly beaten
- 1 cup sugar
- ½ cup butter, cubed
- ⅓ cup lemon juice
- 2 teaspoons grated lemon peel
- 1 pastry shell (9 inches), baked
- 3 cups fresh blueberries
- ⅓ cup sugar
- 1 tablespoon cornstarch
- ¼ cup orange juice

1. In a saucepan, combine the eggs, sugar, butter, lemon juice and peel; cook over medium-low heat,, stirring constantly, until mixture is thickened, about 20 minutes. Cool the mixture for 20 minutes, stirring occasionally. Pour into pie shell.

2. In a saucepan, toss blueberries and sugar. Combine the cornstarch and orange juice until smooth; add to blueberries. Cook over medium heat until mixture comes to a boil, about 8 minutes, stirring gently. Cook and stir for 2 minutes or until thickened. Cool for 15 minutes, stirring occasionally. Spoon over lemon layer. Refrigerate for 4-6 hours.

Grandma's Sour Cream Raisin Pie

The aroma of this pie baking in my farm kitchen oven reminds me of my dear grandma, who made this pretty dessert for special occasions.

—BEVERLY MEDALEN WILLOW CITY, NORTH DAKOTA

YIELD: 8 SERVINGS.

- 1 cup raisins
- ⅔ cup sugar
- 3 tablespoons cornstarch
- ⅛ teaspoon salt
- ⅛ teaspoon ground cloves
- ½ teaspoon ground cinnamon
- 1 cup (8 ounces) sour cream
- ½ cup milk
- 3 egg yolks
- ½ cup chopped nuts, optional
- 1 pie shell (9 inches), baked

MERINGUE

- 3 egg whites
- ¼ teaspoon salt
- 5 tablespoons sugar

1. In a small saucepan, place raisins and enough water to cover; bring to a boil. Remove from the heat; set aside.

2. In a large saucepan, combine the sugar, cornstarch, salt, cloves and cinnamon. Stir in sour cream and milk until smooth. Cook and stir over medium-high heat until thickened and bubbly. Reduce heat to low; cook and stir for 2 minutes longer. Remove from the heat. Stir a small amount of hot filling into egg yolks; return all to the pan, stirring constantly. Bring to a gentle boil; cook and stir for 2 minutes. Remove from the heat.

3. Drain raisins, reserving ½ cup liquid. Gently stir liquid into filling. Add raisins, and nuts if desired. Pour into pie shell.

4. For meringue, in a small bowl, beat egg whites and salt on medium speed until soft peaks form. Gradually beat in sugar, 1 tablespoon at a time, on high until stiff peaks form. Spread over hot filling, sealing edges to crust.

5. Bake at 350° for 15 minutes or until golden brown. Cool on a wire rack for 1 hour; refrigerate for 1-2 hours before serving. Refrigerate leftovers.

Lattice-Topped Apple Pie

You can't beat my mom's yummy apple pie. Pretty as a picture, the golden crust is flaky and the filling has just the right amount of spices.

—ANNE HALFHILL SUNBURY, OHIO

YIELD: 6-8 SERVINGS.

5½ cups thinly sliced peeled apples (about 6 medium)
1 cup sugar
2 tablespoons water
4½ teaspoons quick-cooking tapioca
½ teaspoon ground cinnamon
¼ teaspoon ground nutmeg

PASTRY
2 cups all-purpose flour
½ teaspoon baking powder
½ teaspoon salt
⅔ cup shortening
5 to 6 tablespoons cold water
3 tablespoons butter
2 tablespoons milk
1 tablespoon sugar

1. In a large bowl, combine the apples, sugar, water, tapioca, cinnamon and nutmeg; toss to coat. Let stand for 15 minutes.

2. In a large bowl, combine the flour, baking powder and salt; cut in shortening until crumbly. Gradually add water, tossing with a fork until dough forms a ball. Divide in half, making one half slightly larger.

3. On a lightly floured surface, roll out larger portion of pastry to fit a 9-in. pie plate. Transfer pastry to plate; trim even with edge of plate. Add filling; dot with butter. Roll out remaining pastry; make a lattice crust.

4. Trim, seal and flute edges. Brush with milk; sprinkle with sugar. Cover edges loosely with foil.

5. Bake at 400° for 15 minutes. Reduce heat to 350°; bake 40-50 minutes longer or until crust is golden brown and filling is bubbly. Cool on a wire rack.

Fluffy Cranberry Cheese Pie

This pie has a light texture and zippy flavor that's very festive. And even though it looks fancy, it's easy to make.

—MARY PARKONEN W. WAREHAM, MASSACHUSETTS

YIELD: 6-8 SERVINGS.

CRANBERRY TOPPING
1 package (3 ounces) raspberry gelatin
⅓ cup sugar
1¼ cups cranberry juice
1 can (8 ounces) jellied cranberry sauce

FILLING
1 package (3 ounces) cream cheese, softened
¼ cup sugar
1 tablespoon milk
1 teaspoon vanilla extract
½ cup whipped topping
1 pastry shell (9 inches), baked

1. In a bowl, combine the gelatin and sugar; set aside. In a saucepan, bring cranberry juice to a boil. Remove from the heat and pour over gelatin mixture, stirring to dissolve. Stir in the cranberry sauce. Chill until slightly thickened.

2. Meanwhile, in another bowl, beat cream cheese, sugar, milk and vanilla until fluffy. Fold in the whipped topping. Spread evenly into pie shell. Beat cranberry topping until frothy; pour over filling. Chill overnight.

Sky-High Strawberry Pie

This pie is my specialty. It's fairly simple to make but so dramatic to serve. The ultimate taste of spring, this luscious pie has a big, fresh berry taste. I'm often asked to bring it to gatherings.

—**JANET MOOBERRY** PEORIA, ILLINOIS

YIELD: 8-10 SERVINGS.

- 3 quarts fresh strawberries, divided
- 1½ cups sugar
- 6 tablespoons cornstarch
- ⅔ cup water
- Red food coloring, optional
- 1 deep-dish pastry shell (10 inches), baked
- 1 cup heavy whipping cream
- 4½ teaspoons instant vanilla pudding mix

1. In a large bowl, mash enough berries to equal 3 cups. In a large saucepan, combine sugar and cornstarch. Stir in mashed berries and water. Bring to a boil over medium heat, stirring constantly. Cook and stir for 2 minutes or until thickened.

2. Remove from the heat; add food coloring if desired. Pour into a large bowl. Chill for 20 minutes, stirring occasionally, until mixture is just slightly warm. Fold in the remaining berries. Pile into pastry shell. Chill for 2-3 hours.

3. In a small bowl, beat cream until soft peaks form. Sprinkle dry pudding mix over cream and beat until stiff. Pipe around edge of pie or dollop on individual slices.

Rustic Autumn Fruit Tart

Your guests are sure to love this impressive dessert featuring rich, buttery pastry with apple and pear. It's surprisingly easy.

—**JENNIFER WICKES** PINE BEACH, NEW JERSEY

YIELD: 6 SERVINGS.

- ½ cup butter, softened
- 4 ounces cream cheese, softened
- 1½ cups all-purpose flour
- 2 large apples, peeled and thinly sliced
- 1 medium pear, peeled and thinly sliced
- 4½ teaspoons cornstarch
- ½ teaspoon ground cinnamon
- ¼ teaspoon ground cardamom
- ¼ teaspoon ground nutmeg
- ¼ cup orange juice
- ⅓ cup packed brown sugar
- ½ cup apricot jam, warmed

1. In a small bowl, beat butter and cream cheese until smooth. Gradually add the flour, beating just until mixture forms a ball. Cover and refrigerate for 1 hour.

2. In a large bowl, combine apples and pear. In a small bowl, combine cornstarch and spices; stir in orange juice until smooth. Stir in brown sugar until blended. Add to apple mixture and stir gently to coat.

3. On a lightly floured surface, roll out dough into a 14-in. circle. Transfer to a parchment paper-lined baking sheet. Spoon filling over the pastry to within 2 in. of edges. Fold up edges of pastry over filling, leaving center uncovered.

4. Bake at 375° for 40-45 minutes or until crust is golden and filling is bubbly. Spread with apricot jam. Using parchment paper, slide tart onto a wire rack to cool.

Cran-Raspberry Pie

Jewel-toned fruits team up to pack this lattice-topped pie. It's a lovely addition to holiday meals.

—VERONA KOEHLMOOS PILGER, NEBRASKA

YIELD: 6-8 SERVINGS.

- 2 **cups chopped fresh or frozen cranberries**
- 5 **cups fresh or frozen unsweetened raspberries, thawed**
- ½ **teaspoon almond extract**
- 1 **to 1¼ cups sugar**
- ¼ **cup quick-cooking tapioca**
- ¼ **teaspoon salt**

Pastry for double-crust pie (9 inches)

1. In a large bowl, combine the cranberries, raspberries and extract. Combine the sugar, tapioca and salt. Add to fruit mixture; toss gently to coat. Let stand for 15-20 minutes.

2. Line pie plate with bottom pastry; trim to 1 in. beyond edge of plate. Add filling. Roll out remaining pastry; make a lattice crust. Trim, seal and flute edges. Cover edges loosely with foil.

3. Bake at 375° for 40-45 minutes or until crust is golden brown and filling is bubbly. Cool on a wire rack.

Coconut-Pecan Pie

I grew up on a farm with pecan trees, so we always had plenty of nuts for baking. Here's one of my favorites uses for them.

—BARBARA ANN MCKENZIE
KEYTESVILLE, MISSOURI

YIELD: 6-8 SERVINGS.

- 3 **eggs**
- 1½ **cups sugar**
- ½ **cup butter, melted**
- 2 **teaspoons lemon juice**
- 1 **teaspoon vanilla extract**
- 1¼ **cups flaked coconut**
- ½ **cup coarsely chopped pecans**
- 1 **unbaked pastry shell (9 inches)**

1. In a bowl, beat eggs. Add sugar, butter, lemon juice and vanilla; mix well. Stir in coconut and pecans; pour into pie shell.

2. Bake at 350° for 45-50 minutes or until set. Cool completely. Store in the refrigerator.

Fall Pear Pie

A wide slice of this festive, fruity pie is a great way to end a delicious meal. The mellow flavor of pears is a refreshing alternative to the more traditional pies prepared for the holidays. It's nice to serve a dessert that's a little unexpected.

—KEN CHURCHES KAILUA-KONA, HAWAII

YIELD: 8 SERVINGS.

    8   cups thinly sliced peeled pears
    ¾   cup sugar
    ¼   cup quick-cooking tapioca
    ¼   teaspoon ground nutmeg
    Pastry for double-crust pie (9 inches)
    1   egg, lightly beaten
    ¼   cup heavy whipping cream, optional

1. In a large bowl, combine the pears, sugar, tapioca and nutmeg; let stand for 15 minutes.

2. Line a pie plate with bottom crust; add pear mixture. Roll out remaining pastry to fit top of pie; cut large slits in top. Place over filling; seal and flute edges. Brush with egg.

3. Bake at 375° for 55-60 minutes or until pears are tender. Remove to a wire rack. Pour the cream through slits if desired. Cool.

Strawberry-Pecan Pie

I stock up on locally grown berries for treats like this pie, which pairs them with pecans. I received a ribbon for this at the strawberry festival in nearby Poteet.

—BECKY DUNCAN LEMING, TEXAS

YIELD: 6-8 SERVINGS.

    1½ cups sugar
    ¼   cup all-purpose flour
    1   teaspoon ground nutmeg
    1   teaspoon ground cinnamon
    2   cups chopped fresh strawberries
    1   cup chopped pecans
    Pastry for double-crust pie (9 inches)
    1   to 2 tablespoons butter

1. In a large bowl, combine the sugar, flour, nutmeg and cinnamon. Add strawberries and pecans; toss gently.

2. Line pie plate with bottom crust. Add filling; dot with butter. Make lattice top. Bake at 375° for 50-55 minutes or until crust is golden brown. Cool on a wire rack.

> Granny would roll out her pie crusts into thin layers, and she'd always poke a hole in the middle of one of the smaller crusts. Then she'd bake them until they were light brown and crisp. When they cooled, she'd spread jelly on the crust with the hole. I stood in her kitchen with my chin on the counter and my mouth watering—I could hardly wait for that special treat she made just for me!
>
> **— SHERRIE CALLISON** CABOT, ARKANSAS

Raspberry Ribbon Pie

As a boy, my husband considered this his favorite Christmas dessert. When we married, his mother gave me the recipe. I take it to family gatherings during the holidays and have yet to bring any leftovers home! It's a cool recipe for summer as well.

—VICTORIA NEWMAN ANTELOPE, CALIFORNIA

YIELD: 6-8 SERVINGS.

2 packages (3 ounces each) cream cheese, softened
½ cup confectioners' sugar
Dash salt
1 cup heavy whipping cream, whipped
Pastry for deep-dish single-crust pie (9 inches), baked
1 package (3 ounces) raspberry gelatin

1¼ cups boiling water
1 tablespoon lemon juice
1 package (10 ounces) frozen raspberries in syrup, thawed

1. In a large bowl, beat the cream cheese, sugar and salt until smooth. Fold in cream. Spread half into pie shell. Chill 30 minutes.

2. Meanwhile, dissolve gelatin in water; add lemon juice and raspberries. Carefully spoon half over cream cheese layer. Chill until set, about 30 minutes.

3. Set aside the remaining gelatin mixture at room temperature. Carefully spread remaining cream cheese mixture over top of pie. Chill for 30 minutes. Top with remaining gelatin. Chill until firm.

Peach Cream Pie

The sour cream filling and cinnamon crumb topping complement the fruit flavor in this yummy pie.

—DENISE GOEDEKEN
PLATTE CENTER, NEBRASKA

YIELD: 6-8 SERVINGS.

- 1½ cups all-purpose flour
- ½ teaspoon salt
- ½ cup cold butter, cubed

FILLING

- 4 cups unsweetened sliced peaches (about 6 medium)
- 1 cup sugar, divided
- 2 tablespoons all-purpose flour
- 1 egg
- ½ teaspoon vanilla extract
- ¼ teaspoon salt
- 1 cup (8 ounces) sour cream

TOPPING

- ⅓ cup sugar
- ⅓ cup all-purpose flour
- 1 teaspoon ground cinnamon
- ¼ cup cold butter, cubed

1. In a small bowl, combine flour and salt; cut in butter until crumbly. Press into a 9-in. pie plate.

2. For filling, place peaches in a large bowl; sprinkle with ¼ cup sugar and toss gently to coat. In another small bowl, combine the flour, egg, vanilla, salt and remaining sugar; fold in sour cream. Stir into peaches.

3. Pour into crust. Bake at 400° for 15 minutes. Reduce heat to 350°; bake for 20 minutes.

4. Meanwhile, prepare topping. In a small bowl, combine the sugar, flour and cinnamon. Cut in butter until crumbly. Sprinkle topping over top of pie. Bake at 450° for 15 minutes or until topping is browned. Cool on a wire rack. Store in the refrigerator.

Creamy Banana Pie

When I read that *Taste of Home* was having a banana recipe contest, I knew instantly the recipe I should share. This delectable pie is from a recipe I found years ago, and everyone who tastes it enjoys its delicious old-fashioned flavor.

—RITA PRIBYL WAUKESHA, WISCONSIN

YIELD: 8 SERVINGS.

- 1 envelope unflavored gelatin
- ¼ cup cold water
- ¾ cup sugar
- ¼ cup cornstarch
- ½ teaspoon salt
- 2¾ cups milk
- 4 egg yolks, beaten
- 2 tablespoons butter
- 1 tablespoon vanilla extract
- 4 medium firm bananas, divided
- 1 cup heavy whipping cream, whipped
- 1 pastry shell (10 inches), baked

Juice and grated peel of 1 lemon

- ½ cup apple jelly

1. Soften gelatin in cold water; set aside. In a saucepan, combine the sugar, cornstarch and salt. Whisk in the milk until smooth. Cook and stir over medium-high heat until thickened and bubbly. Reduce heat; cook and stir 2 minutes longer. Remove from the heat.

2. Stir a small amount of hot filling into yolks. Return all to the pan, stirring constantly. Bring to a gentle boil. Cook and stir 2 minutes longer. Remove from the heat; stir in softened gelatin until dissolved. Stir in butter and vanilla. Cover the surface of custard with plastic wrap and chill until no longer warm.

3. Slice 3 bananas; fold into custard along with whipped cream. Spoon into pie shell. Cover and refrigerate until set, about 4-5 hours.

4. Just before serving, place the lemon juice in a small bowl and slice the remaining banana into it. Melt jelly in a saucepan over low heat. Drain banana; pat dry and arrange over filling. Brush banana with the jelly. Sprinkle with grated lemon peel. Serve immediately. Refrigerate leftovers.

Editor's Note: *The filling is very light in color. It is not topped with additional whipped cream.*

Cherry Pie

For a traditional delicious treat, serve this pretty cherry pie.

—FRANCES POSTE WALL, SOUTH DAKOTA

YIELD: 6-8 SERVINGS.

PASTRY
- 1½ **cups all-purpose flour**
- ½ **teaspoon salt**
- ½ **cup shortening**
- ¼ **cup ice water**

FILLING
- 2 **cans (16 ounces each) tart cherries**
- 1 **cup sugar**
- 3 **tablespoons quick-cooking tapioca**
- ¼ **teaspoon almond extract**
- ¼ **teaspoon salt**
- **Red food coloring, optional**
- 1 **tablespoon butter**

1. In a large bowl, combine flour and salt; cut in shortening until crumbly. Gradually add water, tossing with a fork until dough forms a ball. Divide dough in half. Roll out one portion. Line a 9-in. pie plate with the bottom crust; trim pastry even with edge.

2. Drain cherries, reserving ¼ cup juice. In a large bowl, combine the sugar, tapioca, extract, salt, food coloring if desired and reserved juice. Gently stir in the cherries; let stand for 15 minutes.

3. Pour into the crust. Dot with butter. Roll out remaining pastry; make a lattice crust. Seal and flute edges. Bake at 375° for 55-60 minutes. Cool on a wire rack.

Golden Apricot Pie

Our pie has wonderful apricot flavor. The fruit's golden-orange color shows through the lattice top beautifully.

—JO AND JOE MARTIN PATTERSON, CALIFORNIA

YIELD: 8 SERVINGS.

- 2 **packages (6 ounces each) dried apricots**
- 2¾ **cups water**
- **Pastry for double-crust pie (9 inches)**
- 1 **cup sugar**
- 3 **tablespoons cornstarch**
- ⅛ **teaspoon nutmeg**
- 1 **tablespoon butter**

1. In a small saucepan, combine apricots and water; bring to a boil. Reduce heat and simmer for 20-22 minutes. Remove from the heat; cool.

2. Place bottom pastry in a 9-in. pie plate. Drain the apricots, reserving ¾ cup liquid. Arrange apricots in pie shell. Combine the sugar, cornstarch, nutmeg and reserved apricot liquid.

3. Pour over apricots; dot with butter. Top with a lattice crust. Bake at 400° for 50-55 minutes or until crust is golden brown and filling is bubbly.

Praline Pumpkin Pie

This makes a sweet ending to winter meals. The sweet pecans are a delightful contrast to the smooth pumpkin filling.

—SANDRA HAASE BALTIMORE, MARYLAND

YIELD: 10 SERVINGS.

- ⅓ **cup finely chopped pecans**
- ⅓ **cup packed brown sugar**
- 3 **tablespoons butter, softened**
- 1 **unbaked pastry shell (10 inches)**

FILLING
- 3 **eggs, lightly beaten**
- ½ **cup sugar**
- ½ **cup packed brown sugar**
- 2 **tablespoons all-purpose flour**
- ¾ **teaspoon ground cinnamon**
- ½ **teaspoon salt**
- ½ **teaspoon ground ginger**
- ¼ **teaspoon ground cloves**
- 1 **can (15 ounces) solid-pack pumpkin**
- 1½ **cups half-and-half cream**
- **Additional chopped pecans, optional**

1. In a small bowl, combine the pecans, sugar and butter; press onto the bottom of pie shell. Prick sides of pastry with a fork. Bake at 450° for 10 minutes. Cool on a wire rack for 5 minutes. Reduce heat to 350°.

2. For filling, combine the eggs, sugars, flour and spices in a large bowl; stir in pumpkin. Gradually add cream. Pour into pastry shell. If desired, sprinkle chopped pecans on top.

3. Bake at 350° for 45-50 minutes or until a knife inserted near the center comes out clean. Cool on a wire rack for 1 hour. Refrigerate for at least 3 hours before serving. Store in the refrigerator.

COOKIES & BARS

Cookie Jar Gingersnaps

My grandma kept two cookie jars in her pantry. One of the jars, which I now have, always had these crisp and chewy gingersnaps in it.

—**DEB HANDY** POMONA, KANSAS

YIELD: 3-4 DOZEN.

- ¾ cup shortening
- 1 cup sugar
- 1 egg
- ¼ cup molasses
- 2 cups all-purpose flour
- 2 teaspoons baking soda
- 1½ teaspoons ground ginger
- 1 teaspoon ground cinnamon
- ½ teaspoon salt
- Additional sugar

1. In a large bowl, cream shortening and sugar until light and fluffy. Beat in the egg and molasses. Combine the flour, baking soda, ginger, cinnamon and salt; gradually add to creamed mixture and mix well.

2. Shape rounded teaspoonfuls of dough into balls. Dip one side into sugar; place sugar side up 2 in. apart on greased baking sheets. Bake at 350° for 12-15 minutes or until lightly browned and crinkly. Remove to wire racks to cool.

Apricot-Coconut Bars

My family likes snacking on these beautiful rich-tasting bars. This recipe's one I've used and shared for over 30 years.

—**HELEN CLUTS** EDEN PRAIRIE, MINNESOTA

YIELD: 2 TO 2½ DOZEN.

- 1 cup all-purpose flour
- 1 teaspoon baking powder
- ½ cup cold butter
- 1 egg
- 1 tablespoon milk
- 1 cup apricot preserves
- TOPPING
- 1 egg, lightly beaten
- ⅔ cup sugar
- ¼ cup butter, melted
- 1 teaspoon vanilla extract
- 2 cups flaked coconut

1. In a large bowl, combine flour and baking powder. Cut in butter until the mixture resembles coarse crumbs. In a small bowl, beat egg and milk; stir into flour mixture.

2. Spread in a greased 9-in. square baking pan. Spread preserves over crust. Combine topping ingredients; carefully drop by tablespoonfuls over apricot layer. Bake at 350° for 25-30 minutes or until golden brown. Cool on a wire rack; cut into small bars.

Chocolaty Double Crunchers

I first tried these fun crispy cookies at a family picnic when I was a child. Packed with oats, cornflakes and coconut, they quickly became a regular treat at our house. Years later, I still make them for my own family.

—**CHERYL JOHNSON** UPPER MARLBORO, MARYLAND

YIELD: 2 DOZEN.

- ½ cup butter, softened
- ½ cup sugar
- ½ cup packed brown sugar
- 1 egg
- ½ teaspoon vanilla extract
- 1 cup all-purpose flour
- ½ teaspoon baking soda
- ¼ teaspoon salt
- 1 cup quick-cooking oats
- 1 cup crushed cornflakes
- ½ cup flaked coconut
- FILLING
- 2 packages (3 ounces each) cream cheese, softened
- 1½ cups confectioners' sugar
- 2 cups (12 ounces) semisweet chocolate chips, melted

1. In a large bowl, cream butter and sugars until light and fluffy. Beat in egg and vanilla. Combine the flour, baking soda and salt; gradually add to creamed mixture and mix well. Stir in the oats, cornflakes and coconut.

2. Shape into 1-in. balls and place 2 in. apart on greased baking sheets. Flatten with a glass dipped lightly in flour. Bake at 350° for 8-10 minutes or until lightly browned. Remove to wire racks to cool.

3. For filling, beat cream cheese and sugar until smooth. Beat in chocolate. Spread about 1 tablespoon on half of the cookies and top each with another cookie. Store in refrigerator.

Peanut Butter Cookies

This treasured recipe is the only one my grandmother ever put in writing! When my mother got married, she asked Grandma to write down just one recipe for her. That required some real effort, because Grandma was a pioneer-type cook who used a little of this or that until it felt right.

—JANET HALL CLINTON, WISCONSIN

YIELD: 3 DOZEN.

1   **cup shortening**
1   **cup peanut butter**
1   **cup sugar**
1   **cup packed brown sugar**
3   **eggs**
3   **cups all-purpose flour**
2   **teaspoons baking soda**
¼   **teaspoon salt**

1. In a large bowl, cream shortening, peanut butter and sugars until light and fluffy. Add eggs, one at a time, beating well after each addition. Combine the flour, baking soda and salt; add to creamed mixture and mix well.

2. Roll into 1½-in. balls. Place 3 in. apart on ungreased baking sheets. Flatten with a fork or meat mallet if desired. Bake at 375° for 10-15 minutes. Remove to wire racks.

Chocolate Malted Cookies

Like good old-fashioned malted milk? Here's the next best thing! Malted milk powder, chocolate syrup, and chocolate chips and chunks make these the yummiest cookies I've ever tasted. With six kids, I've made a lot of them over the years.

—**TERI RASEY** CADILLAC, MICHIGAN

YIELD: ABOUT 1½ DOZEN.

- 1 **cup butter-flavored shortening**
- 1¼ **cups packed brown sugar**
- ½ **cup malted milk powder**
- 2 **tablespoons chocolate syrup**
- 1 **tablespoon vanilla extract**
- 1 **egg**
- 2 **cups all-purpose flour**
- 1 **teaspoon baking soda**
- ½ **teaspoon salt**
- 1½ **cups semisweet chocolate chunks**
- 1 **cup milk chocolate chips**

1. In a large bowl, beat the shortening, brown sugar, malted milk powder, chocolate syrup and vanilla for 2 minutes. Add egg.

2. Combine the flour, baking soda and salt; gradually add to creamed mixture, mixing well after each addition. Stir in chocolate chunks and chips.

3. Shape into 2-in. balls; place 3 in. apart on ungreased baking sheets. Bake at 375° for 12-14 minutes or until golden brown. Cool for 2 minutes before removing to a wire rack.

Chocolate Marshmallow Bars

I've been asked to share this chocolaty layered recipe more than any other in my collection. It's a longtime favorite of our three daughters and I can't even begin to count how many times I have made them!

—**ESTHER SHANK** HARRISONBURG, VIRGINIA

YIELD: ABOUT 3 DOZEN.

- ¾ **cup butter, softened**
- 1½ **cups sugar**
- 3 **eggs**
- 1 **teaspoon vanilla extract**
- 1⅓ **cups all-purpose flour**
- 3 **tablespoons baking cocoa**

½ teaspoon baking powder
½ teaspoon salt
½ cup chopped nuts, optional
4 cups miniature marshmallows

TOPPING

1⅓ cups semisweet chocolate chips
1 cup peanut butter
3 tablespoons butter
2 cups Rice Krispies

1. In a small bowl, cream the butter and sugar until light and fluffy. Add eggs, one at a time, beating well after each addition. Beat in vanilla.

2. Combine the flour, cocoa, baking powder and salt; gradually add to creamed mixture. Stir in nuts if desired. Spread in a greased 15-in. x 10-in. x 1-in. baking pan.

3. Bake at 350° for 15-18 minutes or until set. Sprinkle with marshmallows; bake 2-3 minutes longer or until melted. Place pan on a wire rack. Using a knife dipped in water, spread marshmallows evenly over the top. Cool completely.

4. For topping, combine the chocolate chips, peanut butter and butter in a small saucepan. Cook and stir over low heat until blended. Remove from the heat; stir in cereal. Spread over bars immediately. Chill.

Turtle Bars

This recipe of my mother's is a must for the holidays. I always have good intentions of taking some to Christmas parties, but my family finishes them too soon!

—**FAYE HINTZ** SPRINGFIELD, MISSOURI

YIELD: ABOUT 8 DOZEN.

½ cup butter, softened
1 cup packed brown sugar

2 cups all-purpose flour
1 cup pecan halves

TOPPING

⅔ cup butter, cubed
½ cup packed brown sugar
1 cup (6 ounces) semisweet chocolate chips

1. In a large bowl, beat the butter and sugar until smooth. Gradually add flour; beat until crumbly. Press firmly into an ungreased 13-in. x 9-in. baking pan. Arrange pecans over crust.

2. In a small heavy saucepan, combine the butter and brown sugar. Bring to a boil; boil for 1 minute or until smooth, stirring constantly. Pour over pecans.

3. Bake at 350° for 18-22 minutes or until bubbly. Sprinkle the chocolate chips on top. Cool in pan on a wire rack for 3 minutes. Spread chocolate but allow some chips to remain whole. Cool completely; cut into small squares.

Hazelnut Shortbread

Traditional shortbread only contains flour, sugar and butter, resulting in a rich, crumbly cookie. This delectable version gets added flavor from chopped hazelnuts, some maple syrup and a touch of chocolate.

—**KAREN MORRELL** CANBY, OREGON

YIELD: 6 DOZEN.

1 cup butter, softened
½ cup sugar
2 tablespoons maple syrup or honey
2 teaspoons vanilla extract
2 cups all-purpose flour
1¼ cups finely chopped hazelnuts
½ cup each white, red, green, yellow and dark chocolate candy coating disks

1. In a large bowl, cream butter and sugar until light and fluffy. Add syrup and vanilla. Beat in flour just until combined; fold in nuts. Shape into two 1½-in. rolls; wrap tightly in waxed paper. Chill for 2 hours or until firm.

2. Cut into ¼-in. slices and place 2 in. apart on ungreased baking sheets. Bake at 325° for 14-16 minutes or until edges begin to brown. Remove to wire racks to cool.

3. In separate microwave-safe bowls, melt candy coating disks; stir until smooth. Drizzle over cookies. Let stand until set.

Icebox Cookies

This cookie recipe from my grandmother was my grandfather's favorite. I keep the dough in the freezer because I love to make a fresh batch when company drops in.

—CHRIS PAULSEN GLENDALE, ARIZONA

YIELD: ABOUT 7 DOZEN.

- ½ cup butter, softened
- 1 cup packed brown sugar
- 1 egg, beaten
- ½ teaspoon vanilla extract
- 2 cups all-purpose flour
- ½ teaspoon baking soda
- ½ teaspoon cream of tartar
- ½ teaspoon salt
- 1 cup chopped walnuts, optional

1. In a bowl, cream the butter and brown sugar. Add egg and vanilla; beat well. Combine dry ingredients; add to the creamed mixture. Stir in the nuts if desired.

2. On a lightly floured surface, shape the dough into three 10-in. x 1-in. rolls. Tightly wrap each roll in waxed paper. Freeze for at least 12 hours.

3. Cut into ⅜-in. slices and place 2 in. apart on greased baking sheets. Bake at 350° for 6-8 minutes. Remove to a wire rack to cool.

Coffee breaks at Grandma's were a local ritual at 10 and 3 o'clock. With a fresh pot of coffee, homemade cookies, open-faced sandwiches or fresh bread with preserves, it was an event. Husbands and wives, children, field workers, neighbors, the postman, the parson... everyone gathered for food and fellowship.

— SUSAN HUPPERT
PALMETTO, FLORIDA

Chewy Brownie Cookies

Bite into one of these chocolaty cookies, and you'll discover they're like chewy brownies inside. Yum!

—JONIE ADAMS ALBION, MICHIGAN

YIELD: 3 DOZEN.

- ⅔ cup shortening
- 1½ cups packed brown sugar
- 2 eggs
- 1 tablespoon water
- 3 teaspoons vanilla extract
- 1½ cups all-purpose flour
- ⅓ cup baking cocoa
- ½ teaspoon salt
- ¼ teaspoon baking soda
- 2 cups (12 ounces) semisweet chocolate chips
- ½ cup chopped walnuts or pecans, optional

1. In a large bowl, cream shortening and sugar until light and fluffy. Beat in the eggs, water and vanilla. Combine the flour, cocoa, salt and baking soda; gradually add to creamed mixture and beat just until blended. Stir in chocolate chips and nuts if desired.

2. Drop by rounded teaspoonfuls 2 in. apart on ungreased baking sheets. Bake at 375° for 7-9 minutes; do not overbake. Cool 2 minutes before removing to wire racks to cool.

Vanilla Crescent Cookies

This recipe originated in Croatia and has been in my husband's family for generations. I was thrilled when my mother-in-law shared it with me.

—**BEVERLY WILLIAMS** RHINELANDER, WISCONSIN

YIELD: 4 DOZEN.

1 cup butter, softened
1 cup confectioners' sugar, divided
1 teaspoon vanilla extract
½ teaspoon grated lemon peel
2½ cups all-purpose flour
¼ teaspoon salt
½ cup finely chopped walnuts
2 tablespoons sugar
1 vanilla bean

1. In a large bowl, cream butter and ½ cup confectioners' sugar until light and fluffy. Beat in vanilla and lemon peel. Combine flour and salt; gradually add to creamed mixture and mix well. Stir in walnuts.

2. Shape tablespoonfuls of dough into crescent shapes. Place 2 in. apart on ungreased baking sheets. Bake at 375° for 10-12 minutes or until edges are lightly browned.

3. Place sugar in a food processor. Split vanilla bean and scrape seeds into food processor. Discard vanilla bean. Pulse mixture until combined. Transfer to a small bowl; stir in remaining confectioners' sugar. Coat warm cookies with sugar mixture. Cool completely on wire racks. Store in an airtight container.

Pecan Squares

These bars are good for snacking when you're on the road or for taking to gatherings. If you love pecan pie, you will surely find them irresistible!

—**SYLVIA FORD** KENNETT, MISSOURI

YIELD: 4 DOZEN.

CRUST
2 cups all-purpose flour
¼ cup sugar
¼ teaspoon salt
¾ cup cold butter

FILLING
4 eggs
1½ cups corn syrup
1½ cups sugar
3 tablespoons butter, melted
1½ teaspoons vanilla extract
2½ cups chopped pecans

1. In a large bowl, combine the flour, sugar and salt; cut in butter until mixture resembles coarse crumbs. Press firmly and evenly into a greased 15-in. x 10-in. x 1-in. baking pan. Bake at 350° for 20 minutes.

2. For filling, in a bowl, combine the eggs, corn syrup, sugar, butter and vanilla. Stir in pecans. Spread evenly over hot crust. Bake 25-30 minutes longer or until set. Cool on a wire rack. Cut into squares.

Caramel-Pecan Dream Bars

These ooey-gooey cake bars pull ever so gently from the pan and hold a firm cut. They're a baker's dream come true.

—CAY KEPPERS NISSWA, MINNESOTA

YIELD: 2 DOZEN.

- 1 package (18¼ ounces) yellow cake mix
- ½ cup butter, softened
- 1 egg

FILLING
- 1 can (14 ounces) sweetened condensed milk
- 1 egg
- 1 teaspoon vanilla extract
- 1 cup chopped pecans
- ½ cup brickle toffee bits

1. In a large bowl, beat the cake mix, butter and egg until crumbly. Press onto the bottom of a greased 13-in. x 9-in. baking pan.

2. In a small bowl, beat the milk, egg and vanilla until combined. Stir in pecans and toffee bits. Pour over crust.

3. Bake at 350° for 20-25 minutes or until golden brown. Cool on a wire rack. Cut into bars.

Peanut Butter Squares

I grew up in Lancaster County, Pennsylvania, and spent a lot of time with my mom and grandmother in the kitchen, making Pennsylvania Dutch classics. This scrumptious recipe, which combines two of our favorite flavors, is one I adapted.

—RACHEL GREENAWALT KELLER ROANOKE, VIRGINIA

YIELD: 4 DOZEN.

- ¾ cup cold butter, cubed
- 2 ounces semisweet chocolate
- 1½ cups graham cracker crumbs (about 24 squares)
- 1 cup flaked coconut
- ½ cup chopped salted peanuts
- ¼ cup toasted wheat germ

FILLING
- 2 packages (8 ounces each) cream cheese, softened

¾ cup sugar
⅔ cup chunky peanut butter
1 teaspoon vanilla extract
TOPPING
4 ounces semisweet chocolate, chopped
¼ cup butter, cubed

1. In a microwave-safe bowl, melt butter and chocolate; stir until smooth. Stir in the cracker crumbs, coconut, peanuts and wheat germ. Press into a greased 13-in. x 9-in. pan. Cover and refrigerate for at least 30 minutes.

2. In a small bowl, combine filling ingredients. Spread over crust. Cover and refrigerate for at least 30 minutes.

3. In a microwave, melt chocolate and butter; stir until smooth. Pour over filling. Cover and refrigerate for at least 30 minutes or until topping is set. Cut into squares. Refrigerate leftovers.

Orange Cocoa Sandies

When I was growing up, I loved to help my mom cut out the appealing dessert recipes from newspapers and magazines. Then we would paste them all into a big book. This recipe is one of our favorites from the collection.

—NELLA PARKER HERSEY, MICHIGAN

YIELD: ABOUT 2 DOZEN.

½ cup butter, softened
½ cup plus 2 tablespoons confectioners' sugar, divided
½ teaspoon orange extract
1 cup all-purpose flour
2 tablespoons baking cocoa
½ cup finely chopped pecans

1. In a large bowl, cream butter and ½ cup confectioners' sugar until light and fluffy; beat in extract. Combine flour and cocoa; gradually add to creamed mixture. Stir in pecans.

2. Roll into 1-in. balls. Place 1 in. apart on ungreased baking sheets. Bake at 350° for 12-14 minutes or until set. Cool for 1-2 minutes before removing to wire racks. Dust with remaining confectioner's sugar.

Grandma's Date Bars

These bars are not only delicious, they're good for those trying to make healthier food choices, as they use no shortening, butter or oil. My great-grandmother, who was born in 1868, made these bars, and the recipe has come down through the generations. Now my children are making them.

—MARILYN REID
CHERRY CREEK, NEW YORK

YIELD: 16 SERVINGS.

1 cup sugar
1 cup all-purpose flour
1 teaspoon baking powder
½ teaspoon salt
1 cup chopped dates
1 cup chopped walnuts
3 eggs, beaten
Confectioners' sugar

1. In a large bowl, combine the first seven ingredients. Transfer to a greased 8-in. square baking pan.

2. Bake at 350° for 25 minutes or until a toothpick inserted near the center comes out clean. Cool on a wire rack. Dust with confectioners' sugar. Cut into squares.

Grandma's Polish Cookies

Our family's traditional khruchiki recipe came down through my mother's side from my great-grandmother. As a child, it was my job to loop the end of each cookie through its hole.

—SHERINE ELISE GILMOUR BROOKLYN, NEW YORK

YIELD: 40 COOKIES.

- 4 cups all-purpose flour
- 1 teaspoon salt
- 1 cup cold butter
- 4 egg yolks
- 1 cup evaporated milk
- 2 teaspoons vanilla extract

Oil for deep-fat frying

Confectioners' sugar

1. In a large bowl, combine flour and salt. Cut in butter until mixture resembles coarse crumbs. In another bowl, beat egg yolks until foamy; add milk and vanilla. Stir into crumb mixture until dough is stiff enough to knead.

2. Turn onto a lightly floured surface; knead 8-10 times. Divide dough into four pieces. Roll each portion into a ¼-in.-thick rectangle; cut into 4-in. x 1½-in. strips. Cut a 2-in. lengthwise slit down the middle of each strip; pull one of the ends through the slit like a bow.

3. In an electric skillet or deep-fat fryer, heat oil to 375°. Fry dough strips, a few at a time, until golden brown on both sides. Drain on paper towels. Dust with confectioners' sugar

Macaroon Brownies

These three-layer brownies make for a pretty presentation on any dessert table. I was first introduced to these coconut-filled brownies when my mother-in-law made them for my bridal shower and wedding reception. After the first bite, I understood why my husband loved them!

—CHRISTINE FOUST STONEBORO, PENNSYLVANIA

YIELD: 4 DOZEN.

- 1 cup butter, softened
- 2 cups sugar
- 4 eggs
- 1 teaspoon vanilla extract
- 2 cups all-purpose flour
- ½ cup baking cocoa
- ½ teaspoon cream of tartar
- ½ cup chopped walnuts

MACAROON FILLING

- 1 package (14 ounces) flaked coconut
- 1 can (14 ounces) sweetened condensed milk
- 2 teaspoons vanilla extract

FROSTING

- ¾ cup sugar
- ¼ cup milk
- 2 tablespoons butter
- 1 cup miniature marshmallows
- 1 cup (6 ounces) semisweet chocolate chips
- 1 teaspoon vanilla extract

1. In a large bowl, cream butter and sugar until light and fluffy. Add eggs and vanilla; mix well. Combine the flour, cocoa and cream of tartar; gradually add to creamed mixture. Stir in nuts. Spread half into a greased 13-in. x 9-in. baking pan.

2. For filling, combine the coconut, condensed milk and vanilla; carefully spread over batter in pan. Top with the remaining batter. Bake at 350° for 40-45 minutes or until a toothpick inserted near the center comes out clean. Cool on a wire rack.

3. For frosting, combine the sugar, milk and butter in a saucepan; cook and stir until sugar is dissolved. Add the marshmallows and chocolate chips; cook and stir until melted. Remove from the heat; stir in vanilla. Cool until frosting reaches spreading consistency, about 25 minutes. Spread over the cooled brownies. Cut into bars.

Swedish Raspberry Almond Bars

When I was a single mom with a young daughter and little money, my Swedish neighbor brought me a batch of these cookies at Christmas. My daughter's 36 now, and I still make these wonderful cookies.

—MARINA CASTLE LA CRESCENTA, CALIFORNIA

YIELD: 2 DOZEN.

 ¾ **cup butter, softened**
 ¾ **cup confectioners' sugar**
 1½ **cups all-purpose flour**
 ¾ **cup seedless raspberry jam**
 3 **egg whites**
 6 **tablespoons sugar**
 ½ **cup flaked coconut**
 1 **cup sliced almonds, divided**
Additional confectioners' sugar

1. In a large bowl, cream butter and confectioners' sugar until light and fluffy. Gradually add flour and mix well. Press onto the bottom of a greased 13-in. x 9-in. baking pan. Bake at 350° for 18-20 minutes or until lightly browned.

2. Spread jam over crust. In a large bowl, beat egg whites until soft peaks form. Gradually beat in sugar, 1 tablespoon at a time, on high until stiff peaks form. Fold in coconut and ½ cup almonds. Spread over jam. Sprinkle with remaining almonds. Bake at 350° for 18-22 minutes or until golden brown. Cool completely on a wire rack. Dust with confectioners' sugar.

Caramel Heavenlies

My mom made these dressy, sweet cookies for cookie exchanges when I was a little girl, letting me sprinkle on the almonds and coconut. They're so easy to fix that sometimes I can't wait until Christmas to make a batch.

—DAWN BURNS LAKE ST. LOUIS, MISSOURI

YIELD: ABOUT 6 DOZEN.

12 whole graham crackers
2 cups miniature marshmallows
¾ cup butter
¾ cup packed brown sugar
1 teaspoon ground cinnamon
1 teaspoon vanilla extract
1 cup sliced almonds
1 cup flaked coconut

1. Line a 15-in. x 10-in. x 1-in. baking pan with foil. Place graham crackers in pan; cover with marshmallows. In a saucepan over medium heat, cook and stir butter, brown sugar and cinnamon until the butter is melted and sugar is dissolved. Remove from the heat; stir in vanilla.

2. Spoon over the marshmallows. Sprinkle with almonds and coconut. Bake at 350° for 14-16 minutes or until browned. Cool completely. Cut into 2-in. squares, then cut each square in half to form triangles.

Iced Anise Cookies

On Thanksgiving, Christmas and Easter we could always expect to see a plate of these scrumptious cookies. My grandmother always kept some on hand for her hungry grandchildren.

—LINDA HARRINGTON WINDHAM, NEW HAMPSHIRE

YIELD: 6 DOZEN.

2⅔ cups all-purpose flour
½ cup sugar
3 teaspoons baking powder
3 eggs
½ cup butter, melted
¼ cup 2% milk
2 teaspoons anise extract
ICING
¼ cup butter, softened
2 cups confectioners' sugar
3 tablespoons 2% milk
½ teaspoon lemon extract
Coarse and colored sugars, optional

1. In a large bowl, combine 2 cups flour, sugar and baking powder. In a small bowl, whisk the eggs, butter, milk and extract. Stir into dry ingredients until blended. Stir in remaining flour until dough forms a ball. Turn onto a floured surface; knead until smooth.

2. Shape dough by rounded teaspoonfuls into thin 6-in. ropes; twist each rope into a "Q" shape. Place on ungreased baking sheets. Bake at 350° for 8-10 minutes or until set. Remove from pans to wire racks to cool completely.

3. For icing, in a small bowl, beat butter until fluffy. Add the confectioners' sugar, milk and extract; beat until smooth. Spread over tops of cookies; decorate with sugars if desired.

Raspberry Coconut Cookies

My mother gave me the recipe for these rich, buttery cookies. Raspberry preserves and a cream filling make them doubly delicious.

—JUNE BROWN VENETA, OREGON

YIELD: 2½ DOZEN.

¾ cup butter, softened
½ cup sugar
1 egg
1 teaspoon vanilla extract
2 cups all-purpose flour
½ cup flaked coconut
1½ teaspoons baking powder
¼ teaspoon salt
FILLING
¼ cup butter, softened
¾ cup confectioners' sugar
2 teaspoons 2% milk
½ teaspoon vanilla extract
½ cup raspberry preserves

1. In a large bowl, cream butter and sugar until light and fluffy. Beat in egg and vanilla. Combine the flour, coconut, baking powder and salt; gradually add to creamed mixture and mix well.

2. Shape into 1-in. balls. Place 1½ in. apart on ungreased baking sheets; flatten with a glass dipped in flour.

3. Bake at 350° for 12-14 minutes or until edges begin to brown. Cool on wire racks.

4. In a small bowl, beat the butter, confectioners' sugar, milk and vanilla until smooth. Place ½ teaspoon preserves and a scant teaspoon of filling on the bottom of half of the cookies; top with remaining cookies. Store in an airtight container in the refrigerator.

DESSERTS

Layered Banana Pudding

My mother gave me this recipe, which an old friend had shared with her. When my children were still at home, we enjoyed this satisfying pudding often, and now I make it for company. There's no comparison between this recipe and the instant pudding mixes from the grocery store!

—**ESTHER MATTESON** SOUTH BEND, INDIANA

YIELD: 8 SERVINGS.

  ½ **cup all-purpose flour**
  ⅔ **cup packed brown sugar**
  2 **cups milk**
  2 **egg yolks, beaten**
  2 **tablespoons butter**
  1 **teaspoon vanilla extract**
  1 **cup heavy whipping cream, whipped**
  4 **to 6 medium firm bananas, sliced**
Chopped walnuts, optional

1. In a large saucepan, combine the flour and brown sugar. Stir in milk until smooth. Cook and stir over medium-high heat until thickened and bubbly. Reduce heat; cook and stir 2 minutes longer. Remove from the heat.

2. Stir a small amount of hot filling into egg yolks; return all to pan, stirring constantly. Bring to a gentle boil; cook and stir 2 minutes longer. Remove from the heat; stir in the butter and vanilla. Cool to room temperature without stirring. Fold in the whipped cream.

3. Layer a third of the pudding in a 2-qt. glass bowl; top with half of the bananas. Repeat layers. Top with the remaining pudding. Sprinkle with nuts if desired. Cover and refrigerate for at least 1 hour before serving.

Pineapple Cheese Torte

This light and yummy pineapple dessert looks prettiest when it's garnished with fresh strawberries. I serve it at summer picnics or family get-togethers. It's a hit any time of year!

—**DIANE BRADLEY** SPARTA, MICHIGAN

YIELD: 12-16 SERVINGS.

PAT-IN-THE-PAN CRUST
  1 **cup all-purpose flour**
  ¼ **cup confectioners' sugar**
  ¼ **cup finely chopped almonds**
  ⅓ **cup butter, softened**
FILLING
  2 **packages (8 ounces each) cream cheese, softened**
  ½ **cup sugar**
  2 **eggs**
  ⅔ **cup unsweetened pineapple juice**
PINEAPPLE TOPPING
  1 **can (20 ounces) crushed pineapple**
  ¼ **cup all-purpose flour**
  ¼ **cup sugar**
  ½ **cup heavy whipping cream**
Fresh strawberries, optional

1. In a bowl, combine crust ingredients until blended; pat into a greased 11-in. x 7-in. baking dish. Bake at 350° for 20 minutes. In a small bowl, beat cream cheese and sugar until light and fluffy. Beat in eggs. Stir in juice. Pour over hot crust. Bake for 25 minutes or until center is set. Cool on a wire rack.

2. For topping, drain pineapple, reserving 1 cup juice. Set pineapple aside. In a small saucepan, combine flour, sugar and reserved pineapple juice until smooth. Bring to a boil. Cook and stir for 1 minute or until thickened and bubbly. Remove from the heat; fold in pineapple. Cool.

3. In a small bowl, beat cream until soft peaks form; fold into topping. Carefully spread over top. Refrigerate for 6 hours or overnight. Garnish with strawberries if desired.

Cherry Cobbler

I've made this recipe for years, adapting it to suit our taste. It's a delicious way to use lots of cherries. I hope you enjoy this tart treat!

—PEGGY BURDICK BURLINGTON, MICHIGAN

YIELD: 6-8 SERVINGS.

- 5 cups pitted canned tart red cherries
- ⅓ cup sugar
- ⅓ cup packed brown sugar
- 2 tablespoons plus 1½ teaspoons cornstarch
- 1 teaspoon ground cinnamon
- ¼ teaspoon ground nutmeg
- 2 tablespoons plus 1½ teaspoons lemon juice

TOPPING
- 1 cup all-purpose flour
- 1 tablespoon sugar
- 1 teaspoon baking powder
- ¼ teaspoon salt
- 2 tablespoons cold butter
- ⅓ to ½ cup milk

1. Drain cherries, reserving 1¼ cups juice; set aside. Discard remaining juice. In a large saucepan, combine the sugars, cornstarch, cinnamon and nutmeg; stir in lemon juice and reserved cherry juice until smooth. Bring to a boil. Cook and stir for 2 minutes or until thickened and bubbly.

2. Add cherries; pour into an ungreased 9-in. square baking pan. For topping, combine the flour, sugar, baking powder and salt; cut in butter until crumbly. Stir in enough milk to moisten. Drop by tablespoonfuls over cherries. Bake at 450° for 10-13 minutes or until golden brown.

Blueberry Grunt

The name may make you smile—and the flavor of this stovetop treat is guaranteed to have the same effect. Make this traditional dessert in a skillet with a tight-fitting lid, and you'll hear it "grunt" as it cooks!

—IOLA EGLE BELLA VISTA, ARKANSAS

YIELD: 6-8 SERVINGS.

- 4 cups fresh blueberries
- 1 cup sugar
- 1 cup water
- 1½ cups all-purpose flour
- 2 teaspoons baking powder
- 2 tablespoons grated orange peel
- ½ teaspoon ground cinnamon
- ¼ teaspoon ground nutmeg
- ¼ teaspoon salt
- ¾ cup milk
- Heavy whipping cream, optional

1. In a skillet, combine blueberries, sugar and water; bring to a boil. Simmer, uncovered, for 20 minutes.

2. In a bowl, combine the next six ingredients; stir in milk just until moistened (dough will be stiff). Drop by tablespoonfuls over blueberries.

3. Cover and cook 10-15 minutes or until the dumplings are puffed and a toothpick inserted near the center comes out clean. Serve warm with cream if desired.

> Making ice cream was the highlight of summer picnics at my great-grandparents' farm. The excitement rose when the cranking became labored, because that meant the dasher would soon be lifted out. For me, no ice cream has ever tasted as good as that sweet treat clinging to the cold metal!
>
> **— BETTE HILLEGASS** BLACK MOUNTAIN, NORTH CAROLINA

Old-Fashioned Ice Cream Roll

When I think of my grandmother, I think of this wonderful dessert. The warm caramel sauce melts the ice cream slightly. Oh, it is so good!

—DARLENE BRENDEN SALEM, OREGON

YIELD: 8-10 SERVINGS (2 CUPS SAUCE).

- 4 **eggs**
- ¾ **cup sugar**
- 1 **teaspoon vanilla extract**
- ¾ **cup all-purpose flour**
- ¾ **teaspoon baking powder**
- ¼ **teaspoon salt**
- ½ **gallon vanilla ice cream, slightly softened**

CARAMEL SAUCE
- 1 **cup packed brown sugar**
- ½ **cup sugar**
- ¼ **teaspoon salt**
- ½ **cup light corn syrup**
- 1 **cup heavy whipping cream**

Chopped pecans, optional

1. Line a greased 15-in. x 10-in. x 1-in. baking pan with waxed paper. Grease the paper; set aside. In a large bowl, beat eggs for 3 minutes. Gradually add sugar; beat for 2 minutes or until mixture becomes thick and lemon-colored. Beat in vanilla. Combine dry ingredients; fold into egg mixture.

2. Spread batter evenly into prepared pan. Bake at 375° for 10-12 minutes or until cake springs back when lightly touched. Cool for 5 minutes. Invert onto a kitchen towel dusted with confectioners' sugar. Gently peel off waxed paper. Roll up cake in the towel jelly-roll style, starting with a short side. Cool completely on a wire rack.

3. Spread cooled cake with ice cream; roll up again. Freeze until firm.

4. For sauce, in a small saucepan, combine the sugars, salt and corn syrup. Cook and stir until mixture comes to a boil. Remove from the heat; cool slightly. Stir in cream. Serve with ice cream roll. Sprinkle with pecans if desired.

Variation: Use strawberry ice cream instead of vanilla and eliminate caramel sauce. Garnish with fresh strawberries and whipped cream.

Homemade Butterscotch Pudding

Homemade pudding stirs memories of grandmothers and their secret knowledge of how to change milk and eggs into creamy concoctions they poured into dessert glasses. The essence of butterscotch adds a caramel-sweet touch.

—TERESA WILKES PEMBROKE, GEORGIA

YIELD: 6 SERVINGS.

- ½ **cup sugar**
- ½ **cup packed dark brown sugar**
- 3 **tablespoons cornstarch**
- ¼ **teaspoon salt**
- ⅛ **teaspoon ground nutmeg**
- 3 **cups 2% milk**
- 3 **egg yolks**
- 2 **tablespoons butter, cubed**
- 2 **teaspoons vanilla extract**

Whipped cream, optional

1. In a large heavy saucepan, combine the first five ingredients. Stir in the milk until smooth. Cook and stir over medium-high heat until thickened and bubbly. Reduce heat to low; cook and stir 2 minutes longer. Remove from the heat.

2. Stir a small amount of hot mixture into the egg yolks; return all to the pan. Bring to a gentle boil, stirring constantly; cook 2 minutes or until mixture is thickened and coats the back of a spoon. Remove from the heat.

3. Stir in butter and vanilla. Cool for 15 minutes, stirring occasionally. Transfer to six dessert dishes. Cover and refrigerate until chilled. Garnish with whipped cream if desired.

Butterfinger Delight

I got the recipe for this wonderful no-bake treat from my mother-in-law because it's my husband's favorite. I'm frequently asked to bring this yummy dessert to get-togethers. Everyone loves it.

—LINDA WINTER ENID, OKLAHOMA

YIELD: 12-15 SERVINGS.

- 1 **cup crushed butter-flavored crackers (about 30 crackers)**
- 1 **cup graham cracker crumbs**
- 4 **Butterfinger candy bars (2.1 ounces each), crushed**
- ¾ **cup butter, melted**
- 1½ **cups cold milk**
- 2 **packages (3.4 ounces each) instant vanilla pudding mix**
- 1 **quart reduced-fat chocolate frozen yogurt, softened**
- 1 **carton (12 ounces) frozen whipped topping, thawed, divided**

1. In a large bowl, combine the first four ingredients; set aside ½ cup for topping. Press remaining crumb mixture into an ungreased 13-in. x 9-in. dish. Chill for 5 minutes.

2. Meanwhile, in a large bowl, whisk milk and pudding mixes for 2 minutes. Let stand for 2 minutes or until set (mixture will be thick). Stir in frozen yogurt and 1 cup whipped topping until smooth. Spread over crust.

3. Top with remaining whipped topping. Sprinkle with reserved crumb mixture. Refrigerate for 8 hours or overnight.

Raspberry Vanilla Trifle

When I was growing up, my English mother made this as the centerpiece at our traditional Christmas Day tea. Presented in a cut glass bowl, it's absolutely stunning.

—JOYCE TOTH WICHITA FALLS, TEXAS

YIELD: 10-12 SERVINGS.

- 2 **cups milk**
- 1 **package (3 ounces) cook-and-serve vanilla pudding mix**
- 1 **loaf (10¾ ounces) frozen pound cake, thawed**
- ¼ **cup seedless raspberry jam**
- ¼ **cup orange juice**
- 10 **soft macaroon cookies**
- 2 **cups fresh or frozen unsweetened raspberries, thawed and drained**
- 1 **cup heavy whipping cream**
- 2 **tablespoons confectioners' sugar**
- ¼ **cup sliced almonds, toasted**

1. In a small saucepan, combine milk and pudding mix. Cook and stir over medium heat until mixture comes to a full boil. Cool. Cut cake into 1-in. slices; spread with jam. Cut into 1-in. cubes. Place cubes jam side up in a 3-qt. trifle or glass bowl. Drizzle with orange juice.

2. Place macaroons in a food processor, cover and pulse until coarse crumbs form. Set aside ¼ cup crumbs for garnish; sprinkle remaining crumbs over cake cubes. Top with berries and pudding. Cover and refrigerate overnight.

3. Just before serving, in a small bowl, beat cream until thickened. Beat in confectioners' sugar until stiff peaks form. Spread over trifle. Sprinkle with almonds and reserved macaroon crumbs.

Fudgy Nut Coffee Pie

My mother served this pretty pie for my birthday dinner one year, and now it's one of my favorites. Fudge sauce, chopped pecans and coffee ice cream top the chocolate crumb crust. Sometimes I garnish the pie with dollops of whipped cream.

—AMY THEIS BILLINGS, MONTANA

YIELD: 8 SERVINGS.

- 1½ **cups confectioners' sugar**
- ½ **cup heavy whipping cream**
- 6 **tablespoons butter, cubed**
- 3 **ounces unsweetened chocolate**
- 3 **tablespoons light corn syrup**

Dash salt

- 1 **teaspoon vanilla extract**
- 1 **chocolate crumb crust (9 inches)**
- ¾ **cup coarsely chopped pecans, divided**
- 3 **pints coffee ice cream, softened**

1. In a small saucepan, combine the confectioners' sugar, cream, butter, chocolate, corn syrup and salt. Cook and stir over low heat until smooth. Remove from the heat. Stir in vanilla. Cool completely.

2. Spread ½ cup fudge sauce over the crust. Sprinkle with ¼ cup pecans. Freeze for 20 minutes or until set. Spread with half of the ice cream. Freeze for 1 hour or until firm. Repeat layers. Cover and freeze for 4 hours or until firm.

3. Just before serving, drizzle remaining fudge sauce over pie and sprinkle with remaining pecans.

Pinwheel Mints

Both my grandmother and my mom used to make these eye-catching confections as a replacement for ordinary mints at Christmas. When I offer them at parties, guests tell me the mints are wonderful, and then ask how I create the pretty swirl pattern.

—**MARILOU ROTH** MILFORD, NEBRASKA

YIELD: ABOUT 3 DOZEN.

 1 **package (8 ounces) cream cheese, softened**
 ½ **to 1 teaspoon mint extract**
 7½ **to 8½ cups confectioners' sugar**
Red and green food coloring
Additional confectioners' sugar

1. In a large bowl, beat cream cheese and mint extract until smooth. Gradually beat in as much confectioners' sugar as possible; knead in remaining confectioners' sugar until a firm mixture is achieved. Divide mixture in half; with food coloring, tint half pink and the other light green.

2. On waxed paper, lightly sprinkle remaining confectioners' sugar into a 12-in. x 5-in. rectangle. Divide pink portion in half; shape each portion into a 10-in. log.

3. Place one log on sugared waxed paper and flatten slightly. Cover with waxed paper; roll into a 12-in. x 5-in. rectangle. Repeat with remaining pink portion; set aside. Repeat with light green portion.

4. Remove top piece of waxed paper from one pink and one green rectangle. Place one over the other. Roll up jelly-roll style, starting with a long side. Wrap in waxed paper; twist ends. Repeat. Chill overnight.

5. To serve, cut into ½-in. slices. Store in an airtight container in the refrigerator for up to 1 week.

Pumpkin Bread Pudding

It may be old-fashioned, but this comforting dessert is never out of style. I got this recipe from an aunt who's a very experienced cook.

—LOIS FETTING NELSON, WISCONSIN

YIELD: 6-8 SERVINGS.

- 4 cups cubed day-old whole wheat bread
- ½ cup chopped dates or raisins
- ½ cup chopped pecans, divided
- 2 cups milk
- 1 cup canned pumpkin
- 2 eggs, separated
- ⅔ cup packed brown sugar
- 1½ teaspoons ground cinnamon
- ¾ teaspoon ground nutmeg
- ¼ teaspoon salt
- ⅛ teaspoon ground cloves

Half-and-half cream or whipped cream, optional

1. Combine bread cubes, dates and ⅓ cup pecans; place in a greased 2-qt. shallow baking dish.

2. In a bowl, combine milk, pumpkin, egg yolks, brown sugar, cinnamon, nutmeg, salt and cloves. In a small bowl and with clean beaters, beat the egg whites until stiff; fold into the pumpkin mixture. Pour over bread cubes and toss gently. Sprinkle with remaining nuts.

3. Bake, uncovered, at 350° for 1 hour or until a knife inserted near the center comes out clean. Serve warm or chilled with cream if desired.

Lemony Apple Dumplings

The first time I made this recipe, my guests included two little girls. They weren't sure about eating a dessert that looked so different. But after just one bite, they proclaimed it "yummy" and cleaned their plates.

—KRISTY DELOACH BAKER, LOUISIANA

YIELD: 4 SERVINGS.

- 1½ cups all-purpose flour
- 1¼ teaspoons salt, divided
- ⅓ cup shortening
- 4 to 5 tablespoons cold milk
- ½ cup packed brown sugar
- 3 tablespoons butter, softened
- ½ teaspoon ground cinnamon
- 4 medium baking apples, peeled and cored
- 1 egg white, beaten

LEMON SAUCE
- ½ cup sugar
- 4 teaspoons cornstarch
- 1 cup cold water
- 3 tablespoons butter
- 4 teaspoons lemon juice
- 2 teaspoons grated lemon peel
- ⅛ teaspoon salt

1. Combine flour and 1 teaspoon salt. Cut in shortening until crumbly. Stir in milk until pastry forms a ball; set aside. Stir brown sugar, butter, cinnamon and remaining salt to form a paste. Divide and press into center of each apple; pat any extra filling on outside of apples.

2. On a floured surface, roll pastry into a 14-in. square. Cut into four 7-in. squares. Place one apple in center of each square. Brush edges of pastry with egg white. Fold up corners to center; pinch to seal.

3. Place in a greased 9-in. square baking dish. Bake at 375° for 35-40 minutes or until golden brown.

4. Meanwhile, combine the sugar and cornstarch in a saucepan. Stir in water. Bring to a boil; cook and stir for 2 minutes or until thickened. Remove from the heat; stir in the remaining ingredients until smooth. Serve sauce warm over warm dumplings.

Berries in Custard Sauce

This refreshing treat showcases the fresh berries of summer. The custard is not overly sweet, so it doesn't overshadow the fruit.

—LEONA LUECKING WEST BURLINGTON, IOWA

YIELD: 6 SERVINGS.

- 1 cup milk
- 1 egg, lightly beaten
- 2 tablespoons sugar

Dash salt

- ½ teaspoon vanilla extract
- 3 cups fresh blueberries, raspberries and strawberries

1. In a saucepan, heat milk over medium heat until bubbles form around sides of pan. Combine egg and sugar in a bowl; stir in a small amount of hot milk. Return all to saucepan. Cook over low heat, stirring constantly, until mixture coats a spoon, about 15 minutes. Remove from heat; stir in salt and vanilla. Chill at least 1 hour. Serve over berries.

Grandma's Chocolate Pudding

My grandmother always made this creamy, very chocolaty pudding when we visited.

—DONNA HUGHES ROCHESTER, NEW HAMPSHIRE

YIELD: 4-6 SERVINGS.

- 1 cup sugar
- ½ cup baking cocoa
- ¼ cup all-purpose flour
- 2 cups water
- ¾ cup evaporated milk
- 1 tablespoon vanilla extract

Dash salt

1. In a saucepan, combine sugar, cocoa and flour. Add water and milk; stir until smooth. Cook over medium heat, stirring constantly, until mixture comes to a boil. Cook and stir for 1-2 minutes or until thickened.

2. Remove from heat; stir in vanilla and salt. Cool to room temperature, stirring several times. Pour into a serving bowl or individual dishes. Serve warm or chill.

Nutty Chocolate Fudge

Many years ago, when I was dating the man who is now my husband, his mother gave me this recipe for his favorite fudge. It's a tasty treat that's so simple to make.

—MAUREEN DREES MANNING, IOWA

YIELD: 2¼ POUNDS.

- 3 tablespoons butter, divided
- 12 ounces German sweet chocolate, chopped
- 2 cups (12 ounces) semisweet chocolate chips
- 1 jar (7 ounces) marshmallow creme
- 4½ cups sugar
- 1 can (12 ounces) evaporated milk
- 2 cups pecans or walnuts, chopped

1. Line a 13-in. x 9-in. pan with foil; butter the foil with 1 tablespoon butter and set aside. Break the German chocolate into 1-in. pieces; place in a bowl. Add the chocolate chips and marshmallow creme; set aside.

2. In a large saucepan, bring the sugar, milk and remaining butter to a boil over medium heat, stirring often. Reduce heat; simmer, uncovered, for 6 minutes, stirring occasionally. Slowly pour over chocolate mixture; stir until mixture is smooth and blended. Stir in nuts.

3. Pour into prepared pan. Let stand at room temperature until cool. Cut into squares. Store in an airtight container in the refrigerator.

General Recipe Index

This handy index lists every recipe by food category, major ingredient and/or cooking method, so you can easily locate recipes to suit your needs.

Appetizers & Snacks

Artichoke Spinach Dip in a Bread Bowl, 8
Blizzard Party Mix, 8
BLT Bites, 14
Caramel Corn, 19
Cheese Rye Appetizers, 7
Cheesy Sun Crisps, 11
Chunky Salsa, 11
Cinnamon-Raisin Granola, 10
Crisp and Nutty Mix, 20
Deviled Eggs with Bacon, 6
Easy Elephant Ears, 9
Easy Hummus, 12
Fresh Vegetable Dip, 16
Horseradish Cheese Spread, 21
Mini Apple Pizzas, 16
Mini Hamburgers, 13
Olive-Stuffed Celery, 21
Pepperoni Pizza Spread, 6
Puffed Wheat Balls, 18
Roast Beef Spirals, 9
Spiced Pecans, 12
Sweet Gingered Chicken Wings, 15
Sweet Minglers, 14
Tangy Meatballs, 10
Tater-Dipped Veggies, 19

Apples

Apple Bran Muffins, 112
Apple Cobbler, 297
Apple Fritters, 35
Apple Raisin Bread, 120
Apple-Topped Oatcakes, 40
Apple Turnovers with Custard, 289
Apple Walnut Cake, 224
Cookie Sheet Apple Pie, 249
Dutch Apple Bread, 111
Herbed Pork and Apples, 182
Lattice-Topped Apple Pie, 251
Lemony Apple Dumplings, 300
Mini Apple Pizzas, 16
Mulligatawny Soup, 51
Nutty Apple Muffins, 113
Oh-So-Good Oatmeal, 32
Overnight Apple French Toast, 28
Roasted Duck with Apple-Raisin Dressing, 163
Rustic Apple-Raisin Bread, 128
Rustic Autumn Fruit Tart, 256
Saucy Apple Cake, 228
Smoked Turkey and Apple Salad, 168
Sour Cream Apple Chicken, 155
Sour Cream Apple Pie, 255
Spicy Applesauce Cake, 241
Streusel-Topped Apple Cheesecake, 24
Summer Apple Salad, 72

Apricots

Apricot Baked Ham, 182
Apricot-Coconut Bars, 268
Apricot Walnut Bread, 107
Golden Apricot Pie, 261
Stuffed Apricot French Toast, 31

Asparagus

Asparagus Ham Rolls, 188
Asparagus with Sesame Butter, 90
Saucy Chicken and Asparagus, 169

Bacon

Bacon Swiss Bread, 113
BLT Bites, 14
Cheese Rye Appetizers, 7
Corn and Bacon Casserole, 87
Creamy German Potato Salad, 66
Deviled Eggs with Bacon, 6
Prosciutto Chicken Cacciatore, 166
Ranch Stuffed Baked Potatoes, 94
Sheepherder's Breakfast, 29
Spinach Bacon Quiche, 37
Tasty Tossed Salad, 65

Bananas

Banana Brunch Punch, 12
Banana Chip Pancakes, 35
Banana Cupcakes, 223
Banana Fruit Compote, 64
Banana Nut Layer Cake, 238
Banana Split Cream Puffs, 296
Creamy Banana Pie, 260
Layered Banana Pudding, 290

Bars & Brownies

Apricot-Coconut Bars, 268
Caramel Heavenlies, 284
Caramel-Pecan Dream Bars, 278
Chocolate Chip Brownies, 281
Chocolate Date Squares, 270
Chocolate Marshmallow Bars, 274
Frosted Cookie Brownies, 272
Fudge Brownies, 267
Grandma's Date Bars, 279
Lemon Bars, 273
Macaroon Brownies, 282

Alphabetical Index

This handy index lists every recipe in alphabetical order so you can easily find your favorite dish.

Photo Credits

COOKING UTENSILS IN CROCK, page 4
Graeme Dawes/Shutterstock.com

WOMAN LEANING OVER COUNTER, page 4
Susan Colbert

COFFEE GRINDER, page 22
Ronald Sumers/Shutterstock.com

WOMAN FLIPPING EGGS, page 22
Everett Collection/Shutterstock.com

KITCHEN UTENSILS, page 42
Danie Nel/Shutterstock.com

WOMAN AT STOVE, page 42
Everett Collection/Shutterstock.com

VINTAGE DISHES, page 62
Karuka/Shutterstock.com

FARM FRESH EGGS, page 62
Kathy Ridder

DISHES ON WOOD SHELVES, page 80
patpitchaya/Shutterstock.com

CANNING, page 80
Rose Cunningham

ROLLING PIN, page 102
Nik_Merkulov/Shutterstock.com

MAKING POTATO PANCAKES, page 102
Melanie Longenecker

ROCKING CHAIRS, page 130
Rob Byron/Shutterstock.com

MOM'S KITCHEN, page 130
Mary Compagnomi

VINTAGE SILVERWARE, page 152
Gyorgy Barna/Shutterstock.com

PULLING OUT TURKEY, page 152
Mike Simko

RICE, page 178
Bienchen-s/Shutterstock.com

WOMAN AT STOVE, page 178
Everett Collection/Shutterstock.com

SPICES, page 200
Vasil Vasilev/Shutterstock.com

WOMAN CUTTING FOOD, page 200
Everett Collection/Shutterstock.com

CUPCAKE LINERS, page 220
alexsalcedo/Shutterstock.com

PULLING FOOD FROM OVEN, page 220
Gene Marsh

MAKING PIE, page 244
jocic/Shutterstock.com

WOMAN TRIMMING CRUST, page 244
Everett Collection/Shutterstock.com

VINTAGE STAR COOKIE CUTTER, page 264
Donna Smith Photography/Shutterstock.com

COOKING POPCORN, page 264
Donna Deem

TEACUP AND SAUCERS, page 286
Cheryl E Davis/Shutterstock.com

WOMAN COOKING AT STOVE, page 286
Everett Collection/Shutterstock.com